GENDER IN HISTORY

Series editors:
Pam Sharpe, Patricia Skinner and Penny Summerfield

The expansion of research into the history of women and gender since the 1970s has changed the face of history. Using the insights of feminist theory and of historians of women, gender historians have explored the configuration in the past of gender identities and relations between the sexes. They have also investigated the history of sexuality and family relations, and analysed ideas and ideals of masculinity and femininity. Yet gender history has not abandoned the original, inspirational project of women's history: to recover and reveal the lived experience of women in the past and the present.

The series Gender in History provides a forum for these developments. Its historical coverage extends from the medieval to the modern period, and its geographical scope encompasses not only Europe and North America but all corners of the globe. The series aims to investigate the social and cultural constructions of gender in historical sources, as well as the gendering of historical discourse itself. It embraces both detailed case studies of specific regions or periods, and broader treatments of major themes. Gender in History titles are designed to meet the needs of both scholars and students working in this dynamic area of historical research.

Murder and morality in Victorian Britain

Myth and materiality in a woman's world: Shetland 1800–2000
Lynn Abrams

History Matters: patriarchy and the challenge of feminism
(with Notre Dame University Press)
Judith Bennett

Gender and medical knowledge in early modern history
Susan Broomhall

'The truest form of patriotism': pacifist feminism in Britain, 1870–1902
Heloise Brown

Artisans of the body in early modern Italy: identities, families and masculinities
Sandra Cavallo

Women of the right spirit: Paid organisers of the Women's Social and Political Union
(WSPU) 1904–18
Krista Cowman

Masculinities in politics and war: gendering modern history
Stefan Dudink, Karen Hagemann and John Tosh (eds)

Victorians and the Virgin Mary: religion and gender in England 1830–1885
Carold Engelhardt Herringer

Living in sin: cohabiting as husband and wife in nineteenth-century England
Ginger S. Frost

Murder and morality in Victorian Britain: the story of Madeleine Smith
Eleanor Gordon and Gwyneth Nair

The military leadership of Matilda of Canossa, 1046–1115
David J. Hay

The shadow of marriage: singleness in England, 1914--60
Katherine Holden

Women police: Gender, welfare and surveillance in the twentieth century
Louise Jackson

Noblewomen, aristocracy and power in the twelfth-century Anglo-Norman realm
Susan Johns

The business of everyday life: gender, practice and social politics in England, c.1600–1900
Beverly Lemire

\ *The independent man: citizenship and gender politics in Georgian England*
Matthew McCormack

MURDER AND MORALITY IN VICTORIAN BRITAIN
THE STORY OF MADELEINE SMITH

✦ Eleanor Gordon and Gwyneth Nair ✦

Manchester University Press
Manchester and New York

distributed exclusively in the USA by Palgrave

Published by Manchester University Press
Oxford Road, Manchester M13 9NR, UK
and Room 400, 175 Fifth Avenue, New York, NY 10010, USA
www.manchesteruniversitypress.co.uk

Distributed exclusively in the USA by Palgrave
175 Fifth Avenue, New York,
NY 10010, USA

Distributed exclusively in Canada by UBC Press
University of British Columbia, 2029 West Mall,
Vancouver, BC, Canada V6T 1Z2

British Library Cataloguing-in-Publication Data
A catalogue record for this book is available from the British Library

Library of Congress Cataloging-in-Publication Data applied for

ISBN 978 0 7190 8069 2 *paperback*

First published 2009

First reprinted 2011

Printed by Lightning Source

Contents

List of illustrations

Acknowledgements

We should like to thank all those who have helped us in the preparation of this book. We are grateful to staff at Glasgow City Archives, Glasgow University Special Collections, the Mitchell Library Glasgow, the National Archives of Scotland, Staffordshire Libraries (Leek), and East Renfrewshire Libraries for their assistance.

We are also indebted to individuals who have assisted specific aspects of our research. Colin Aldebert of Grigor, Donald, solicitors, Glasgow, was invaluable in helping us to track down Smith family papers. George Toulmin and Bill Greenwell were generous in sharing information about Madeleine's school days and later life respectively. The owners of *Rowaleyn* welcomed us into their home, and the late Anne Jacques offered information about the Wardle family. We also thank Sandy Hobbs, Jennifer Scherr and Eileen Yeo for their continued interest and support.

We are grateful to Emma Brennan, our cheerful and understanding editor, and her colleagues at Manchester University Press.

Finally, special thanks go to our families and friends for their patience and their encouragement as they have followed with us the complexities of the story of Madeleine Smith.

Introduction

In the Edinburgh courtroom, the excited chatter died abruptly. The trapdoor to the dock swung upwards, and the prisoner gradually appeared: first a bonnet, then a smudge of veil, then a head held high and a straight back. The spectators in the crowded galleries craned forward for a better view and then, as the accused took her place, settled back to savour the drama. All Scotland had eagerly anticipated this trial, for it had startlingly unusual features. The accused was female; she was young and attractive; and she came from a class that rarely was exposed to the gaze of the court. What was more, there had been rumours that shocking sexual details were to be revealed during the trial.

The prisoner calmly taking her place in the dock was Madeleine Smith. There was nothing particularly unusual about her, nothing to set her apart from scores of other young middle-class women in her native Glasgow in the 1850s. Observers agreed on only a few features. She was not very tall, and quite slightly built. Her hair was brown and straight and her eyes were dark, though some thought they were blue and others brown. She was fair skinned and pink cheeked, with a long straight nose. Indeed there was a consensus that her features were rather sharp, and her manner rather pert. She was vivacious, stylish and attractive, but not beautiful.

Neither was there anything particularly unusual in her background and way of life. The daughter of well-to-do parents, she enjoyed the social life of the Glasgow 'season' and the more rural pleasures of the family summer home at Rhu, near Helensburgh on the Clyde. So, as a journalist later said, the country was riveted by 'the discovery that such unsuspected dramas as this [Madeleine's story] may underlie the calm and decorous aspect of society'.[1] For in the spring of 1857, when she was just 22, Madeleine Smith was arrested on suspicion of poisoning a Jersey-born clerk, Pierre Emile L'Angelier, who had died suddenly at his Glasgow lodgings. Two discoveries precipitated this: the clerk was found to have had a quantity of arsenic in his body, and numerous letters from Madeleine among his possessions.

Madeleine Hamilton Smith was born in Glasgow in March 1835. The city in the early nineteenth century was a burgeoning, bustling place. But Glasgow was not just growing: it was reinventing itself by turning its back on the narrow wynds off the High Street and Saltmarket, running from the cathedral down to the river. Instead, it looked west and sought to build a late-Georgian city of classical elegance and spaciousness. Although there was some expansion elsewhere, Glasgow's centre of gravity was shifting westwards, and both offices and homes for the new middle class were built in wide streets on a grid system. The undulating nature of the land to the immediate west, on Blythswood Hill and Garnet Hill, of necessity added a pleasing irregularity to the architecture of the grid blocks, and variety to the vistas presented as one looked along the streets.[2] By the 1850s, admiring observers could note that:

> The West End is a city of palaces ... but also the older parts of town are being renovated and brushed up ... old and narrow houses are being pulled down and edifices in the large spirit of the day are being erected ... the universally substantial and neat appearance of the streets squares and buildings; the new halls churches and public edifices ... [mean that] it is fast becoming a one of the most sumptuous ... superb cities in the world.[3]

Madeleine's grandfathers both played a key role in this development of the city. Her maternal grandfather was David Hamilton, once a pupil of Adam, and one of the most revered of Glasgow architects. Hamilton loved classical proportions and Georgian restraint. In the 1820s he designed a new frontage for the eighteenth-century mansion house which became the Royal Exchange and set it in what is still the most elegant square in Glasgow – Royal Exchange Square. This was close to his home and office on Buchanan Street.

The builder who took on the realisation of Hamilton's plans had quite recently arrived in the city from Alloa. He was called John Smith, and his partner was his son James. The Royal Exchange was designed in 1827 and completed by 1829, although the Square took longer to build. The families of the architect and the builder were clearly in close touch, and in March 1833 James Smith married Hamilton's daughter Janet.

Much has been made of the supposed social imbalance of this relationship, with Janet Hamilton seen as having married 'beneath herself'. Yet the difference was in reality not so very great. David Hamilton, though famous, had himself begun as a mason. John Smith had been a prominent figure in Alloa, and his wife's brother was head of the Royal Bank now housed in the Square and adjoining the Exchange. Both families were headed by men who were talented, energetic and self-made.

Royal Exchange Square (Figure 1) was new, imposing and stylish. It lay at the heart of the commercial centre of the city, very much at the hub of city life. The Smith building firm had its offices in the Square too, and the young Smith couple lived here for a time after their marriage. Much

1 Royal Exchange Square, designed and built by Madeleine's grandfathers

later, Madeleine was to write that 'We are to call at our old quarters in the Square on Wednesday ... see us come out of Mrs Ramsay's' [3rd April 1855]. George Ramsay was a porter to the Royal Bank in Royal Bank Place, which forms one arm of the Square.[4] So it seems likely that the family was indeed in 'quarters' in this area for at least a short while.

However, although the Smith offices remained in the Square, it seems that the young couple soon set up home in Regent Street, a few hundred yards to the west, almost at the top of Blythswood Hill. Their first child, Madeleine, was born here on 29th March 1835. James Smith soon began to call himself an architect as well as a builder. The Smiths' life was a privileged one, but not undemanding . They were solidly, respectably middle class. They lived at the heart of a great city, seeing all around them the family's tangible mark upon it, and reminded daily of their contribution to its splendour. Yet hard work was not always enough to keep a man in his position: he had to speculate, to take risks. The Smiths, father and son, like many others, in time over-reached themselves, and both were made bankrupt for a while in the early 1840s.

James and Janet Smith went on to have in all five children who survived infancy – three girls and two boys. Although they lived for a time outside the city during Grandpapa Smith's attempts to become a country gentleman, they were essentially Glaswegian. They spent much of the year in apartments in the centre of the city and, like other middle-class Glaswegians, rented a house in the country or at the coast for the summer. Eventually they came to own the splendid house called *Rowaleyn*, designed by James and built at Rhu, above Helensburgh on the Clyde coast, although they continued to rent in town for the winter season.[5] Mr Smith opened offices in St Vincent Street, one of the key streets in the new town grid. The children were growing up, Mr Smith's architecture practice was blossoming, and life seemed set on a predictable and prosperous course.

So in many respects the Smith family were typical of their time, place and class. Certainly they never appeared in any way unusual to their neighbours. Yet it was this very ordinariness that seemed alarming: if shocking things could be going on unbeknownst in the Smith household, could any respectable couple ever feel so confident about their own family? Local newspapers voiced this fear. A cruel light had shone on the Smith household. 'Suddenly the curtain has been lifted, and nothing has been descried but a pious and well-ordered household.' 'What may be going on,' they agonised, 'in the inmost core of all that is apparently pure and respectable?'[6] So no one was safe: 'But what family might not suffer from such a disaster?' Was the disaster that Madeleine, having spent a couple of years away at school in London, had, home again at the age of 19, met a penniless clerk with whom she carried on a secret and sexual relationship for two years? Or perhaps the disaster was that when he was found to have died from arsenic poisoning, Madeleine was arrested for his murder. Or perhaps the real disaster was that indiscreet letters that she had written to him over this period were discovered and became the talk of the country and beyond.

The trial of Madeleine Smith for the murder of her lover in 1857 became a world-wide cause célèbre. The case has continued to attract widespread interest, spawning a number of publications, a Hollywood film, several plays and at least one stage musical. The one hundred and fiftieth anniversary of the trial in 2007 saw a raft of publications which revisited the case,[7] most of which focused on the 'whodunnit' aspect. Indeed, most of those who have written about the case have focused on the murder mystery and the psychological dynamic of the relationship between Madeleine and her lover, Emile L'Angelier. The continued fascination with the case stems partly from the fact that the verdict was 'not proven', a uniquely Scottish verdict which, in popular parlance is thought to mean 'We think you did it, but we can't prove it'.

However, the case provides a rich source for the social and cultural historian whose interests lie beyond the question of Madeleine's culpability. The Madeleine Smith affair offers us a window into the day-to-day life of a young middle-class woman who, despite her involvement in an extraordinary event, was in most other ways unexceptional and typical. Although Madeleine's affair and trial were extraordinary, they could also be viewed as 'out of the ordinary' in the sense that they were enacted in the context of a typical middle-class Glaswegian life of the mid-Victorian period. Extraordinary events and the documents which they generate freeze in time the day-to-day life which frames them and have often been used as a means of illuminating the humdrum and the ordinary.[8] The voluminous legal documentation of the Madeleine Smith case, including the criminal precognitions, the trial evidence and the extensive press coverage will be used to provide insights into not only the relationship but also the social background against which it was played out. Richard Altick, who wrote perceptively about this and other murder cases, argued that 'Murder trials, if held to the light at the proper angle, are an almost unexcelled mirror of an epoch's mores'.[9] Our intention is to angle that mirror in such a way as to reflect the many different ways in which Madeleine's contemporaries viewed the case and what this tells us about Victorian life, morality and gender relations.

One of the few academic studies of the Madeleine Smith case[10] shares the view that Madeleine was typical of her class and that her behaviour can help us to understand her social and class contemporaries. However, in common with much other academic work, Mary Hartman's premise is that in the high Victorian period middle-class young women led a highly circumscribed life and had limited access to the public spheres of city and social life. Our approach shares the view of much recent academic work which questions the potency of the ideology of separate spheres and highlights the extent to which it not only was negotiated but also jostled with competing discourses in shaping the mental universe of the Victorians.[11] There is a rich vein of scholarship which has highlighted the business and economic opportunities available to women in the Victorian period,[12] the ways in which middle-class women drew on religious discourses and inflected them with a radical edge to sanction a political and public role for themselves,[13] and the role which middle-class women played in the city and in the creation of middle-class culture and identity.[14] There were, of course, great inequalities of power between Victorian men and women. However, despite these inequalities middle-class women exercised agency and had scope to make their own choices, shape their experience and make their own histories.

We do not aim to write a straightforward narrative life history, but rather a thematic biography which uses the Madeleine Smith story to reconstruct the lives of Madeleine and her peers. However, as well as offering unique glimpses of Victorian middle-class life and reconstructing the full and sometimes frenetic social life of the Smiths, the book also tells the story of a fascinating and controversial figure. Madeleine's life was long, full and varied. As well as standing trial for her life at the age of 22, she subsequently carved out a life in Bohemian London of the late-Victorian period and emigrated to the United States, where she continued to court controversy.

At the heart of the book are the 250 or so letters which Madeleine wrote to her lover, covering the period from when the pair first met in the spring of 1855 until Emile's death in March 1857. Previous accounts of the Madeleine Smith case have drawn on the sixty or so letters which were produced at the trial as evidence and which have been the basis of every publication since. The remaining two hundred letters have been virtually untapped.[15] Because their meetings were necessarily clandestine and infrequent, letters flew between the couple. Only Madeleine's have survived. Her hurried outpourings, breathless and disjointed, sometimes disingenuous, sometimes barely coherent, chart not only the course of the affair but also all other aspects of her daily life – her relationships, her social life, her city.

Glasgow permeates the letters.[16] Madeleine wrote about its shops, theatres and concert halls; about the homes she visited, the streets where she strolled. She was bound up in the very fabric of the city: her father and grandfathers had literally made significant parts of it. While she was writing, the sumptuous MacLellan Galleries were being built on Sauch-iehall Street to her father's design. Madeleine, too, looked to the west of the city rather than its increasingly squalid east. She mentions going west as far as the almost-separate village of Partick for household shopping, and to the smart new suburb of Hillhead for dining with friends. Other social visits centred on the north and west of the city's core, to Hill Street, Cambridge Street and Renfrew Street – an area where the Smiths had lived for some time and which was still residential rather than commercial in character, despite its centrality. Most of all, Madeleine walked on Sauchiehall and Buchanan Streets, shopping, greeting old acquaintances and, fatally, meeting new ones.

The same streets were mentioned time after time: Madeleine's city was a very clearly defined one. But she never records going east or south of the

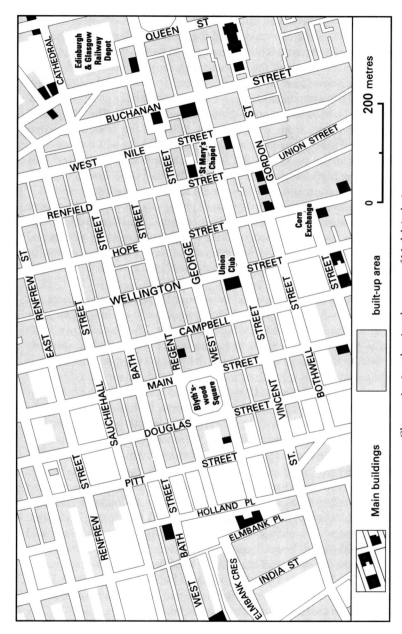

2 Glasgow in 1857, showing the extent of Madeleine's city

Argyle Arcade off Buchanan Street (Figure 2). For a middle-class woman, the older parts of the city centre and the pandemonium of the Broomielaw on the river were unknown territory. In terms of area, Madeleine's Glasgow was less than half the city: although the middle class had not yet moved their homes from the city centre, already their social, cultural and commercial life was withdrawing to enclaves within it.

Madeleine's letters are not the only untapped source. The trial papers include statements from witnesses not called at the trial, supporting evidence and even L'Angelier's black leather wallet. In addition we have tracked down the papers of the family solicitors and uncovered new details about Madeleine's subsequent life. We have also drawn on fresh contemporary sources to provide context to this fascinating story.

By drawing on these diverse and previously unexplored sources, we can follow the Smith family as they browsed the fashionable shops; went to balls, plays and concerts; dined with friends; enjoyed picnics and yachting trips. We can see the workings of the 'well-ordered household', as well as be party to its undercurrents of domestic tension and the romantic secret at its heart.

At the core of Madeleine's life was a murder mystery – had there not been, most of what we know would have been lost to us. Emile L'Angelier died, and Madeleine stood trial for his murder. Their secret love affair began in the spring of 1855. By the autumn of 1856, Madeleine seems to have tired of the relationship. Early in the new year she became engaged to William Minnoch, a much more suitable match. She tried to break off her unofficial engagement to L'Angelier and asked him to return her indiscreet and passionate letters. He refused. Worse, he hinted that he might show them to her father. Madeleine was distraught and wrote begging him not to expose her to shame. However, when he continued to refuse she reverted to her previous affectionate manner and asked him to visit her, as he had done before, in the servants' quarters of the family's rented winter home in Blythswood Square. A letter from her requesting such a meeting was forwarded to L'Angelier at Bridge of Allan, a fashionable spa town in Stirlingshire where he had gone for a few days to improve his health. Back in Glasgow, he went out for the evening – no one knows where – and returned in the small hours desperately ill. His landlady called the doctor and next morning his friend Mary Perry, a single, middle-class woman of nearly 40 who had befriended him, was sent for. Before she arrived, Emile L'Angelier died. Doctors were suspicious and ordered a post mortem, which revealed that he had died of arsenic poisoning.

Of course, Madeleine's letters, incredibly rich though they are, cannot simply be read at face value. They need to be seen as cultural constructs which express Madeleine's attempts to create an identity, entertain her lover and narrate her own love story. They are the product of a conversation and are shaped by the interaction between two people, although we hear only one voice. But other sources can enhance, contradict or confirm the picture drawn by the letters: trial testimony, the statements made by members of the Smith household and others, contemporary newspapers and so on can all augment them. In particular, the lengthy accounts of the trial and extensive editorial commentary it provoked in newspapers are immensely revealing of mid-Victorian attitudes not only towards Madeleine but on subjects as diverse as national identity, class inequality and single-sex education.

Furthermore, in recovering the particulars of Madeleine's long life after the trial, and from the way that the continuing interest in her story has led to its being retold by succeeding generations of commentators, we can chart the evolution of the Madeleine Smith story and how it has been reworked and shaped by contemporary preoccupations and concerns. Each retelling of the story can shine a light on Victorian times, and also on the times in which it was written. The Madeleine Smith story has taken many forms, yet one remarkably enduring feature, common to all accounts, is the influence of the notion of 'separate spheres' as a means of understanding Victorian gender relations.

So the story of Madeleine Smith becomes much more than a murder mystery. It challenges many assumptions about Victorian social life, sexuality, and family and gender relations. The way in which Madeleine and her family lived out the rest of their lives confirms Oscar Wilde's dictum that it is only in fiction that the good end happily and the bad unhappily.

Notes

1 *Manchester Guardian*, 11th July 1857.
2 F.A. Walker, 'Glasgow's New Towns', in Peter Reed (ed.), *Glasgow: The Forming of the City* (Edinburgh University Press, 1993).
3 *Hamilton Advertiser*, 13th September 1856.
4 Glasgow Post Office Directory, 1840.
5 Rhu was at the time known as Row, and we adhere to the contemporary spelling.
6 *Glasgow Citizen*, 18th July 1857; *Dumbarton Herald*, 16th July 1857.
7 Jimmy Campbell, *A Scottish Murder: Rewriting the Madeleine Smith Story* (Tempus, 2007); Mary Craig, *French Letters: The True Story of Madeleine Smith* (Black and White Publishing, 2007); William Knox, *Lives of Scottish Women* (Edinburgh University Press, 2006); Douglas MacGowan, *The Strange Affair of Madeleine Smith: Victorian Scotland's Trial of the Century* (Mercat Press, 2007);
8 Emanuel Le Roy Ladurie, *Montaillou* (Penguin Books, 1990); Carlo Ginzburg, *The*

Cheese and the Worms: The Cosmos of a Sixteenth-century Miller (Routledge & Kegan Paul, 1980); Natalie Zemon Davis, *The Return of Martin Guerre* (Harvard University Press, 1983).

9   *The Times*, obituary, 20th March 2008.

10   Mary Hartman, 'Murder for Respectability: The Case of Madeleine Smith', *Victorian Studies*, 16 (1972–73), pp. 381–400.

11   Eleanor Gordon and Gwyneth Nair, *Public Lives: Women, Family and Society in Victorian Britain* (Yale University Press, 2003); Amanda Vickery, 'Golden Age to Separate Spheres? Review of the Categories and Chronology of Women's History', *Historical Journal* 36, 2 (1993), pp. 383–414.

12   See essays in Jon Stobart and Alastair Owens, *Urban Fortunes: Property and Inheritance in the Town 1700–1900* (Ashgate, 2000); Eleanor Gordon and Gwyneth Nair, 'The Economic Role of Middle-Class Women in Victorian Glasgow', *Women's History Review*, 9, 4 (2000), pp. 791–814.

13   Clare Midgley, *Women against Slavery: The British Campaigns, 1780–1870* (Routledge, 1992) Kathryn Gleadle, *British Women in the Nineteenth Century* (Palgrave, 2001); Megan Smitley, '"Women's Mission": The Temperance and Women's Suffrage Movements in Scotland c.1870–1914 (unpublished PhD thesis, University of Glasgow, 2002); Sue Innes and Jane Rendall, 'Women, Gender and Politics', in Lynn Abrams, Eleanor Gordon, Deborah Simonton and Eileen Janes Yeo (eds), *Gender in Scottish History since 1700* (Edinburgh University Press, 2006), pp. 43–83.

14   Gordon and Nair, *Public Lives*; L. Walker, 'The Feminist Re-mapping of Space in Victorian London' in I. Borden et al. (eds), *The Unknown City: Contesting Architecture and Social Space* (MIT press, 2000), pp. 297–309; Linda Nead, *Victorian Babylon: People, Streets and Images in Nineteenth-Century London* (Yale University Press, 2000).

15   Peter Hunt, *The Madeleine Smith Affair* (Carroll & Nicholson, 1950) and later Douglas MacGowan, *Murder in Victorian Scotland* (Praeger, 1999) are the only writers to draw on more than the trial letters. However, even they did so only to a limited extent.

16   Jack House, *Square Mile of Murder* (Chambers, 1961) makes the point that four of 'the world's greatest murder cases', including this one, took place in a very small area of Glasgow's West End.

I

Papa's house

'Papa's house is not economically kept – but he does not complain so I suppose he can afford it', Madeleine wrote to L'Angelier in January 1856. By this time, James Smith had achieved success as an architect and he could indeed afford for his family to live well, whether in Glasgow or in the country. The summer of 1855, the first summer of Madeleine's relationship with Emile, was also the first that the family had spent at the new country house he had designed at Row, above Helensburgh on the Clyde estuary.[1] A new pattern of residence began, which meant summers – stretching from April or May right through to October or November – were spent at Row and the winter season in rented accommodation in Glasgow. The Smiths had always rented in Glasgow, as most people did at a period when house buying was not nearly so prevalent as it was to become. Indeed the fact that they owned their summer house – rather than renting afresh each year – was somewhat unusual.

Although their homes had never been as palatial as the house at Row, Mr and Mrs Smith throughout their married life had lived comfortably in pleasant surroundings. The apartments in West Regent Street, Madeleine's birthplace, were of a comfortable size. An inventory of one of these apartments taken in the 1860s details a drawing room, a dining room, three bedrooms, a kitchen and a 'lobby'. Even at that date, however, there was no bathroom.[2] The then resident, a widow named Agnes Logan, had household goods valued at £458, which included a great deal of silver and cut glass, rosewood furniture, oil paintings and a great number of books. The apartment was lit by both gas and candles, and had bell pulls in the principal rooms for summoning a servant. Mrs Logan was elderly and had lived there for some time, so it is likely that her home was not furnished very differently from that in which Madeleine had been born thirty years earlier.[3] In 1871 there were six rooms in total at number 167, the Smiths' old home, which sounds very much like Mrs Logan's house in size.[4] Madeleine's sister Bessie was also born there two years later, but the family moved shortly afterwards, so it is unlikely that Madeleine would have retained anything but the haziest of recollections of her birthplace.

It also seems to have been the case that they lived at least for a time in Royal Exchange Square, where Mr Smith had his business. It was not particularly unusual for domestic and business life to be conducted side by side. Madeleine's grandfather David Hamilton lived and worked in nearby Buchanan Street and there is an account of his premises in the period 1838 to 1843.[5] His offices and the servants' rooms and kitchen were on the ground floor; on the first floor were a library and a large room that combined drawing room and dining room; the bedrooms were at the back of this floor and on the second. The furnishings were tasteful and the library was that of a cultivated man. Because of the dual nature of the premises, Mrs Magdaline Hamilton would on most days call in to the office and chat with the apprentice draughtsmen, often bringing her daughters; and the young men felt that they were living almost *en famille*. Much later, one of the apprentices was to see this as an 'old-fashioned' arrangement. Clearly, the separation of home and work that is argued to have been such a key feature of middle-class life under industrial capitalism had not yet taken place in the Glasgow of the 1830s and 1840s. In fact, that separation was never as complete as has often been assumed, with domestic and business life intertwined for most families throughout the century.[6]

So there is a good chance that, at least for a time, the Smiths lived 'over the shop', so to speak, at the commercial heart of the city. However, they had moved again by early in 1839. This time they were slightly further from the centre, though hardly suburban. For some years James Smith and his father had kept a workshop in Renfrew Street, which lay on the other side of Sauchiehall Street, towards Garnethill (see Figure 2). Now the family moved to Bedford Place, a section of Renfrew Street not far from the workshop. This was probably the first home that Madeleine would have remembered. From here it was possible to look down at the bustle of Sauchiehall Street and the rest of the newly developed retail centre of the city beyond it. The homes were genteel but not opulent. As an address, it was less exalted than Royal Exchange Square, but perhaps offered more space for a growing family. A son, Jack, was born here, and so was another baby boy, David, who died in his first month.

They were still here in the autumn of 1840, but at some time in the next six months James Smith moved his family yet again. Now, for the first time, they were to live outside Glasgow city centre. Madeleine's grandfather John Smith, the builder, had become the tenant of Birkenshaw House in 1836.[7] This lay to the south-west of Glasgow, into East Renfrewshire. Then, in 1839, he bought the 'mansion house' and 'adjoining farm', with 27 acres of land, for £3,000.[8] His architect son had a house – Birkenshaw Cottage – built on this land for himself, presumably to his own design, and probably drew up the plans for his father's improvements to the main house.

This was an idyllic place for the Smith children to grow up. There was plenty of space, and gardens and 'romantic walks' had been laid out which still exist in Rouken Glen Park.[9] What a contrast it must have been from the noise and crowds of the city! Grandpapa Smith enjoyed the life of a country squire and – it seems – the proximity of his grandchildren. Madeleine later remembered 'when I was very young – about 5 years … my Grand Papa's farm' [8th October 1856]. The cottage was a few hundred yards away from the main house: were the children allowed to run to Grandpapa's through the wooded grounds, or did they have to walk there accompanied by their nursemaid?

The 'mansion house' no longer survives, but photos suggest that at least some of the alterations and additions made to it were done at this time, and probably to James Smith's designs. The house certainly had features reminiscent of the style he later employed in designing his own house at Row – mock-baronial turrets and gables abounded. The 'cottage', though more modest, still represented a step up for James Smith. At the census of 1841 he and his wife Janet were recorded there with three children – Madeleine was 6 (although the enumerator's return mistakenly says 4), Bessie 4, and Jack 2. There were three female domestic servants to help run the house and look after the children. In the main house lived the Smith grandparents, now in their mid fifties, two uncles and a maiden aunt. So Madeleine was surrounded by indulgent relatives at a very happy period in the family's life. She always retained a fondness for the country over 'the Town' and an interest in animals and gardens, and her Papa was similarly influenced; fifteen years later he wanted 'a large place where we could have farms' [31st October 1856].

But the idyll was not to last. When both John and James Smith were declared bankrupt in September 1843 the whole property was sold and Madeleine's parents and their growing family were forced to move yet again.[10] They headed back to the city, in fact to Sauchiehall Street, at its very heart. Here they rented an apartment at number 230, a classically elegant building which was Georgian in spirit if not in date, with tall windows in a regular façade that must have allowed such Glasgow sun as there was to flood in. The change from Birkenshaw Cottage could hardly have been greater. Here there was no garden in which to roam and play; no pet animals to feed; and less domestic space to be shared with – by now – four younger siblings. Madeleine felt the change greatly, and just as she remained fond of the country, so she continued to speak disparagingly of Glasgow and its inhabitants. Nevertheless, for a curious child there were compensations in being situated on one of the two or three main shopping streets, with a never-ending panorama of comings and goings in the street below. And despite her protestations to the contrary, Madeleine did always delight in some aspects of metropolitan life.

Most homes in Sauchiehall Street were apartments above shops or, less frequently, offices. John Wilson, a bookseller who died in 1868, lived at number 239, in a flat presumably over his shop. It had a hall, dining room, parlour, kitchen and two bedrooms.[11] In 1861, apartments in Sauchiehall Street could vary considerably in size, even within the same building; some had only a couple of rooms, while others had about six, as Wilson had. All of his rooms had a fireplace, and the dining room and parlour had gas lighting. In the kitchen was a range with oven and boiler for cooking and heating water; but there was no bathroom, and the family washed at basins in their bedrooms. Furnishings (at least in 1868) were solid and comfortable, but not lavish. There were a 'cottage piano', a tester bed, an eight-day clock and a barometer – as well as, of course, plenty of books. This gives us a flavour of the Smith home twenty years earlier, for although the latter may have been somewhat better appointed, it must have been a similar size. They were not living in the height of luxury, and felt cramped after the space they had become accustomed to, both indoors and out, at Birkenshaw.

Sauchiehall Street was widened around 1846 and became an elegant as well as busy thoroughfare. The Smiths may have moved into a brand new building, if number 230 was built at the time of the improvements. However, it is possible that they moved away for a while at this time and came back to a refurbished home, for the Post Office Directory of 1848 lists James Smith's home address as 11 Greenlaw Place, Paisley Road, Govan, a couple of miles south-west of the centre. This address was the home of Madeleine's Smith grandparents from at least 1851 until the death of Grandpapa in 1853, so it seems as though the younger family moved in with them for a time. The Smiths, senior and junior, had come down in the world, and their plight illustrates the sometimes precarious nature of middle-class finances in the mid-nineteenth century. No doubt it was a pleasant enough home, but it had neither the social cachet and attractions of Birkenshaw nor the centrality of Sauchiehall Street. It was too far from the centre to allow any sense of engaging with the vibrancy of the burgeoning city; yet it was too suburban to provide the almost-rural seclusion of Birkenshaw.

Not surprisingly, then, by 1849, with the bankruptcy discharged, they were back at the old address in Sauchiehall Street. No doubt Madeleine, now 14, was in many ways glad to be back right next to the shops, concert halls and theatres of the city centre. In 1851 Mr and Mrs Smith and all five children were settled in Sauchiehall Street.[12] They had three servants – a general maid, a kitchen maid and a house maid. This was a fairly standard middle-class complement, although elsewhere one of the three might have been the cook. It seems unlikely that Mrs Smith cooked, so perhaps the kitchen maid did, or perhaps there was a cook who came on a daily basis. Certainly the Smiths had a live-in cook from at least 1855 to 1857, so they may simply have been 'between cooks' at the time of the census. With at least five adults and five children to accommodate, the apartment must indeed have been quite large; but even so, there was not a great deal of space or privacy for individuals.

Nigel Morland tells us, without supporting reference or evidence, that the Smiths spent the summer of 1853 at Glenap, near Girvan in Ayrshire.[13] This is entirely credible: it was just the sort of seaside venue favoured by the Glasgow bourgeoisie for long summer stays. As yet, in the early 1850s, the Smiths did not have a summer house of their own, so they would have had to rent. This was not a problem, as from early spring the Glasgow newspapers were full of adverts for villas to let and for removal firms who would transport the whole panoply of belongings which middle-class families felt it essential to have about them over the summer. The essentially temporary nature of such rentals, though, meant that their Glasgow residence felt like 'home'; and for some years, after the peripatetic early years of their marriage, the Smiths made the Sauchiehall Street flat their fixed base.

However, some time in 1852, when Madeleine was away at school, they once again retraced their steps and moved back to Renfrew Street. Number 164 was again in Bedford Place, just a few doors from their earlier home. There seems to have been no obvious reason for the move, one of only a few hundred yards. Bedford Place was a little quieter, a step removed from the clamour of Sauchiehall Street; but the Smiths were long accustomed to that. Extensive building work was about to begin very close by their house: James Smith himself had designed the new MacLellan Galleries which were to occupy the next block. Perhaps he had no wish to live quite so close to the building site. And the Bedford Place homes were – unusually for the city centre – houses rather than flats, and with eight or nine rooms were somewhat bigger than the Sauchiehall Street flats.[14]

Whatever the reason, the household was on the move yet again. Packing and unpacking figured prominently in the life of the middle-class housewife, and all such families owned trunks, crates and boxes to enable such frequent flittings. The Glasgow middle class was astonishingly peripatetic, moving not only between town and seaside, but also from one rented property to another within the city. The Smiths were not unusual in the number of removals they made. It is noteworthy that they stayed in the central area of the city, close to Mr Smith's office, which from the late 1840s was at 123 St Vincent Street. It is often argued that the Victorian bourgeoisie were eager to distance themselves from the contamination of commerce and to set up home in the suburbs, where domestic life could be separated from the world of business.[15] This does not seem to have been especially important to the Glasgow middle classes in general or to the Smiths in particular. Even the newly built residential terraces of the Claremont and Woodside estates to the west were barely a stone's throw from Sauchiehall Street. Apart from their brief interludes outside the city, all the family's homes were clustered within a few hundred yards of each other.

In the summer of 1854, however, James Smith began to put into practice a plan he had probably had for some time. He would continue to rent in town, but instead of also leasing a summer holiday home he would design and build a magnificent house in the country which would advertise both his skills as an architect and his success as a businessman. In September he completed the purchase of a piece of land at Row. The hamlet had a pier and was well served by boats from Glasgow. Mr Smith's land was situated up the hill, inland from the pier, and had a fine view back down over the water.

The house he designed for his family was very different from the buildings he had been designing in the city. The latter were classical in inspiration, characterised by restraint and symmetry. Here, where he was his own client, he could indulge his personal taste, which was for a much more ornate, Scottish baronial style, harking back not to the eighteenth century but to an imagined medieval world of gables and turrets, spiral stone staircases and heraldic shields (Figure 3). Nevertheless, within that tradition he incorporated some more modern features, like the tall windows the family had been used to in Sauchiehall Street and a round cupola over the main stairwell, which lit the stairs and the first floor landing, with its pedimented arches. Principal rooms on the ground and first floors had bay windows – another relatively modern touch – which also maximised the light. Thus *Rowaleyn*, as the house was named, emerged as a hybrid, marrying baronial style with the larger, lighter rooms of the nineteenth century. These were indeed magnificent, with marble fireplaces and elaborate plaster cornices. In all, there were at

3 *Rowaleyn*, built to Mr Smith's design as the family's summer residence

least fifteen rooms, including kitchen, housekeeper's room, laundry and so on.[16] The house and its setting were certainly imposing, and proclaimed to the world that the Smiths had 'arrived'.

Madeleine, with some understatement, referred to *Rowaleyn* as 'a very nice place'. She and the rest of the family first went to stay there in the spring of 1855; they were there at the beginning of April, when her first letters to L'Angelier were written. The house had been built and furnished astonishingly quickly, given its size and opulence and the fact that the land had been bought only in the previous autumn. Shortly after he moved in, Mr Smith bought more land next door. 'Papa had last week bought the place next to us and of course that makes ours very much larger' [18th May 1855]. The grounds were now quite extensive, both down the hill towards the pier and uphill at the back. Carriages came up the drive from the coast road, through a stone gateway and up a sweeping curve that approached the house only obliquely. There was, however, a footpath leading more directly to the side of the house, which Madeleine instructed L'Angelier to take (see Figure 7). 'Come up by our gate. Come in and take the narrow path on the *left hand* and wait there' [3rd October 1856].

Up the hill, behind the house, was what Madeleine referred to as 'the park', and sometimes she would meet Emile there.[17] 'I am quite accustomed to go out after 10 at night by myself,' she said [19th October 1855]. On other occasions they met nearer or even in the house. This was made easier by its layout and by the location of Madeleine's room, at least from the spring of 1856. In fact, it sounds as if there was some general reallocation of rooms each time the family returned to Row for the summer, for in April 1856 she wrote that 'I found the room allotted for me near papa's was not to my mind, I told them so and have taken possession of a room on the low flat. I could just step out from my window any night to see *you*.' The low flat – or ground floor – housed the kitchen and other domestic offices in a semi-basement at one end; but the other end, thanks to the slope of the land, was more elevated and culminated in a pretty room giving onto the terrace just opposite the path which L'Angelier climbed through the grounds. Madeleine could indeed just step out from her window, or actually invite Emile inside, which she had to do in June 1856, since, as a result of two attempted break-ins, a watchman would be patrolling the grounds at night.

Only the servants shared this floor with Madeleine. The kitchen end was reached by a winding stone staircase, romantic but perhaps impractical. Her sister Janet fell down these 'back stairs' one day, so they were used by the family as well as by the servants. Some at least of the servants also slept down here, and Mama had planned for summer 1857 that Madeleine was 'to change my bedroom to the larger one the servants have' [5th November 1856]. It is not entirely clear how many servants were maintained at Row, but there were a housekeeper, two gardeners and at least three other female domestics. When the family went back to Glasgow in the autumn the housekeeper was retained to look after the house. 'I do so pity the poor housekeeper, she is to remain here all winter for there are such a lot of rooms that it must be rather a charge for her' [27th October 1856]. But three other female servants were to be 'let go', while one went with them to Glasgow.

Some at least of the female servants shared a bedroom, even in a house as large as *Rowaleyn*.[18] The laundry maid was taken ill in 'the servants' room' one night and Madeleine, by her own account, was called to tend to her – which would be logical, since she slept on the same floor. The cook and the maid Christina Haggart later shared a similar semi-basement room in the Smiths' Glasgow home. In fact it was not only servants who routinely shared a bedroom: a fellow employee of L'Angelier in Dundee reported that they shared a room there; and another friend said that they shared a bedroom when L'Angelier visited him. Siblings, like Madeleine and Janet, shared not only a room but also a bed. In fact, single beds were something of a rarity.[19] Madeleine only had her bedroom at Row to herself while Janet was still at school in Glasgow, or when, in Papa's absence, Janet went to sleep with Mama.

The main reception room at *Rowaleyn* was the drawing room, a spacious room lit by three windows and looking out over the drive. Madeleine sometimes wrote letters here, and broke off when she saw a visiting carriage approaching up the curving drive. There were also a dining room and a library. Madeleine found the latter had become disordered during their absence. 'Yesterday I was busy with the library. It was changed so I had all the books to place right' [11th April 1856].

Already, barely a year after moving in, Mr Smith had made improvements to the house – 'All the house is changed and a great deal more of money expended on it which is great stuff' [11th April 1856]. These were probably to the interior and the furnishings: but in addition a cottage was built on the extra land that he had acquired. This was named Woodcliff and had nine rooms, so was hardly a cottage except in the Victorian sense of country dwelling. Indeed, Madeleine gave up her plan for Emile and herself to rent it on the grounds that it was far too large (as well as too close to her family). It was to be rented out at £100 p.a., another problem for the young couple. Woodcliff was separate from the main estate, and in fact remained in the family's possession long after *Rowaleyn* was sold. But a gardener's cottage, stables and a coachman's house were all built as part of *Rowaleyn* itself.

There were in fact two gardeners to tend the extensive gardens.[20] 'We have got a new hot house put up here but not a vinery this year' [11th April 1856]. This was probably where they grew the melons which Madeleine said were 'rather a favourite of mine' [3rd July 1856]. One gardener was going to help Madeleine make a collection of ferns, that very Victorian pastime also pursued by L'Angelier when he was visiting friends in England. In fact, there were all the trappings of Victorian country house life. The gardener was asked to supply flowers for the house and even to send them up to Glasgow whenever a party was planned.[21] The coachman was on hand to take Madeleine into Helensburgh or on visits around the neighbourhood. The post – of vital importance to Madeleine – was dealt with on the usual country-house system whereby letters were brought and collected by servants from the hall: Madeleine was anxious that Bessie might take Emile's letters 'out of the post bag', and so arranged for a servant to collect them from the Post Office in the village.

Madeleine loved this privileged and leisured life, as well she might. She particularly enjoyed playing a pastoral role, in a sort of Marie Antoinette dilettante fashion. In spring 1856 she decided that she would 'have a donkey as a pet this season' [24th April 1856]. In May she reported having 'got a new employment – the Hen Yard. I go there every morning. You can fancy me every morning at 10 o'c seeing the Hens being fed and feeding my donkey.' But quite soon she had got rid of the donkey and by August she had 'a pet lamb, Fanny, I got it from the under gardener'. These were short-lived enthusiasms, and Madeleine never seems to have been particularly fond of these less-than-traditional pets. (The donkey, she feared, 'had little affection'.)

Dogs were perhaps a better bet, but seem to have enjoyed little more success in engaging her affections. The first, called Milo, arrived in May 1855 but was soon gone again. She could not get the next, Toby, who came in August, to answer to 'Milo'. In any case, 'It is not in the least pretty it is much too large for a pet' [8th August 1855]. By the end of the month she had 'seen Milo away'. The following summer Madeleine acquired two terriers – Sambo, a gift from her father, and Pedro, which the coachman got for her. Pedro was in favour for a while: he 'is the most affectionate I ever saw' [9th August 1856]. In August she was to get a pure Skye terrier from the Highlands; and in October she acquired a large Newfoundland dog, Major. By November she had parted with all the dogs except Major. Like the farm animals, the dogs were amusing for a while and then were discarded without a thought. Of course, after the first few months of their relationship Madeleine also began to call L'Angelier her 'little pet'.

The house at Row came to be called 'home'. Indeed the family had given up the Bedford Place house on moving to *Rowaleyn*. However, they needed to be in Glasgow for at least part of the year. In fact, the Glasgow middle class were in this respect less like the English bourgeoisie with their suburban villas than they were like the aristocracy, spending the season (in this case the winter) in town and the summer in the country. Over the summer, *Rowaleyn* was a base from which to come and go – not just for Papa, with his job in the city, but also for the boys and Janet, with work and school keeping them in town during the week. Mr Smith was able to spend considerable periods in the country too: 'Papa has not been a night in town for some time' [29th April 1856]. The excellent steamer service from Glasgow enabled him to commute when necessary; indeed, everyone routinely went up and down to Glasgow. There was no attempt to withdraw permanently from the city, and no question but that the whole family would go back to town in the autumn.

The only question was – where in the city would they spend the winter? As late as the end of October 1855, according to Madeleine, this had still not been settled. The house they had hoped to have, in Blythswood Square, would not after all be available, as the gentleman who lived there was ill and unable to move out. House agents were used to find a suitable property to rent. Possibilities were discussed in Newton Place, to the west of Charing Cross, and Madeleine's personal favourite, Bath

Street, in the most central district. However, the house that was decided upon was the home of a John Kinnear at 16, India Street. This was not quite as central as Bath Street, but lay just off its western end. Nevertheless, it was too quiet for Madeleine: 'India St is very quiet – I don't like it much' [20th November 1855].

The house was a terraced town house, with steps up to the front door bridging a semi-basement area, and particularly fine, tall windows over a wrought-iron balcony at the first floor. There were two principal rooms, one either side of the front door, on the ground floor. One of these we know was the dining room, whose curtains Madeleine would open as a signal to L'Angelier before letting him in at the front door. She also referred to the breakfast room, but this was probably the same as the dining room. The other principal room was the drawing room. Here in India Street, too, Madeleine shared a bedroom with Janet.

Mr Kinnear and his family must presumably have moved out for the season. There is a sense of a constant round of musical houses being played by the whole middle class of the city. 'Lodgings' and 'quarters' were taken, presumably furnished, by families as well as by single men such as L'Angelier. Madeleine's two brothers took lodgings in Glasgow, at a cost of 15 shillings a week, in spring 1856, when the rest of the family decamped to Row. Twice a year, for the Smiths, came the upheaval of packing and moving belongings. Madeleine portrays herself, as well as the servants, as busily involved in this – as no doubt she was. 'A great lot of things leave [Row] tomorrow in carts. I have been in the stable packing till 10 o'c tonight' [31st October 1856]. The house at Row, she says, was 'in confusion'. There were servants to be sacked (one at Row had 'got into a consumption' and so 'of course' could not be kept on 'as she could not work') and others to be appointed. The faithful Christina Haggart came from Row to India Street, and three others were taken on, including a cook and a page, William Murray.

Although the India Street house looked pleasant and smart, it was not only Madeleine who found it less than ideal. Mr Smith was apparently so ashamed of the 'dirty house' they were in that he would not have a large party at Christmas 1855. With four servants to clean it, the house can hardly have been literally dirty, but perhaps it was a little shabby in its decor. Nevertheless, the family settled in and adopted a set regime of breakfast at 10 a.m., luncheon at 2 p.m. and dinner at half past six. Even so, Madeleine said she was always last at breakfast; she never was an early riser.

By late March of 1856, the family was again making arrangements to move back to Row. This time, it seems, they had tried to avoid the last-minute rush that had left them with the India Street house. In addition,

Jack and James would need to be in town over much of the summer, so the plan had been to get another city house sooner rather than later. But in the end they had to take lodgings for those who had to remain in the city. 'I have been with her [Mama] for the last 4 hours looking for lodgings for the boys. We don't get our house in town till May and then it has to be painted so it shall be August before they get into it' [21st March 1856]. Some digs were secured on 5th April – Madeleine thought them both small and, at 15 shillings, expensive. At the same time, Papa went down to Row to make sure everything was ready for the family. The others travelled to Row on 9th April by boat, and had a 'very very wet passage'. Madeleine by this time regularly referred to *Rowaleyn* as 'home'. It was, after all, their only fixed base. Yet she was sad to leave town: 'I cannot express my feelings at leaving today. I was so foolish as to burst into tears just before starting' [9th April 1856].

Even *Rowaleyn* was not necessarily their permanent home. Already in 1856 there was talk of a possible move. Papa went to look at some property near Edinburgh, 'and if he can get a nice large place, Row will be sold. But he won't sell it till he gets another' [31st October 1856]. Perhaps *Rowaleyn* had been something of an advertisement for his architecture practice and was never intended to house the family for ever. Meanwhile, the house that was being painted ready for the autumn was at 7 Blythswood Square. Although it was an elegant and expensive square, this was again in the centre of the city. The Smiths rented the ground floor and semi-basement of the house, which stood on the corner of the Square and Mains Street leading down to Bath Street, with Sauchiehall Street just beyond it. It was not only painting that needed to be done before the family moved in. Papa said that the house was infested with rats, and he had had some floorboards lifted and asphalt laid.[22] Thus it was November before the family actually moved in.

Number 7 was divided into two apartments, one (the Smiths') with an entrance onto the Square, the upper one entered via Mains Street around the corner. Madeleine had complained that they would be able to keep only two or three servants because the apartment was so small. But the address was a good one and the other houses were very grand. Number 1, on the north-west corner of the Square, was for sale in January 1856 for a sum in excess of £3,500.[23] It had a large dining room and drawing room, each twenty-six feet by eighteen feet, as well as a smaller 'ante-drawing room' and parlour, six bedrooms and a dressing room. Also listed were a kitchen, laundry, store room and pantry – but no bathroom. So, even half of a comparable house was not excessively small, though it must have seemed so after the splendours of *Rowaleyn*.[24]

Because of the testimony at the trial, we know much more about the details of domestic life here in Blythswood Square than at any of the many other homes that the Smiths had over the years. A contemporary floor plan shows the layout of the rooms. As at India Street, there were steps up to the front door, over the basement area, although here everything was on a slightly larger scale (Figure 4). Inside the front door, the drawing room and dining room were behind each other, off to the right. Further back, beyond the stairs, were three bedrooms and – unusually for the city centre – a bathroom. Stairs led down to the 'sunk floor'. Here were the kitchen, pantry and wine cellar, as well as a decent-sized bedroom shared by the maid and cook, and a tiny room for the boot boy. In addition, there was a bedroom next to the kitchen that came to be shared by Madeleine and Janet. Ironically, Madeleine was originally opposed to the famous semi-basement room: 'He [Papa] wants me to take a bedroom on the low flat in Blythswood Square and I don't want' [13th October 1856]. But, because the back door from this floor led out to an enclosed area and then a lane, she came to realise the potential for continuing to see L'Angelier. Here, as she had at India Street, she could take him into the laundry or the kitchen.[25]

4 No. 7 Blythswood Square, where the Smiths lived through the winter of 1856–57 and where Madeleine would talk with Emile late at night as he stood outside the window of her basement room

Madeleine and Janet shared a bed here, too, a 'French bed' situated behind the door, its end towards the window. There was a fireplace where a fire always burned, and a press or built-in cupboard where clothes were kept. The sisters washed in a bowl at a washstand 'of the usual kind,' which stood between the window and the fire.[26] Madeleine always washed and dressed in this room, despite the presence of a bathroom on the floor above. Christina Haggart emptied the washbasin – and probably also was responsible for filling and emptying the bath upstairs, as it is unlikely that running water was available even in this rather grand town house.[27] Madeleine kept her cosmetics in a dressing case and used them when she was getting ready to go out, as well as pomade and soap, which were on the washstand.[28]

This bedroom lay immediately below the dining room and was the largest bedroom in the house. In fact, that occupied by Mr and Mrs Smith was just about the smallest. The two reception rooms were large; each had two windows, those of the drawing room to the front and those of the dining room to the side, overlooking Mains Street. These were the 'public rooms'.

Madeleine illustrated that this was more than a titular description when she referred on several occasions to having to leave the drawing room when she felt herself unfit for appearing 'in public'. 'I was in no state of mind to be in the Drawing room', she wrote after a confrontation with Mama in March 1856. This, of course, referred to the drawing room at India Street; but in all the Smith homes the drawing room had a public function. It was here that friends were entertained. At *Rowaleyn*, dancing took place in the drawing room. In India Street and Blythswood Square, friends of Jack came to play cards there. As well as the more formal and extensive social engagements that we shall describe elsewhere, there were pastimes that formed part of domestic life and which may or may not have involved those outside the immediate family. As well as cards and billiards, 'There is another great game in our house – the "race course". A lot of money is lost and won on that game' [28th May 1856].

There must have been some furniture provided in the rented houses at India Street and Blythswood Square, but the Smiths added to it, for instance by acquiring a piano for the drawing room in the former. (Never doing things by halves, they had 'got the large one he [Banks] used to play on in the exhibition' [15th January 1856].[29]) Madeleine and her sisters played duets in the drawing room, and she pressed flowers, did drawings and wrote letters there.

The drawing room was for family amusements, but also for public display. Mama had received a gift of 'pretty drawing room ornaments' from Paris, brought back as a present by Papa's business partners the Houldsworths. A lifetime later, Janet still retained in her drawing room a 'Rosewood and brass cabinet with Sèvres miniatures' which were probably these very ornaments.[30] She also had a rosewood semi-grand piano and a music stand: possibly this too was the same piano, for it was noted that most of Janet's furnishings were old. At any rate, the tradition of music making in the drawing room had continued. So had that of games playing, for there were also carpet bowls and a card table. And the drawing room had remained a place for entertaining often large numbers: the family drawing room had by the early twentieth century accumulated thirty-two chairs, a sofa, nine stools and eleven tables. This was the accretion of decades, but at its core was the furniture of Madeleine's youth.

In Janet's dining room in 1922 were the relics of the family's days of lavish entertaining – a telescopic dining table with two extra leaves and a set of twelve chairs, as well as other odd chairs which could be pressed into service. The silver and cut glass was stored here too: there were twenty-four 'fruit plates', numerous decanters and wine glasses, silver forks and spoons literally by the dozen, some of them 'with ivory handles initialled "S"'. There were silver accessories for every conceivable culinary eventuality – entrée dishes, toast racks, egg stands, cruet sets. Much of this must have predated the trial, if we are to believe that the Smiths did little entertaining after it.

Dining rooms were not just used for entertaining, but for all family meals. In Blythswood Square breakfast was taken in the dining room, and afterwards Madeleine stayed at the table, ostensibly writing orders for the servants but actually writing to L'Angelier. Luncheon, according to Bessie, was served here too. Family prayers, where the servants and family members came together on Sunday evenings at nine o'clock, were also held in the dining room. There was a press or built-in cupboard where some items such as cocoa were kept ready for use in the room.

Drawing and dining rooms were large – at least twenty-five feet square at *Rowaleyn* – and needed to be, to house all the furniture and ornaments.[31] There were side tables, card tables, tea tables; a plethora of chairs, stools, sofas; there were vases, boxes, cabinets and screens. As skirts got ever more voluminous, it must have been tricky for women to manoeuvre their way around without leaving a trail of devastation. Walls were covered with paintings, engravings and mirrors.

Part of what was on display in the public rooms was the family itself – its wealth, its accomplishments and its lineage. Still surviving in Janet's drawing and dining rooms in 1922 were two small silver salvers inscribed 'James Smith Esq', one poignantly dated 1856, when, unknown to their recipient, the storm clouds were gathering. The most valuable items she possessed were two oil paintings, one of Papa and one of grandfather David Hamilton; and a portrait of the 'late Duke of Hamilton'. It has not been established that there was any family connection between the Hamiltons and the Duke, but it rather looks as though the Smiths were at least tacitly suggesting it.

It is often argued that the 'consumer revolution' which took place in Britain from the eighteenth century was in considerable part fuelled by women,[32] although an uncritical equation of women with the urge to frivolous consumption has rightly been criticised.[33] With their increasing withdrawal from public life, it is alleged, women concentrated on the domestic domain, and its adornment (as well as their own) became a key part of their responsibilities. Their job was to reflect the good taste and the spending power of the family in the furnishings and décor of the home. While we do not accept the consequent argument that men were uninvolved in this aspect of domesticity – James Smith, after all, was the architect of the family's main home – it *was* the case that women were aware of the messages given by the public rooms of the house. Yet the tradition in Scotland had been more for a display of solid, enduring, often inherited, 'good' furnishings with family and sentimental connections, than for a concern with the newly fashionable.[34] As far as the Smiths were subsequently concerned, this war between nostalgia and fashion was no contest. Janet's dining and drawing rooms were heavily Victorian in style: they were a public display of the private virtues of family, hospitality, sentimentality and industry; they were opulent but stolid.

By contrast, bedrooms were relatively sparsely – indeed spartanly – furnished. In the 1860s, flats like those the Smiths had lived in at West Regent and Sauchiehall streets had no gas lighting in their bedrooms, which were furnished in a fairly utilitarian way with bed, wardrobe and washstand only. Bedrooms were for sleeping, washing and dressing, and only occasionally for family chats, as when Jack would come to sit with Madeleine in her room at Row. Janet's testimony later stressed that, although their room in Blythswood Square had a press, it was usually full of clothes and boxes. There was no crockery, bread, wine or food kept in the room. Christina Haggart confirmed that there were no cups or biscuits, and that Madeleine was not in the habit of drinking or eating in her room.

The room was cosy, though, for a fire burned there day and night, and there were blinds at the windows to prevent passers-by looking down and in.[35] Not all the bedrooms were as cosy: even in December, Mama did not have a fire in her bedroom, so when Papa was away, Janet declined to leave the warmth of the basement and move in with her. Madeleine sat up by the fire, writing her love letters. She preferred to use a quill pen, but sometimes had to make do with a steel one borrowed from Bessie. Both sisters seem to have used portable writing slopes.

Even at the new and palatial *Rowaleyn*, Madeleine wrote by candle-light. 'I must stop as my candle is just going out' [n.d. September 1856]. The public rooms would have had oil lamps, and in Glasgow there were 'gasoliers' by this date. But candles were good enough for bedrooms. To modern eyes, there is a distinct lack of luxury about many aspects of what was, in most ways, a very privileged and lavish lifestyle. Perhaps this was universal, or perhaps the Smiths were simply old fashioned. As late as 1922, the family home still had marble washstands in the bedrooms.

Similarly, there is little sign of the supposedly gargantuan meals enjoyed by the Victorian middle class. No doubt sumptuous dinners could be supplied for visitors, but Madeleine was certainly no great eater. One of her few consistent statements across the correspondence with Emile was that she rarely ate breakfast. At Row she had 'no breakfast for two months, not even a cup of tea, nothing until lunch at 1 o'clock' [27th July 1856]. According to Bessie, she sometimes took tea, and sometimes coffee, for breakfast, and sometimes cocoa for luncheon.[36] She herself said that she enjoyed coffee at lunchtime, although in November 1856 the doctor had suggested she take 'something called piecemeal' which she said was 'very nasty'. Meals were often skipped. One problem was that breakfast at Row was served at 7.30 a.m., but Madeleine by her own admission did not get up until nine – or even later: 'I am just up, half past 10 o'c – you are horri-fied' [20th October 1856]. Having gone to church with Papa one Sunday without breakfast, Madeleine found she was unable to leave until 4 p.m., by which time she was very hungry and ate lunch and dinner in one.

Dinners with guests were more formal – and presumably larger. The women of the family dressed for dinner, at least at *Rowaleyn*, which could be something of a rush if they had been out all day. Dinner 'when we have friends' was at 7.30 p.m., a little later than usual. During the hot weather at Row, Mama and Bessie took a siesta in the afternoon, rising at five, just in time to dress for dinner – which, when held *en famille*, must have been around six, as it was in town, unless the requisite dressing was an inordinately lengthy procedure. Madeleine complained when, coming home from a day out 'on the water', she found that Mama had guests and that, instead of going to bed, she had to dress (i.e. change) and join them [18th August 1856].

Madeleine portrays herself as very rarely drinking alcohol, though she recommended porter to L'Angelier: 'Is the Porter making you fat? You would be the better of a little bit of stoutness' [n.d., autumn 1856]. In return, he suggested that she might take a glass of port. She felt that was far too much. '[I]f I was to take as you say a glassful of Port wine I would not be unable to stand [sic] – two spoonfuls of port is enough for me' [8th December 1856]. It is noteworthy that they both recommended alcohol for medicinal purposes. Another Victorian Glaswegian, J.J. Bell, wrote amusingly on the way his grandmother and her friends drank whisky with the same single-minded concern for health.[37] In general, Madeleine felt that Glaswegians drank far too much, that they 'are so vulgar and mercenary and so much addicted to drinking' [30th June 1855].

There clearly was a culture of drinking. Inventories of the goods of the Glasgow bourgeoisie show that very extensive cellars were kept, including wines and spirits of every imaginable kind.[38] Every middle-class household possessed the trappings for serving alcohol – wine coolers, punch bowls, toddy ladles, bottle labels, decanters, and glasses in their dozens.[39]

Excessive drinking, 'unladylike' or not, was not in fact confined to men. Madeleine mentions Mrs Baird, widow of a lawyer and mother to the young clerks who were instrumental in introducing Madeleine and Emile. Alcohol seems to have cost her friendships and even financial stability: 'Aunt tells me Mrs Baird's furniture was all sold yesterday. M. was telling me why she did not call so often for her – I could not believe the reason. M. says the last time she saw her she was in a very excited state and M. has heard from many people she takes brandy. Did you ever hear this?' [18th May 1856]. Thirty years later, another murder case would reveal the drinking habits of another middle-class woman, Florence Bravo, who was clearly an alcoholic consuming a bottle of sherry a day in addition to some wine.[40] One wonders how widespread the practice was.

Nor, of course, was the culture of excessive drinking confined to the middle classes. Madeleine complained that the post mistress at Row got drunk every night, and so there were mistakes with the post. And when the gardener's daughter was born in July 1856 she supposed that he would go and drink for a day. In fact, initially the temperance movement concentrated almost exclusively on the drinking habits of the lower orders; but eventually middle-class campaigners did look nearer home and recognise the Mrs Bairds and Mrs Bravos in their midst.

Managing the servants was one of the jobs Madeleine alleged that she did as part of her role as housekeeper. 'I can assure you it is no easy work to manage such a large household,' she told L'Angelier, and indeed it cannot have been. It 'takes up a great part of my time' she commented later. The work involved has routinely been underestimated, despite several valuable studies illustrating the contrary, by those determined to see the middle-class housewife as bored, caged and indolent.[41] Madeleine repeatedly portrayed herself as taking over the running of the household from her mother. Hence Mrs Smith has been seen as a perpetual semi-invalid. Yet, when Madeleine first made this claim it was not because of Mama's poor health at all, but rather, on account of her busy and demanding social life. 'I take the entire charge of the house as Mama is too much occupied with friends to have time to attend to it' [23rd May 1855]. Later, according to Madeleine, Mama was simply 'tired of' such domestic responsibilities. Mrs Smith was occasionally reported to be unwell, but no more frequently than other members of the family. If anything, Papa seems to have been the more sickly of the two.

If we are to believe her own accounts Madeleine wrote orders for the servants, both in town and at Row, where she said the staff were 'first rate'. She planned menus, paid household bills, dealt with the agents about renting a house, and saw the pianist Banks about buying his piano. She managed the servants, sometimes, as in the case of the boy William Murray, by 'giving him a blow up every day', but at other times by being on hand to tend the sick laundry maid at Row, or dealing with the after-math of a serious accident to the cook at India Street. 'There has been a horrid affair in the house tonight. Our cook's clothes took fire and she is much burned the bosom and face. I was the only one who could help the dr. to dress it. I dressed it myself for the second time at 12 o'clock tonight – but after I did it I fainted – the first time I ever fainted. I was so sorry for it looked so stupid to have so little nerve' [25th January 1856]. Madeleine was not often open to the charge of lacking nerve, and there is a convincing ring about her account.

However, Mary Hartman is unconvinced that Madeleine played any substantial role in household management. She cites Madeleine saying (in a letter to Mary Perry) 'I have taken the charge of Mama's house for the last two years', but is scathing about this, arguing that Madeleine 'exagger-ated the occasional help she provided' and adding that she had failed to mention the half a dozen servants.[42] The servants, of course, did do the majority of the manual work of the household; but Hartman also takes too little account of how much organising, shopping, planning, sewing and budgeting was done by the bourgeois housewife, as well as some measure of hands-on housework.[43]

The truth probably lies somewhere between Hartman's dismissal of any real housekeeping on Madeleine's part and Madeleine's own, no doubt exaggerated, portrayal of herself as a busy and efficient household manager. She was keen to impress L'Angelier with her domestic skills, especially those of budgeting, to show that his relative poverty would be no bar to their happiness.

There was talk during 1856 of Madeleine and and L'Angelier getting lodgings to live in, at least initially. She had heard that there were lodgings available for 12 shillings a week 'a little out of town' (the developing suburb of Hillhead had been mentioned earlier). 'How nicely the 12/- would suit us at Hillhead.' So, with food, they could live for £1 a week, she thought, though she did acknowledge that £52 a year was 'quite a lot' [26th May 1856]. It was, at the time, double what L'Angelier actually earned.

On other occasions a more rural idyll was favoured. 'Some day darling we may have a cottage and garden' [25th April 1856]; 'I like your plan of taking a cottage on the rail to Glasgow from Helensburgh it would be so nice to live in the country' [6th July 1856]. Perhaps she was harking back to the just-remembered Birkenshaw Cottage. Madeleine did acknowledge that they might have to 'live economically for a year or two', but remained unrealistic about the problems of maintaining a home on ten shillings a week. 'I cannot think why Miss P. thinks it is easier to do housekeeping for a large house than a small one. I fancy you and I would be so easily managed' [16th January 1856].

As part of her housekeeping role, Madeleine did spend time in the service areas of the family's houses (unlike Bessie, who, according to Madeleine, never ventured beyond the drawing room). In the apartments at Regent and Sauchiehall streets these were simply a kitchen, with probably a shared wash-house outside at the back. At Row and in Blythswood Square there were laundries near the kitchens. As befits the much grander house, the service rooms at *Rowaleyn* are more numerous, including a butler's pantry and housekeeper's room, though some of these may well be later additions.

Even middle-class kitchens in Glasgow were not particularly well equipped. The West Regent Street houses had kitchen fires, but as late as 1860 no oven or range – merely a spit to turn meat before the fire. The houses in the splendid Monteith Row, further to the east of the city, which were designed by David Hamilton, had in 1845 a 'grate and jack' in the kitchen, not an oven or range.[44] Mrs Beeton, writing in 1859–60, recommended a vast array of utensils for the middle-class kitchen. Judith Flanders similarly cites long lists of suggested kitchen equipment from the high-Victorian period.[45] But inventories of actual Glasgow homes suggest that, although they were equipped with every conceivable item for serving food to the family and their guests, the picture behind the scenes was much less lavish and kitchen equipment was often rudimentary.

So Madeleine moved between the opulence of the public rooms and the austerity of the private ones, at home in each. She was a restless person, filled with nervous energy. Unlike the rest of the family, she did not take a siesta during summer heatwaves at Row. She ran and jumped when out with the dog Major, walked miles with her brother Jack, and rowed a small boat until her hands and arms hurt. She loved it when the carriage horse bolted – 'It is great fun, we go so fast' – and once sprained her ankle when she impetuously 'jumped from the carriage when the horse was going fast. I wanted to speak to someone and did not tell the man to pull up' [15th September 1856]. So when we picture her at home, either in the grand house at Row or in the less spacious apartment in Blythswood Square, it is as a slight figure darting up the stairs from her bedroom, past the servants' quarters where she would perhaps pause for a word, either conspiratorial or admonitory, with Christina Haggart. She would check her appearance in one of the many mirrors that made the hall and drawing room bright with the reflections of the gas globes, before slipping into one of the leather and mahogany chairs at the dining table. Whether or not there were guests, the table glittered with cut glass and silver, and everyone was dressed for their part.

Sometimes, when she was excitedly playing cards or billiards, or rolling back the drawing room carpet for dancing, or arranging the flowers sent up by the gardener, the picture is enviable and strikingly modern. At other times, as she struggled, with her quill, to finish her letter by a guttering candle before a dying fire, we are reminded how little some aspects of life had changed since pre-industrial times.

The material culture of the Victorian bourgeoisie was a strange mixture of the sumptuous and the spartan. The 'public rooms' were indeed intended for public view, and were full of costly and elaborate furnishings. They were for entertaining guests, but also for the coming together of the household. Even when there were no visitors, it seems that the family dressed up to dine together and to play games or make music together afterwards. In this sense, the drawing and dining rooms remained 'public' at all times. Elizabeth Wilson argues that, as part of a sharpening division between public and private, nineteenth-century clothes 'increasingly marked the distinction between being at home and being on display in public.'[46] Yet with the Smith women (and probably men) dressing up for family dinners and for appearing in the drawing room, the distinction appears more subtle than that: there were 'public' and 'private' areas of the home, and indeed times of the day. Passers-by could see into the public rooms: L'Angelier had spotted Bessie at the window in Blythswood Square, and in India Street young men were in the habit of standing about under the windows. 'Our horrid servant boy told P last evening that there were

young men in the custom of standing under the dining room window
and *it was not you he meant.* But he had seen someone I suppose for fun
looking at the windows' [n.d. December 1855].

There was in fact little really 'private' space, for most people shared
a bedroom. Nevertheless, bedrooms were not intended to be seen by
outsiders (it was particularly shocking that Madeleine had taken L'Angelier
into her room) and were correspondingly austere in their appointment.
Servants' bedrooms were especially spartan. If kitchens and their equipment were fairly rudimentary, wash-houses and pantries were even more
so. These areas were not so much below stairs as backstage, where servants
and family alike prepared for the theatre of the public rooms and the
performance of domestic life that was carried out there.

Such was the material context of Madeleine's early years. Much as
she professed a fondness for the rural life, Madeleine was a child of the
smoky, bustling city and was at home among the jostling crowds, the
traffic, the noise and smells. In many ways it was a comfortable and cosy
home life, with good food, solid furniture and the trappings of recognised good taste. Yet many of the family homes were without bathrooms
or lavatories; washing was done in a basin in front of a dying fire; letters
were written by the light of a guttering candle. Rooms were often cold,
and everywhere the dust and dirt of the city crept in and clung to curtains
and carpets.

This was the world that, for most of her childhood, was familiar and
comfortable to Madeleine. But then, in 1851, at the age of 16, she set off
for boarding school.[47] This is often described as 'in London'; but in fact
Clapton, where Mrs Alice Gorton kept her school, was still essentially
a village lying outside the urban sprawl of the capital. It was a long way
from home. Tradition holds that Mrs Gorton's school was chosen on the
recommendation of Dr Buchanan of Dumbarton, whose daughter Mary
Jane was already at the school. Mary Jane and Madeleine did become
friends, and the two families were on visiting terms in 1855. So this seems
as plausible a way as any other for the Smiths to have heard about the
school. There were no other Scottish girls there.

Madeleine must have had some education before this. Later Janet
had a 'governess' – who may have come to the house on a daily basis –
and then went as a weekly boarder to Mrs Steward's school in Newton
Place, Glasgow from about the age of 12. Her older sisters Madeleine and
Bessie probably attended a local school for some time before heading off to
London – for Bessie too went to Mrs Gorton's some time between May 1853
and May 1854, though she was back in Glasgow by the spring of 1855.

Alice Gorton was a widow of about 55 who had run the school with her sister and daughters for more than ten years.[48] The family were closely involved in education: in April 1851 Mrs Gorton was temporarily not at her own school but at that run by her daughter and clergyman son-in-law in Edgware. This was a large establishment with nearly seventy boys in residence. The Clapton girls' school was much smaller: in 1851 there were twenty-two resident pupils, mostly aged between 13 and 19. They came from all over England, which suggests that the school had something of a reputation, and were clearly all from prosperous backgrounds. The school was housed in a solid, terraced villa at 11 Clapton Terrace (since renamed), with stables and a mews at the back.

Mary Hartman speculates much on the regime and curriculum of Mrs Gorton's school and draws uncritically on the unsubstantiated detail offered by earlier biographers. She argues that such schools encouraged secrecy and dissimulation, and that the education was 'miserable'.[49]

The education provided at Clapton may have been narrow, but it was good in basics. In her scores of letters Madeleine rarely makes spelling errors, and then usually with proper names unfamiliar to her, which she renders phonetically. Her punctuation is erratic, but this seems to arise from haste rather than ignorance. Her handwriting is very distinctive – very large, hard to read: it certainly does not look like the overly schooled hand of many Victorians. Did Mrs Gorton's teachers try to change it? English was taught at the school, together with French (by a French woman) and music. There were six teachers resident there in 1851, and for other subjects masters would have come in daily.

There is no evidence that the life of the school particularly promoted secrets and lies. The emphasis was probably as much on the social as the academic, it is true. At least, that is the way Madeleine chose to remember it. 'When I was at school in London I was not at all attentive to my classes. I was very much taken out with Society and you know one cannot attend classes and go about visiting. I only wish I have my school days to go over again' [18th June 1855]. She may have been trying to impress L'Angelier with her metropolitan sophistication, but the girls certainly did attend social events. Madeleine had, she said, never been to a wedding in Scotland but went to many in London. She also claimed to have visited the Great Exhibition of 1851.

Subsequent writers have mentioned an enamoured curate among Madeleine's flirtations at school.[50] Mrs Gorton is supposed to have reported that her pupil, though bright, could be provoking and sulky.[51] But no evidence for any of this survives, if indeed it ever existed, although it is taken up and repeated by most later writers on the case. L'Angelier's over-excited imagination had been caught by some gossip he had heard about girls' boarding schools – or maybe he was encouraging Madeleine to incriminate herself. She was having none of it:

> What queer creatures you must think young ladies at school. For a moment do you think their conversations are what you said. Believe me, I never heard a young lady while I was at school (nearly three years) speak on the subject you mentioned. But perhaps it was different with me when at school – I always had a bedroom to myself. And I was a Parlour Boarder. Do not think they are so bad. Some may be but not all. [n.d. 1856]

Madeleine suggests that 'parlour boarders' were a cut above the rest, though it is doubtful that she always had a bedroom to herself: in 1851, the year she went there, the house in Clapton had thirty-two residents in all, and it is probable that even teachers did not get a single room. However, she does seem to have remained somewhat aloof. She was friendly with Mary Jane Buchanan, but later Augusta Giubelei, a pupil-governess, recalled that although 'Miss Smith and Miss Buchanan were intimate such as might be expected among girls coming from the same part of the country', she could not 'remember any other girl intimate with Miss Smith'. She herself 'never talked much with her'.[52] Mary Jane later said that their time at the school overlapped by only twelve months.[53]

Madeleine did not readily make female friends, though she did later mention one or two with whom she corresponded and whom she may have met at school. But she loved social events and came home to Papa's house from Mrs Gorton's in the summer of 1853 ready to plunge into Glasgow's social round; ready to flirt, to fascinate and to fall in love.

Notes

1 Now Rhu.
2 GCA T-HB/493, Trust of Mrs Agnes Adam or Logan, Victoria Place, West Regent Street, died 20th January 1866.
3 It would not, however, have been lit by gas when Madeleine was born, gas being installed in private houses only from the 1840s. Jenni Calder, *The Victorian Home* (Batsford, 1977), p. 19. Some houses in West Regent Street were larger. One was on sale in 1856, described as having the same drawing room and dining room, but with five bedrooms, kitchen, bathroom and laundry. *Glasgow Herald*, 14th January 1856.
4 Glasgow Census 1871.
5 Autobiography of Thomas Gildard, cited at www.amostcuriousmurder.com/Story. htm.
6 Eleanor Gordon and Gwyneth Nair, *Public Lives: Women, Family and Society in Victorian Britain* (Yale University Press, 2003).
7 Typescript, East Renfrewshire Library. We are grateful to the local history librarian, Maud Devine, for this.

8   GCA AGN 256.
9   *The Extra*, 28th October 1993. East Renfrewshire Library as above.
10 GCA AGN 256. The estate was sold to John Slater, a Glasgow merchant, for £4255.
11 GCA T-BK 165/9, Testamentary papers of John Wilson, died 1868.
12 Glasgow Census 1851.
13 Nigel Morland, *That Nice Miss Smith* (Souvenir Press, 1988), p. 18.
14 Glasgow Census 1861.
15 L. Davidoff and C. Hall, *Family Fortunes: Men and Women of the English Middle Class, 1780–1850* (Routledge, 1987), p. 181; John Gillis, *A World of their Own Making* (Oxford University Press, 1997), p. 71.
16 The number of rooms with a window is given in the 1861 Census as 15, and in the 1871 Census as 21. Major extensions were only carried out in the early twentieth century, so this increase may represent redivision as much as addition to the house.
17 It afforded fine views down to the estuary, but not the sight or sound of the riotous Helensburgh ceilidh depicted by David Lean as backdrop to Madeleine's seduction in his 1950 movie.
18 The number of bedrooms is not clear, and considerable changes have since taken place in the layout of the upper floors, but in Madeleine's day there were perhaps eight or even ten bedrooms.
19 Gordon and Nair, *Public Lives*, p. 127.
20 William Campsie, gardener, and Robert Eliot, under gardener, were listed as potential witnesses. NAS JC 126/1031/1, Box.3
21 NAS AD 14/57/255, Precognition of Robert Oliphant, Helensburgh.
22 NAS AD 14/57/255/3, Criminal precognitions of James Smith senior.
23 *Glasgow Herald*, 28th January 1856.
24 A half-house of 'street flat and sunk flat' comparable to the Smiths' at number 20 was rented at £90 p.a. *Glasgow Herald*, 16th January 1856.
25 NAS AD 14/57/255/3, Precognition of Christina Haggart; NAS AD 14/57/255/19, Precognition of Janet Hamilton Smith.
26 Ibid.
27 Judith Flanders, *The Victorian House* (HarperCollins, 2003) p. 286.
28 NAS AD 14/57/255/49, Precognition of Janet Hamilton Smith.
29 This is Andrew Banks, professor of music, 402 Parliamentary Rd (Glasgow Post Office Directory, 1856/7). He had played at the Bath Street Exhibition.
30 Inventory of Janet Smith, 1922. Kindly supplied by McGrigor Donald, solicitors, Glasgow.
31 In Woodside Terrace, built in the 1840s to the west of the city centre, Andrew MacGregor's drawing room measured 30 ft by 33 ft. GCA TD 66/5/9.
32 Neil McKendrick, J. Brewer and J.H. Plumb, *The Birth of a Consumer Society: The Commercialization of Eighteenth-century England* (HarperCollins, 1984).
33 Amanda Vickery, 'Women and the World of Goods; A Lancashire Consumer and Her Possessions, 1751–81', in John Brewer and Roy Porter (eds), *Consumption and the World of Goods* (Routledge, 1993), pp. 274–304.
34 Stana Nenadic, 'Middle Rank Consumers and Domestic Culture in Edinburgh and Glasgow, 1720–1840', *Past and Present*, 145 (November 1994), 122–56.
35 NAS AD 14/57/255/3, Precognition Christina Haggart; and F. Tennyson Jesse, *The Trial of Madeleine Smith* (William Hodge and Co., 1927).

36 NAS AD 14/57/255/3, Precognition of Bessie Smith.

37 J.J. Bell, *I Remember* (Porpoise Press, 1934).

38 Gordon and Nair, *Public Lives*, chapter 4.

39 All these, for instance, were listed in the inventory of Agnes Logan of West Regent Street in 1860. She also had a 'gardwine and bottles' – presumably a tantalus.

40 James Ruddick, *Death at the Priory: Love, Sex and Murder in Victorian England* (Atlantic Books, 2001).

41 Flanders, *The Victorian House*, still subscribes to this view. Revisionist arguments have been put forward since the work of Patricia Branca, *Silent Sisterhood: Middle Class Women in the Victorian Home* (Croom Helm, 1975).

42 Mary S. Hartman, *Victorian Murderesses: A True History of Thirteen Respectable French and English Women Accused of Unspeakable Crimes* (Schocken Books, 1977), p. 59.

43 Gordon and Nair, *Public Lives*; Amanda Vickery, *The Gentleman's Daughter* (Yale University Press, 1998).

44 GCA TD 559/4, inventory of valuation of John Stewart, 10 Monteith Row, 1845.

45 Flanders, *The Victorian House*, pp. 74–5.

46 Elizabeth Wilson, *Adorned in Dreams: Fashion and Modernity* (Virago, 1985), p. 27.

47 There seems to be a general agreement that this is the date at which she went – though it was probably in the autumn, as she was at home in Glasgow in April 1851, when the Census was taken.

48 We are grateful to George H. Toulmin for supplying details on the Gorton family and on the fabric of the school.

49 Mary Hartman, 'Murder for Respectability: The Case of Madeleine Smith', *Victorian Studies*, 16 (1972–73), pp. 381–400.

50 Henry Blyth, *Madeleine Smith: A Famous Victorian Murder Trial* (Duckworth, 1975), p. 12.

51 Morland, *That Nice Miss Smith*, p. 16.

52 NAS AD 14/57/255/80, Precognition of Augusta Walcot nee Giubelei.

53 NAS AD 14/57/255, Precognition of Mary Jane Buchanan.

2

My own beloved darling husband

ierre Emile L'Angelier was handsome, and he knew it. He was not good looking in a rugged, masculine way; rather, his demeanour and appearance were those of a sensitive aesthete. In fact, during Madeleine's trial he was described by one newspaper as having a 'pretty face'.[1] The only photographic representation of L'Angelier captures him in a sideways pose, legs elegantly crossed and gazing soulfully at some point off camera (Figure 5). Anyone encountering Emile L'Angelier on one of his regular strolls along Sauchiehall Street could not help but be struck by his appearance. The term 'dandy' could have been coined to describe him. Although he was short and slightly built (his feet were even described as 'dainty'), his dress and demeanour gave him an exotic aspect which set him apart from his contemporaries. He sported a luxuriant moustache which was artfully groomed, his dark hair was carefully combed into a side parting and brushed smoothly down, with his natural curls allowed to emerge at the nape of his neck. His dress was stylish and rather dashing; he wore his cravat loosely knotted over his collar and hanging in two long, soft, symmetrical folds.

L'Angelier's route to Glasgow from his native Jersey had been circuitous. As a young boy he had worked in his father's modest seed shop in Jersey and then gone on to train in all aspects of the nursery trade at another Jersey firm which was larger and more modern than his father's.[2] The young Emile was both hard working and charming. No doubt it was these qualities which drew him to the attention of a wealthy Scottish client, Sir Francis Mackenzie of Gairloch, who offered him a position on his estate in Ross-shire in the Scottish Highlands. Mackenzie suggested that Emile complete a training at Dickson's and Co., an Edinburgh nursery, before joining the estate staff.[3] L'Angelier arrived in Edinburgh in 1842, aged 19. However, he never made it to the Highlands of Scotland; his patron died suddenly and, although Emile continued at Dicksons for a further

+= 37 =+

5 Emile, c. 1856

three years, he grew homesick and decided to return to Jersey in 1846. He remained only a short time in Jersey before leaving for Paris to stay with relatives of his mother's. By this time Emile had abandoned his career in market gardening and for the next five years he worked as a clerk in Paris. The death of his younger sister brought him back to Jersey, but it was only a short while before he took up his travels again and returned to Scotland, going first to Edinburgh, then to Dundee, before settling in Glasgow in mid 1852.[4]

L'Angelier had been living in Glasgow for three years by the time he and Madeleine began their affair. He was just 32 and she was barely 20. He was employed as a warehouse clerk in the firm of Huggins and Co., earning a modest 10 shillings a week. Despite his lowly status, income and address, L'Angelier's social circle included a number of Glasgow's prosperous and well connected. He counted among his friends Auguste de Mean, Chancellor to the French Consulate in Glasgow, several young scions of Glasgow's bourgeoisie, and Mary Perry, a well-heeled spinster who attended the same church as L'Angelier. His expansive social network derived partly from his outgoing and friendly manner, but also from the fact that he was most probably a social climber who cultivated friendships with his social superiors.

We do not know exactly when or where L'Angelier first set eyes on Madeleine (Figure 6). We do know that he pursued her indefatigably and was determined to get to know her. He inveigled his way into the company of a family who were acquaintances of the Smiths and on several occasions tried unsuccessfully to persuade them to introduce him to her. Eventually his persistence paid off and in the early spring of 1855 he managed to contrive an introduction to her through a mutual friend, Robert Baird. Did L'Angelier fall madly in love with Madeleine at first sight, or was he impressed by her social connections as much as by her looks? He certainly knew very little about Madeleine as a person. He had never been in her company, never spoken to her, knew nothing about her temperament, and while she had a pleasing appearance, she was not a great beauty. Given that she was the daughter of one of Glasgow's most prominent citizens, it is likely that he knew her by repute before he actually saw her. Perhaps it was the heady mix of physical attraction and social cachet which proved so seductive to L'Angelier.

Although L'Angelier is often portrayed as the pursuer in the relationship, Madeleine's correspondence suggests a more complex story. She claimed to have 'got an old note-book three years old, and in going over it many of the pages had the name L'Angelier on them. Now, that is long before I knew you' [29th April 1856]. Elsewhere she confirms that she had indeed watched and admired L'Angelier from as early as 1853 – 'You were looking so well today, just like the Mr L of three years back' [31st March 1856]. She later confessed: 'I shall tell you what I have never told you – while I was in town last winter the happiest part of the day was when I saw you pass in the morning. I watched you passing with pleasure' [7th May 1855]. At one point she even wrote: 'I did love you before we were introduced' [29th December 1855].

6 Madeleine, 1856

Madeleine and her sister Bessie frequently went out together and they often strolled along the busy shopping centre of Sauchiehall Street, sometimes shopping or simply engaging in the age-old mating ritual of 'seeing and being seen'. Madeleine's correspondence with Emile suggests that he had indeed caught her eye when she was out and about with Bessie: 'The way we used to look at you, I feel ashamed of it now' [18th May 1855]. His exotic appearance would probably have been attractive to Madeleine, who believed that she had finer sensibilities than her 'vulgar' Glaswegian contemporaries from whom she set herself apart, at least metaphorically. L'Angelier, with his aura of 'otherness', would have reflected Madeleine's own sense of alienation from those around her and her consummate belief in her uniqueness. The version of Madeleine as complicit in the development of the relationship, rather than being a passive prey, sits more readily with what we know of her personality; she was a spirited and wilful young woman who enjoyed the attentions of the opposite sex. It takes no great leap of the imagination to envisage her flirting with L'Angelier from a distance and encouraging his attentions.

The first meeting between Madeleine and L'Angelier took place in March 1855. He had spotted her entering a draper's shop in Sauchiehall Street with her sister Bessie. He persuaded his companion, Robert Baird, who was an acquaintance of the Smiths', to follow them into the shop, strike up a conversation and then invite them out to be introduced to him.[5] A flirtation rapidly blossomed and thereafter the two met up regularly in various venues around the city centre. The relatively free and easy nature of these early encounters did not last long. L'Angelier may have regarded himself as an eligible bachelor, but he was a seriously unsuitable match for a young middle-class woman whose social circle included many of the most eminent members of Glasgow society. Not only was he an impecunious clerk whose social origins were several notches beneath the Smiths', his French background was a further disability, even though, technically, he was a British subject. When Madeleine's parents found out about the relationship – 'Some friend was *kind* enough to tell P. that you were in the habit of walking with us' – they ordered her to stop seeing L'Angelier [3rd April 1855]. Madeleine wrote to him on 18th April, putting an end to the correspondence. Emile's response was to intercept Madeleine on Hill Street in Glasgow on 20th April and to pass her a note. This was a declaration of his love and a proposal of marriage. Madeleine later claimed that 'I did not expect a declaration of your love so soon. In fact I had been so used to flirtations that I thought it was all flirtation on your part' [8th December 1855]. It seems that she rapidly accepted him, for that night, she said, she became his intended wife [19th April 1856].

It seems that Madeleine's parents did not know the extent of her involvement. Nevertheless, her father was angry that she was 'walking out' with a gentleman who was outside of the family's social circle, while her mother berated her for seeking a liaison with a 'poor ... clerk' when she should 'look higher'. Her younger brother Jack, with whom she enjoyed a warm and friendly relationship, joined in the chorus of opprobrium. Even Bessie, who had initially been her co-conspirator, turned against her and took her parents' side. Faced with this tide of hostility to her relationship with L'Angelier, Madeleine did what came naturally to a headstrong and self-willed young woman; she lied and resorted to subterfuge, resolving to continue the relationship clandestinely.

The practical difficulties of the two lovers meeting up and the secretive nature of the relationship meant that their prime form of communication was the letters they wrote to each other. It is difficult to say how often Madeleine and L'Angelier actually met in the two years which the relationship lasted. However, they did write to each other frequently, on average about three times a week. Only two of L'Angelier's letters survive in draft, because Madeleine destroyed all of them, or returned them, presumably to ensure that they did not fall into the hands of her parents. However, L'Angelier meticulously saved all the letters written by Madeleine in her distinctive, large, florid handwriting.

She wrote the first letter from the family's summer residence in Row in the early spring of 1855. It was to be the beginning of an extraordinary correspondence. The letters provide an exceptionally rich source for the historian. They are all extant, just as they were written, with no intervening editorial hand to excise what has been perceived as uninteresting, repetitive, or which does not fit a particular narrative. During the two years of the correspondence the Crimean war raged, and yet national and international events are rarely referred to in Madeleine's letters, other than through a personal lens. Instead the letters are filled with the details of the everyday life of Madeleine and her family, although mainly they dwell on the intimacies and choreography of her relationship with L'Angelier, their plans for the future and how to overcome the obstacles to their true happiness.

Unlike other sources, private letters are often free from the layers of artifice which characterise more official historical sources. Private correspondence is a very intimate medium – particularly secret correspondence when the writers believe that no one other than the intended recipient of the letter will read it. Therefore it would be tempting to read these letters as unmediated sources which, like time capsules, can take us back to the past and provide a window into the hearts and minds of the writers. However, even such intimate correspondence as that between Madeleine and L'Angelier can be viewed as a cultural practice which conformed to a set of rules and conventions. Etiquette manuals and formal education provided advice and instructions on the correct form of letter writing, even love letters.[6] Moreover, letter writers drew on wider cultural conventions when constructing an identity for themselves in their letters. Dominant discourses of masculinity and femininity influenced how letter writers presented themselves and they might also draw on the devices of contemporary literature and other writing forms to help fashion an identity. Madeleine's letters certainly drew heavily on common tropes found in the romantic and melodramatic literature of the period when she was constructing a narrative of her relationship with L'Angelier. However, although her letters sometimes read as though heavily scripted, and reveal Madeleine's socially constituted self, they also reflect her own particular understanding and adaptation of cultural conventions. She might have employed certain rituals of letter writing and drawn on the narrative conventions of imaginative writing, but she adapted them for her own purposes and imprinted them with her own personality. So not only do her letters tell us something about the society in which she lived, they tell us how she interpreted, accepted and rejected the social rules and conventions of her world.

In the early stages of their relationship, Madeleine was keen to present herself as the dutiful and obedient pupil of L'Angelier. She constantly promised to obey him, to learn from him, and looked to him to correct her faults and provide her with moral and intellectual guidance. In her first letter to L'Angelier she bemoaned her lack of knowledge of botany – 'I wish I understood Botany for your sake' – and promised to try 'to break myself of all my *very* bad habits' [n.d. 1855]. Once their relationship had developed and they regarded themselves as engaged, Madeleine would refer to L'Angelier as 'My dear husband' and implore him 'to give your foolish wife advice so I may try and improve' [21st February 1856]. Eager to please him, she announced, as though catechised: 'I shall practice music and drawing and I shall read useful books. I shall not read Byron anymore. I shall not spend my time idly' [30th January 1856].

She seemed to take delight in parading her obedience to Emile: 'I shall be thine own dear dutiful wife'; 'I shall make it my study to please you in all things [...] it is the duty of a wife to study her husband in all things'; 'I shall love and obey you. It is my duty as your wife to do so. I shall do all you want me'; 'I shall feel happy in doing what you wish me to. To please you will be my greatest pleasure' [18th August 1855]. Madeleine was clearly drawing on a well-established model of conjugal idiom to represent their relationship. Her constant avowals of obedience and deference to L'Angelier were typical of an uncompromisingly patriarchal model of marital relationship which was beginning to be challenged by the middle of the century. She made it clear to L'Angelier that she would have no truck with the more egalitarian ideas about the relationship between men and women which were becoming popular among her contemporaries: 'I have a very poor opinion of my sex. There is no doubt man is a superior being and that is the reason why I think a wife should be guided and directed in all things by her husband' [6th August 1856]. Madeleine acknowledged that her views were not popular among other women in her circle: 'I get few ladies who agree with me. They all think "woman" is as good and clever as a man' [ibid.].

Madeleine may have been sincere in her protestations of undying obedience to Emile and her belief in his moral and intellectual superiority. However, there is every reason to believe that she was constructing an identity for herself which she thought Emile would approve of. The content of her letters should be seen as a product of the interaction between her and L'Angelier and as a response to his letters. Therefore to a great extent L'Angelier as well as Madeleine shaped what she wrote about and what she said. His two surviving letters reek of priggish self-righteousness and suggest a controlling personality: 'You are not stupid Mimi – and if you disappoint me in information, and I have cause to reproach you for it, you will have no one to blame but yourself. I have given you warning long enough to improve yourself'.[7] Judging from her responses to his letters, L'Angelier's idea of a love letter consisted of a series of instructions about how Madeleine should behave, what she should read and what she should wear. Two months into the relationship Madeleine was writing, 'I cannot promise always to wear high dresses but I shall have them made higher for the future. ... I shall not encourage any gentleman. I never tasted toddy in my life. The very smell of it is offensive to me. I think it is a most unladylike thing. It is only fit for men. Now in these three things I can please you. So in your next letter tell me another three' [7th May 1855].

Fryn Tennyson Jesse, a first-wave feminist, writing about Madeleine in the 1920s, was shocked by the eagerness with which Madeleine wanted to please L'Angelier and cited a litany of her declarations to illustrate Madeleine's submissiveness: 'I must be very stupid in your eyes. You must be disappointed in me. I wonder you like me in the least'; 'if I do anything wrong and you check me I shall never, never do it again. I shall be all you could wish. You shall love me and I shall obey you.'[8] Tennyson Jesse found this kind of behaviour so alien and unpalatable as to be pathological and came to the conclusion that Madeleine was an 'unconscious Masochist'.[9] Indeed Madeleine's letter of 24th November 1855 to L'Angelier seemed to provided irrefutable evidence for this analysis when she wrote, 'It will take a long time beloved to make me what I know you would like me to be [when married] you will be there to give me some grand rows.' The only way in which Tennyson Jesse could make sense of Madeleine's letters was to see her as relishing her role as slave to L'Angelier and L'Angelier equally happy to be master of her. The language of deference and submission which Madeleine used confirmed Tennyson Jesse's belief that the relationship between the two was based on classic sadomasochism whereby L'Angelier

gained sexual gratification from inflicting mental pain and Madeleine
gained it by enduring it:

> This sordid little Abelard [L'Angelier], playing the schoolmaster, this
> sensation loving Heloise, determined to be mastered into submission,
> were playing a game which would land them in self-disgust, but she
> found too alluring to be resisted.[10]

Tennyson Jesse's psycho-sexual interpretation of their relationship is colourful and partly convincing. However, the truth is probably
more prosaic. Madeleine was well aware of L'Angelier's opinions and
was probably telling him what he wanted to hear and tailoring her
discourses accordingly. The language of obedience and submission was
almost certainly performance, designed to please L'Angelier. Sometimes
Madeleine adopted another nineteenth-century discourse: that of angel
in the house. Echoing the prescriptive literature of the early nineteenth
century, she also promised to provide a haven for him where he would
not only be obeyed, but also be comforted and cosseted: 'When we are
married, it will be my constant endeavour to please you and to add to your
comfort. I shall try to study you, and when you are a little out of temper,
I shall try and pet you, dearest – kiss and fondle you' [3rd July 1856]. The
writers of advice literature to young women would have been heartened
by the way Madeleine seemed to embrace enthusiastically their dictums:
'Is a man not more happy with a wife? Is she not a happiness and comfort
to him? A solace to him in his sad hours?'[11]

As Tennyson Jesse observed, despite Madeleine's posturing, 'I know
from experience that the world is not lenient in its observations', she was
not a sophisticated young woman. Just 20, only recently returned from
finishing school and thoroughly bourgeois by birth and upbringing,
Madeleine had very little experience of anything, let alone how to conduct
a love affair. She therefore made full use of the cultural material to hand
in order to express herself and imagine her relationship with L'Angelier.
Not only did she draw freely from advice literature; her sources ranged
from religious imagery and language to contemporary novels. Sometimes
her prose had biblical echoes – 'I shall throw aside all my childish amusements and make a dutiful steady loving wife to you' [2nd March 1856],
or the letter she wrote to Emile asking his forgiveness for her 'unkind'
letter:

> Emile, I wish I could convince you that I live but for you alone …
> Whatever your lott [sic] may be, I shall be thine, and however humble
> your home shall be mine. I shall share your couch, no matter where.
> I have thought well of all this, and I shall never repine though my

husband is poor – no, it shall be my duty to make him happy, make him forget all the sorrows of the past, and look to a bright, happy future. [n.d. June 1856]

It is not surprising that the language used here is almost evangelical, with the reference to a 'bright, happy future' sounding very much like a nineteenth-century hymn. Madeleine, in common with most middle-class Victorians, would have been well versed in the language of the Bible. Evening family prayers and regular church attendance were staple features of the Smith household, albeit sometimes foisted upon a reluctant Madeleine.

On other occasions Madeleine seemed to be more influenced by the novels of the period. Sometimes her idiom was self-consciously melodramatic: 'I shall leave all, sacrifice friends, relations, family and everything for your sake, for the love I have for you' [June 1856]. Her letters are studded with this kind of artifice and often read as a well-scripted melodrama. Their tone suggests that despite L'Angelier's attempts to ensure that she read only 'improving' literature, she was familiar with the romantic fiction of the period.

Victorian fiction has acquired a reputation for its melodrama, complicated and unrealistic plots, unlikely coincidences and exaggerated sense of right and wrong. The fiction of the 'women's novelists' is usually singled out for this kind of criticism, exactly the kind of light reading which Madeleine may very well have indulged in. When Madeleine was growing up the fiction which was popular with her gender and class was the novels of the early generation of women's novelists such as Mrs Gaskell and Mrs Frances Trollope. In these stories, the reader was invited to feel sympathy for the 'fallen woman' of the lower classes, or was urged to beware of false emotion and the traps in which it might enmesh her. Essentially, these were didactic tales which appealed to the reader's sense of compassion and charity.[12] This type of novel had its fair share of melodrama and female heroines and would certainly have appealed to Madeleine. However, the way she positioned herself in terms of her relationship with L'Angelier suggests that her influences may have been that generation of women novelists of the 1850s and 1860s whose fiction was pejoratively labelled 'sentimental'.[13]

These novels usually followed a familiar pattern and had as their central character a female protagonist who was either misunderstood or victimised or felt persecuted by those around her. Sally Mitchell's neat contrast of the heroines of the earlier genre of women novelists and those of the 1850s and 1860s claims that 'The fallen woman of the 1860s is much more likely to be someone with whom the reader will identify, who

suffers, not because she is wrong but because everyone else is'[14] – a sentiment with which Madeleine would have strongly identified. When her
father ordered her to stop seeing L'Angelier, Madeleine complained how
alone and misunderstood she felt by each member of her family:

> [My father] hates you with all his heart. He despises you … he cares not
> for what I say … I do not think he understands the warm love of young
> people. He has forgotten all his youthful passions … [28th November
> 1856].

Of her mother she wrote: '[My mother] hates you. [She'd] rather see
you [sic] dead than, beloved, your wife' [29th January 1856]. When she
tried to talk to her brother Jack of her love for L'Angelier, his comment
was, 'I am ashamed of you. Do you know he is only a clerk in Huggins.'
According to Madeleine, Bessie, her erstwhile ally in her secret liaisons
with L'Angelier, resorted to humiliation, claiming that Emile had deliberately ignored Madeleine in the street, and crowing, 'I knew it would come
to this. I have no doubt that he is after some other girl. So you are cut. *So
you are cut.*'[15] At this stage in the relationship, Madeleine succumbed to
the combined pressure of her parents and siblings and wrote a letter to
L'Angelier resolving to break off their relationship. She cast them as persecuted lovers, their destiny frustrated by a cold, unyielding world ruled
by convention and moral codes rather than by love and passion. Both
the language and the narrative reek of classic Victorian melodrama and
sentimentality and one has a sense that Madeleine relished the opportunity to wallow in the role of star-crossed lover as she composed what she
intended to be her last letter to L'Angelier:

> Get married. You will never get one who will love you as I have done.
> I must banish your image from my heart. It almost breaks my heart to
> return to you your likeness and chain – *I* must not keep them. Write me
> a parting note – the last one I can ever receive …
>   Be happy. Forget me and may she whom you call your wife be a
> comfort unto you. May she love and esteem you. [n.d. September 1855]

Madeleine's letters frequently refer to her feelings of being misunderstood by her family and out of place in her city and her social circle: 'I am
weary of this sort of life – to be quiet and near you would please me better'
[18th May 1856]. Her response to her family's disapproval of their relationship was to write: 'I feel all alone in the world … I could die and no-one
would shed a tear for me but you' [n.d. 1856]. If Madeleine cast herself
as the alienated outsider constrained by family pressures and bourgeois
conventions, it was a role she took to heart and played with great relish.

So to a great extent Madeleine's letters tracked along certain well-defined paths, using conventional and ready-made modes of expression drawn from a variety of genres to communicate her feelings to L'Angelier. She also drew on established narrative forms to plot their relationship. Madeleine favoured telling the story of their relationship as a melodrama, and the roles which best fitted this narrative were those of doomed lovers. She may have been parroting a script for much of the time, but she also inscribed her own personality and motivations into that script, and the performance of it was entirely individual. Madeleine's letters tell us much about the public discourses of marriage, courtship, love and literary conventions. However, they are more than simply a product of these discourses. There are many instances when we glimpse another Madeleine: the flirt, the self-willed young woman, the dutiful daughter and the conventional young bourgeois. Therefore her letters may have conformed to various rhetorical modes, but they reveal more than mere artifice or the power of discourse to shape individual subjectivity. Nestling among the romantic and melodramatic forms is a clear indication of Madeleine's personality and emotional make-up and how she negotiated and interpreted dominant cultural forms.

For all her cloying phrases and simpering admiration for L'Angelier, the terms of affection which she most often uses – 'dear pet', 'sweet pet', 'dear little pet' – are tinged with a patronising tone. Were these terms of endearment common to all Victorian wives, or did Madeleine regard L'Angelier with more condescension than he would have cared to imagine? There were many occasions when Madeleine could not suppress the natural arrogance of her class and station, nor indeed her personality. Her tone was often peremptory. Even her in her first letter to L'Angelier, when she was intent on pleasing him and claiming to 'wish you were near us', she forbade him from visiting her at the family's summer residence, as her parents were probably going to be there. She instructed him, almost regally, 'So of course you do not come to Row. We shall not expect you' [n.d. 1855]. Issuing orders came relatively easily to Madeleine: 'I forgive you from my heart for that picture – never do the same thing again' [n.d. September 1856]. Although she often complimented him on his appearance, she was not averse to being critical of him. She asked him 'why do you wear such wide trousers? They quite spoil your neat little figure' [24th November 1855]. She informed him that his long hair made him look 'not near so good looking' [August 1856]. At times she could be staggeringly insensitive when puncturing his vanity: 'Is your cousin back yet. I should like to know him he is so like you *only a little better looking*' [n.d., c. April 1856].

Although much of the language which Madeleine used was deferential, the relationship between them was more complex than this suggests. Madeleine's letters are riddled with references to flirting, or rather, persuading L'Angelier that she had given up flirting: 'I shall not flirt. My flirting is all over now' [8th June 1855]. This is obviously a response to repeated injunctions by L'Angelier that she remain faithful to him: 'I feel confident you will trust me with society. I made a promise to you that I would not flirt that promise I shall keep' [15th June 1855]. However, even a superficial reading of the letters suggests that Madeleine was engaging in more than mere compliance. She was an inveterate flirt and she squandered few opportunities to remind Emile of the fact. Her frequent references to flirting were probably a ploy to make him jealous rather than to reassure him. On one occasion, when L'Angelier had chided her about her conduct, she assured him that she 'had flirted with no one this year'. Madeleine realised that this was no great testimony to her fidelity, as it was only 14th January, so added in parenthesis: '(or rather since we were engaged.)' [14th January 1856]. Her denials of having flirted are usually set alongside references to the attentions she had been receiving from rival suitors: 'I got 4 such pretty valentines this morning. I don't know where they came from and I don't care'; 'I write to one or two gentleman friends – but if you wish it I shall give it up' [14th February 1856]. If her intention was to quell Emile's jealousy rather than inflame it, it is unlikely that she would have made so many references to the fullness of her social calendar and the many young men she encountered. Somewhat disingenuously, she complained to him of the many visitors who came to see the family at their summer house in Row:

> We have had a great many friends with us last week (four young men) (Englishmen) but I tried not to flirt with them. I did not tell you how much I enjoyed my visit to the Trossachs. I never enjoyed a trip more (it would have been perfect if you had been with me). [8th August 1855]

> Living in the house with me are two very smart young fellows, both of them 6 feet tall you know they won't please my fancy. [31st January 1856]

Small of stature, and some might say no longer particularly young, L'Angelier must have seethed inwardly at this well-aimed barb. However, Madeleine excelled at fanning the flames of Emile's jealousy and relished in goading him, albeit under the cloak of innocent tittle-tattle. The festive season was a particularly active social period for the Smith family, and thus one when it was difficult for the two to meet. Madeleine was only too happy to keep L'Angelier abreast of her activities:

McK has been with us this evening – came in without invitation. Papa seemed pleased – he has got the length of calling him 'John'. What shall be the next. Thank God he leaves in two weeks. Everyone is speaking to me about him. I cannot fancy why they have fixed me. It used to be B [Bessie]. He is to dine with us on Wednesday ... I do not intend to go to the Ball in January – I shall go out as little as I can. I dislike so many parties now. I believe we are to have a small dance on Wednesday. [30th December 1855]

The list of her references to her active social life and the 'young gentlemen' who populated it, is lengthy: 'I have not kissed McKenzie since we have become engaged' [n.d. April 1856]; 'I write to one or two gentlemen friends' [18th June 1855]; 'When at Loch Katrine I had a most beautiful flower sent to me, one of the waiters brought it to me, but I fancy you would think it *flirting* if I took it so I left it in the Hotel' [8th August 1855]; 'dear Emile I have been very bad this week. I have never gone to bed till long after 12. But I know you will pardon me' [8th July 1855]. One year into their relationship she wrote to L'Angelier: 'Trust me I shall not flirt this summer. I have had enough of it' [25th April 1856]. Despite her 'reassurances' to him that 'I am behaving so well just now sweet pet as you would like to see me, no flirting' [23rd July 1856], Emile, understandably, was not convinced and repeatedly questioned her about her flirting. In view of her confession that she was 'easily led away by foolish temptations', his suspicions are perhaps unsurprising [30th March 1856].

Although Madeleine was born to flirt, this intricate dance with Emile's emotions cannot be explained solely by her coquetry. Flirting seemed to be part of the ritual of courtship, at least among Madeleine's contemporaries. The period of courtship was one in which a woman, however briefly, reigned supreme.[16] She was the one who was sought after, while the man had to prove his commitment and his worthiness as a successful suitor. For some women, like Madeleine, the temptation to capitalise on this welcome if fleeting reversal of gender power relations was too great and they may have abused their temporary ascendancy and indulged, as L'Angelier complained of Madeleine, 'in playing with affections ... pure and undivided'.[17]

What Madeleine meant by 'flirting' is not entirely clear. The behaviour which constitutes flirting is not only culturally specific, but varies from individual to individual. A quiet smile or raised eyebrow may be deemed outrageous flirting by one person and common courtesy by another. We do know that by 'flirting' Madeleine meant more than simply chatting with the opposite sex: 'I will be quite civil but won't flirt' [3rd July 1856]. Whatever behaviour she deemed to be flirting, the intention was clear: to attract the attention of men. She and her sister Bessie enjoyed indulging in this form of sexual teasing. Affecting the voice of a repentant sinner, Madeleine confessed to Emile that:

> I shall do all I can to prevent my sister being fast – alas Emile that was what put me in such a conspicuous place in the mouths of young men at one time we tried to make ourselves conspicuous and we liked to get talked of by gentlemen. If I did succeed in that – and I assure you I am sorry for it now – I never did any other thing but flirt and I do regret it much. I weep to think of my folly. [26th June 1856]

In order to vaunt her virtuousness, she drew attention to Bessie's persistent bad behaviour: 'B. still likes to be talked of – a young gentleman Harvie who has been staying with us (from Stirlingshire) told her on Friday night that she was spoken a good deal of and not in the best way – meaning she was a flirt' [26th June 1856]. However, according to Madeleine, Bessie shrugged off this reproach: 'She told him she was delighted to hear of it and that she would do all in her power to get more spoken of.' Either Bessie revelled in her bad reputation or she was possessed of a waspish tongue.

Her response provided Madeleine with another opportunity to pose as redeemed and repentant: 'Fine character this. I am sorry for her, but she will live to regret it all as I have done.' Once again Madeleine was providing L'Angelier with exactly what he wanted to hear. Was he convinced of her fidelity and devotion to him? Madeleine's responses to his letters suggest that he was perennially anxious about her behaviour and not entirely convinced of her ingenuousness. He complained perceptively: 'Sometimes I do think you take no notice of my wishes and desires, but say "yes" for mere matter of form.'[18]

L'Angelier and Madeleine regarded themselves as 'engaged' from very early on in the relationship and set their wedding date for September 1856. It seems to have been fairly common practice among courting couples to become engaged. Yet it did not necessarily signal serious intent to marry. Both L'Angelier and Madeleine had professed to have been engaged before. It is likely that these engagements were unofficial 'understandings' to which sometimes only the 'betrothed' couple were privy. She warned L'Angelier not to mention to her father that she had once been engaged: 'Don't mention my previous engagement to him' [September 1855]. On the other hand, L'Angelier's previous engagements had been common knowledge. On one occasion he had been engaged to a young woman from Fife, who had broken it off in favour of someone else. According to the accounts of his acquaintances at the time, he talked of having a broken heart and committing suicide, although he remained hale and hearty enough to become involved with several other women and 'engaged' to at least one other. Madeleine told L'Angelier that she had previously been engaged, but she was anxious to assure him that it was not the 'real thing': 'I do not wish you to mention to me that I was engaged before. Mention it to *no one*. You are my first and only love. I was very foolish at one time – it was all my own fault – no-one was to blame but myself' [24th August 1855]. She had previously told him that she had 'loved before but I never loved one better than you. When I do set my affections on anyone I am true to them' [18th May 1855].

Her engagement and love affairs may have been fabrications on her part and a way of proving her credentials as an experienced paramour rather than an ingénue. However, once she realised that L'Angelier was not impressed by her romantic history, she had to recast quickly the episode as a mistake and contrast it with her 'true love' for him. Whether or not Madeleine had been 'engaged' previously, she made frequent references to acquaintances who had been engaged: '[Minnoch] had a second-rate looking girl with him of the name of Christie. John McKenzie was engaged to her for two years' [19th December 1856]; while she informed L'Angelier that 'Miss Grierson is engaged to a clergyman' [21st December 1855].

A common function of engagements was to provide a proving ground to test the depth of the lovers' affection. But they could also serve as a mechanism to sanction the kind of intimacies between young people which would otherwise have occasioned censure. When Christina Haggart, Madeleine's maid, recounted to the court that her fiancé Duncan McKenzie had visited her in her bedroom, as if by way of justification she remarked to the procurator fiscal: 'I am engaged to be married to him on June next.'[19] In the eyes of Madeleine and Emile, their engagement probably permitted them physical and verbal intimacies which would have been otherwise unacceptable. During their 'engagement' they addressed each other as husband and wife: 'My Own Beloved Darling Husband'; 'Ever thine, thy own fond wife'; 'My Dearest and Beloved Wife, Mimi'. The use of these terms suggests that they regarded their relationship as intimate as any married couple's and thus paved the way for its consummation.

The notoriety of the Madeleine Smith case arose as much from the revelations of their sexual encounters as from the fact that the young daughter of a respectable and prosperous businessman had been accused of murder. However, in the first nine months or so of their relationship Madeleine's letters are full of the typical innocent, romantic exchanges one would expect from a young woman in the throes of a love affair: 'My love for you is now past expression. I dote on you' [16th October 1855].

She and Emile exchanged 'likenesses', trinkets and locks of hair, and she revelled in telling him how her love for him overshadowed everything else and dominated her waking and sleeping hours: 'I forget so many things ... Mama often says she is sure I am in love' [8th August 1855].

During the first summer of their affair they were able to meet only irregularly. Madeleine was based at the family's summer residence in Row, although she made occasional forays into town to visit friends and attend functions and various social events. On one of these visits she was able to meet L'Angelier secretly and have tea with him at his friend Miss Perry's house. However, most of their meetings were at Row, in the large grounds of the family home, late at night when everyone had gone to bed. These assignations left plenty of scope for the two to indulge their romantic passion for each other. However, at this stage the evidence suggests that their encounters were well within the limits of conventional courtship.

By the time Madeleine had returned to Glasgow in November for the winter season, there are indications that L'Angelier was encouraging Madeleine to be less inhibited in the expression of her feelings for him: 'I shall try and not appear shy to you. I will be frank with my dear little husband' [24th November 1855]. By December she was more explicit about physical intimacy and referred to him 'fondling' her, while in January 1856 she wrote to him in the early hours of the morning: 'I can fancy you in bed asleep. I wish I were aside you.' It was during this period that Madeleine would on occasion take Emile inside the house at India Street when her parents were away. Her maid, Christina Haggart, was usually her accomplice in arranging these daring trysts. On at least one occasion Madeleine used Christina's bedroom to entertain L'Angelier, and there is a suggestion that they also made use of the bed to indulge in some petting: 'I am to sleep with B tonight, dear Emile knows who I would rather sleep beside, do you pet. I shall receive no embrace this night, no dear bosom to lay my head on. Some day pet' [9th April 1856]. In these early months of 1856 L'Angelier was certainly encouraging her to experience the delights of a full physical relationship. However, she valiantly resisted his attempts at seduction: 'I shall not yield to you, you shall marry me pure and innocent as the day in which I was born. You shall never deprive me of my honour, I shall be firm on this point. Dearest I know you shall love me better for it. August or September shall soon come, how I long for that time to pass' [n.d. 1856].

In the spring and summer of 1856, when Madeleine and her family had taken up residence once again in Row, Emile's visits seemed to become more frequent. As in the previous year, they met up in the extensive grounds of the house, late at night when the rest of the family was

7 The path which L'Angelier took to meet Madeleine in the grounds of *Rowaleyn*

asleep (Figure 7). Not only were they able to meet in the grounds: as we have seen, Madeleine was even able to take him into her bedroom on the lower ground floor of the house. There was a brief period of anxiety when her parents decided she should be moved to one of the upstairs bedrooms when she contracted a chest cold. Madeleine, however, managed to forestall them.

During April and May her letters became increasingly explicit about their physical relationship, and although they had still not consummated their relationship, it was clear that they were indulging in serious foreplay, which gave both of them pleasure: 'My sweet husband how I shall kiss you and pet you. So you promise only to *love* me once a night make no such promises – I shall never ask you to *love* me but when *you feel inclined* – so if you kill yourself it shall be your own doing my sweet fond husband' [18th May 1856]. Less than a week later Emile visited Row again and, in spite of the cool night air, they enjoyed another passionate encounter:

> truly glad to see you last night. My husband, my own true husband, I am your wife. No-one can ever separate us now ... last night I did burn with love – but we were good – we withstood all temptations. Well it is better. Some day we may *love* without fear or risk. We shall then be happy. I trust you got no cold. I got none, CH had hot coffee for me when I got in. I am sure I don't know what I should do without her. [23rd May 1856]

Their love making had obviously bordered closely on full consummation and had left L'Angelier wondering whether Madeleine had had other lovers. It also opened the door to more frank exchanges about physicality:

> You could not write too free for me your wife. No darling it is not too free. I am very well, not the least pain now. I shall tell you when I am *ill*. Darling we were wrong, but God I trust shall forgive me – I loved you so. My heart burned with love for you. I swear to you I never was intimate with any other but you. Any love I ever felt was a childish love and farther than a long time ago young gentlemen giving me a kiss I never was intimate with any one. [28th May 1856]

Madeleine's reference to being '*ill*' is probably a reference to menstruation and a response to L'Angelier asking her to tell him when she had her period as a sign that she was not pregnant. At their next meeting at Row on the evening of 6th June, Madeleine's resolve to wait until marriage before having sexual intercourse with Emile failed her. The letter she wrote to him after they had made love was remarkably explicit: 'I did not bleed last night, but [had] a good deal of pain during the night.' She went on to express the pleasure and enjoyment she had experienced, betraying only a hint of shame at having breached the ultimate sexual taboo for respectable single women: 'Beloved, if we did wrong last night, it was in the excitement of our love. Yes, beloved, I did truly love you with my soul. Oh, if we could have remained, never more to have parted, But we must hope the time shall come' [7th June 1856]. If there was any regret on Madeleine's part at making the ultimate sexual transgression, it was not enough to prevent the sexual liaison continuing, nor was it solely at Emile's behest.

It was almost one month before they were able to meet up again and Madeleine took the unprecedented step of taking Emile into her room at Row on the basis that she was afraid of being seen outside. They once again had sexual intercourse, and although Madeleine expressed concern that she might become pregnant – 'We must not indulge again. What if anything was to occur – what would they say' – she also confessed: 'Darling it is hard to resist the temptations of Love. My heart burns this night with love for you. I grow excited while I write to you' [3rd July 1856]. Her subsequent letters to Emile reveal a healthy appetite for *love*: 'Oh! to be with you this night. But I fear I should ask you to *love* me, and that would not do. No no we must not till we are married. It is hard to restrain one's passions' [15th July 1856]; 'You will *love* me but I suppose I must not be too hard on my little husband or would kill him in no time' [27th October 1856]. At the end of October she complained that her lips were painful from kissing so often, but a few days later she informed him: 'Lips all right. I wish I could get them bad in the same way this night' [3rd November 1856]. Far from reluctantly succumbing to pressure from an insistent lover, once Madeleine had taken that final step, she exhibited a lusty appetite for intercourse: 'Oh to be with you – to have you loving me. I fear we shall get very thin from want of sleep, but we shall be happy' [n.d. 1856].

The only respect in which Madeleine seems to conform to the cultural stereotypes of a Victorian of her gender and class is in her penchant for euphemisms. Although she talked frankly and freely about sex, her language was never sexually explicit or coarse. She used 'ill' to mean menstruation, 'love' underlined, italicised or in capital letters to denote sexual intercourse, or alternatively she would talk of being 'intimate'. However, every time and culture has its own forms of euphemism. Even modern-day society, which is regarded as open and liberal in terms of attitudes to sex, has its own stock of euphemisms: 'going to bed' with someone; 'period' or the 'curse' for menstruation. Victorians may have been excessively euphemistic. However, this is not the same as being repressive and it is perhaps the conflation of euphemism and repression which has given the Victorians their reputation for being a sexually repressed society.

When excerpts from the letters were read out at Madeleine's trial, Victorian society was shocked to the core. It was not the fact that a woman had enjoyed sexual intercourse which caused the collective sexual frisson. Many scholars have long debunked the myth that the Victorian woman was passionless or regarded sexual gratification as something which she provided rather than received.[20] However, if women enjoyed sexual intimacy it was expected that it would be confined to the marital bed, as would any expressions of sexual fulfilment. But here was a young, unmarried, middle-class woman not only indulging in and enjoying premarital sexual intercourse, but writing about her experience in candid and sensual terms. Rarely were so many Victorian sexual taboos simultaneously and publicly broken. We cannot know whether Madeleine was *sui generis* in terms of her experience of premarital sexual relations. She certainly was not unique in her unqualified enjoyment of them, nor did she regard herself as such. The evening after she had displeased Emile by refusing his sexual advances she wrote, 'It was a punishment to myself to be deprived of your *loving me*, for it's a pleasure, no one can deny that. It is but human nature. Is not every one that *loves* of the same mind?' [14th August 1856].

Emile was twelve years older than Madeleine, more experienced in liaisons with the opposite sex and a 'foreigner'. *Ipso facto*, at her trial there was a strong body of opinion which saw Madeleine as the innocent victim of a heartless seducer. In the absence of L'Angelier's 'voice' it is difficult to know what kind of man he was. We can gain some glimpses into his personality through the prism of her letters and from the two letters which he wrote to her in draft form. They do not paint an edifying picture. He emerges as an insecure but controlling figure who was determined to make an advantageous marriage. He had already had one unsuccessful attempt at marrying someone better off: several acquaintances spoke of his disappointment over a broken relationship with a lady from Fife. When living in Edinburgh in the early 1850s he appeared to those in the same lodgings as 'a vain, lying fellow … very boastful of his personal appearance, and parties admiring him, ladies particularly. He boasted of his high acquaintances repeatedly, and the high society he had moved in.'[21] Yet the letters suggest that he was not simply a gold digger and had some genuine affection for Madeleine, although one wonders whether his love would have remained constant if she had been disinherited and disowned by her family.

The copy of a letter which L'Angelier had written to Madeleine after their first full sexual encounter provides some illuminating insights into his personality and motivation. In the first instance, the fact that he had kept a copy suggests a lack of spontaneity and that the letter had been carefully drafted with a specific purpose. In his opening sentence he expressed regret at what had happened but made it clear that he did not accept sole responsibility: 'My dearest and beloved Wife Mimi, – Since I saw you I have been wretchedly sad. Would to God we had not met that night – I would have been happier. I am sad at what we did, I regret it very much.' Although he seemed to accept a portion of the blame – 'We did wrong. God forgive us for it. Mimi, we have loved blindly' – he went on to reproach Madeleine for submitting to him: 'Why Mimi, did you give way after your promises?' Adopting a tone of sorrow rather than anger he again scolded her later in the letter: 'I was not angry at your allowing me, Mimi, but I am sad it happened. You had no resolution. We should indeed have waited till we were married, Mimi. It was very bad indeed. I shall look with regret on that night.' In a staggering piece of self-exoneration, he concluded the recriminations by shifting the blame squarely onto the shoulders of Madeleine's parents: 'It is your parents' fault if shame is the result; they are to blame for it all.'

Despite his regret about having had sexual intercourse with Madeleine and his vow not to do so again until they were married, he continued to press his sexual advances upon her, and even became annoyed when she refused him: 'Emile you were not pleased because I would not let you *love* me last night. Your last visit you said "You would not do it again till we were married." I said to myself at the time, well, I shall not let Emile do this again' [14th August 1856]. Emile's unreasonableness knew no bounds. He was displeased when she would not submit to his sexual demands, yet when she acquiesced he castigated her for her lack of virtue: 'Yes, I did feel so ashamed after you left of having allowed you to see my (any name you please to insert). But as you said at the time, I was your wife' [14th August 1856].

L'Angelier capitalised on the fact that they had made love by telling Madeleine that she now had no choice but to marry him: 'You are right Mimi, you cannot be the wife of any one else than me.' He chivvied her to speak to her brother and her mother to convince them to take their side and plead their case to her father. When he was not resorting to moral blackmail – 'Think of the consequences if I were never to marry you. What reproaches I should have, Mimi. I shall never be happy again' – he simply threatened to leave her: 'Unless you do something of that sort, Heaven only know when I shall marry you. Unless you do, dearest, I shall have to leave the country ...' There is no doubting Emile's determination to marry Madeleine. What we do not know is whether love, social status or money was his main motivation.

Emile's two letters expose his sexual hypocrisy, but we also catch glimpses of other unredeemed features of his character which were to be repeatedly refracted through Madeleine's letters. He was self-pitying: 'I got home quite safe after leaving you, but I think it did my cold no good.' He was melodramatic: 'Truly dearest, I am in such a state of mind I do not care if I were dead.' And he could match Madeleine's attempts to arouse jealousy: 'I can assure you it will be many days before I meet such nice people as the Seaverights, especially the daughter. I longed so much to have introduced you to her, to see the perfect Lady in her, and such an accomplished young person.'

However, it is the controlling aspects of L'Angelier's character which are most striking and which repeatedly surface in the letters. Indeed the leitmotif of their relationship is Emile's attempts to control Madeleine's behaviour. To some extent this can be explained by his insecurity, which may have been part of his psychological make-up, but which was undoubtedly exaggerated by the circumstances of their relationship. Madeleine had a large social circle and an extremely full social calendar. If she chose to, she could have been out almost every night of the week. Indeed, there were weeks when this was the case. Her family also entertained frequently, sometimes on a large scale. Emile, on the other hand, although gregarious, had a more limited social circle. He also lacked the means to match Madeleine's social activities. While she was gracing the floors of the city's ballrooms, attending concerts and plays and entertaining the soldiers of the 72nd Regiment, he admitted that his evenings were often 'very long and dreary'. His powerlessness over how she spent most of her time, coupled with the knowledge that she was frequently in the company of young men of her own station and class, no doubt compounded his insecurities and anxieties.

The list of 'do's and 'don't's which he issued to Madeleine is not only endless but comprehensive. Barely had their relationship begun than he was interrogating her about her behaviour and chiding her for using 'fast expressions' [16th July 1855]. He was particularly exercised about her going out to balls and socialising:

> your *cross* letter I have read about a dozen times – I shall often read that letter, it shall do me good to read it ... Allow me to correct you – the last Ball I did not go because I knew *you do* not *want* me. It was *not* that I could not go for at the last hour I was asked to go not only by Papa, but by a Party. But for your sake dearest I did not go. [28th March 1856]

In a statement more honoured in the breach than in the observance she promised: 'I trust never again to incur your displeasure by going to a Glasgow Ball' [30th March 1856]. Once they had consummated their relationship, L'Angelier became more insistent that Madeleine should curb her socialising and behave as a married woman and not a single one:

> We must not be separated all next winter, for I know, Mimi, you will be as giddy as last. You will be going to public balls, and that I cannot endure. On my honour, dearest, sooner than see you or hear of you running about as you did last, I would leave Glasgow myself. Though I have truly forgiven you, I do not forget the misery I endured for your sake ...
>
> ... I cannot help doubting your word about flirting. You promised me the same thing when you left for Edin., and you did nothing else during your stay there ... I do trust you will give me no cause to find fault again with you on that score, but I doubt very much the sincerity of your promise. Mimi the least thing I hear of you doing, that day shall be the last of our *tie*, that I swear. You are my wife, and I have the right to expect from you the behaviour of a married woman – or else you have no honour in you; and more, you have no right to go anywhere but where a women [*sic*] could go with her husband.

In the circumstances, one might have expected L'Angelier to be jealous, particularly when he knew that his grip on the relationship was tenuous. However, it is the extreme nature of the demands which he imposed which seems abnormal. He took exception to Madeleine and

Bessie going about town, was outraged that when they visited Edinburgh they had no chaperone, and even made her promise to confine her outings into town to mornings. His behaviour became more controlling once they had made love and he seems to have issued a series of questions and demands which obviously began to irritate her:

> Now I shall answer your questions.
> I have not flirted for long so won't do it.
> I shall study watercolours if I can get P. to allow me. I shall study anything you please to name.
> I shall not go to a Glasgow Ball without asking your consent. Is that fair?
> I cannot promise to go out only twice a week.
> I shall go into Sauchiehall St, Buchanan St as little as possible and as early as I can.
> I cannot promise not to go with B. I must go out with her when I have no other one. Janet is at School (I do not think it fair for people to speak of B. as they do for she is not so bad. You may have heard wrong statements of her as your friends have misinformed you more than once regarding myself so they may of her)
> I shall write you as often as I can and as lovingly as I can but to tell the truth I cannot write so lovingly as others. [22nd August 1856]

He went to absurd lengths to control her: forbidding her from wearing certain kinds of clothing, reproving her for not practising her drawing and music daily, and most bizarrely, objecting to her going out rowing: 'I have never been out in a small boat since I promised.' Small wonder that Madeleine was driven to cry: '*Emile you are not reasonable*' [8th October 1856].

There is no doubt that L'Angelier must have found the situation intolerable. He was resolved to marry Madeleine, yet he was disapproved of by her family. Their meetings were limited to the occasional clandestine rendezvous, while Madeleine swanned around Glasgow enjoying the company of a host of young men many of whom her father, and perhaps Madeleine too, would have regarded as ideal suitors. Even in the light of these extenuating circumstances, his behaviour appears excessive.

Of course our impressions of L'Angelier are filtered mainly through Madeleine's construction of him in her letters. However, it is an impression which seems to be confirmed by his two surviving draft letters. He was clearly intent on procuring Madeleine as his wife and desperate to ensure that she did not slip out of his hands into those of a more financially and socially appropriate suitor. It is tempting to see him as a manipulative fortune hunter motivated by material gain rather than by romantic love.

However, perhaps his misfortune was that he was in thrall to both.

Did Madeleine tolerate his appalling conduct because she was deeply in love with him and was just as firm in her resolve to marry him? It is equally difficult to determine Madeleine's 'true' feelings for L'Angelier. Her letters are so layered with artifice that it is difficult to penetrate the performance aspect and discern how she really felt. At the beginning of the relationship Madeleine was probably infatuated with him. He was older, exotic in appearance and quite different from most of the young men she met. She claimed to regard Glasgow and Glaswegians as 'vulgar' and was probably flattered by the attentions of someone she considered as sophisticated and cosmopolitan. However, when her parents found out about the relationship only a few weeks after it had begun, she curtly wrote to him: 'I think that you will agree with me in what I am proposing, viz., that for the present the correspondence had better *stop*' [18th April 1855]. However, Emile managed to persuade her to continue with the relationship, and in the ensuing months Madeleine's feelings for him seemed to grow stronger. L'Angelier, meanwhile, was using every lever he could to induce her to tell her father about their relationship and intention to marry. He even considered taking a position in Lima, intending that Madeleine would accompany him, if they could not conduct their affair with the blessing of her family. While Madeleine made clear that she could not go with him to Peru, she responded as one would expect of a love-struck young woman, begging him to stay and declaring her undying love for him:

> For my sake do not go … I have not felt well since I got your last letter, and I try to appear cheerful before my family, and it is not easy to appear in good spirits when there is a pain at the heart. It will break my heart if you go away. You know not how I love you, Emile. I live for you alone. I adore you. I never could love another as I do you. Oh! Dearest Emile, would I might clasp you now to my heart. [4th September 1855]

The prospect of his imminent departure persuaded her to confront her father again and she promised to write to him, 'tell him all' and face his wrath: 'I shall try and bear with all the threats he will hold out – I am not easily frightened – he will find out that his Daughter has a mind of her own' [11th September 1855]. She seems to have been genuine in her resolve to confront her father and issued L'Angelier with a raft of instructions on how to deal with what she predicted would be an implacable père Smith:

> I shall write Papa on Monday. – so he will get it on Tuesday. He will most likely send for you. Be careful what you tell him – not a word about seeing me on Sundays. Don't mention my previous engagement to him

Don't show him any of my letters. Burn them all. No eye shall ever see mine from you. Do keep cool and composed when you see him. I know his temper – fiery like my own. [15th September 1855].

Although Madeleine kept her promise to inform her father of the relationship, she clearly had to steel herself to do it. In the following forty-eight hours the flurry of letters she sent to L'Angelier reveals her inner turmoil and her conflict of loyalties:

Dearest Emile,
I have written this morning and will post it with this. I have not slept for two nights –thinking of what we are to do. He will send for you. He will be angry. But do keep your temper for Mimi's sake – allow as I have done that we have been to blame in not informing him of it before this. We shall succeed I am sure. God grant we may. For we love each other is not that enough. [Posted 18th, probably written 17th September 1855]

Despite these protestations that love would conquer all, her resolve crumbled when faced by her family's opposition and she executed a complete volte-face:

Dear Emile can you ever forgive me – But you know it is not my fault – Papa would not hear of it. We part … – Burn all my letters before you leave. I hope you will succeed in the land you are going to. I shall ever look back on the days spent with you as the happiest of my life …
I was wrong to conceal it so long from Papa. He has been most kind to me – say not a word against him to anyone … You who I lived for art lost to me forever ah forever …
I was forbid to write to you. But I could not. I write without their knowledge at present. Dearest Emile you only think me cool but if you only knew what I have suffered you would forgive me. It was not intended that we should ever be happy. I shall love you as long as I live. Has Papa written to you? I never asked any questions at him – adieu for the present love.
Believe me Your
Mimi
[18th September 1855]

Her next letter, probably written a few hours later was an anguished *cri de coeur* in which she begged Emile to contact her and suggested that she had not reconciled herself to the relationship's ending:

For the love of Heaven write me, if it should only be a line. I know you must hate me, write me by return. No-one shall know. Perhaps Papa has written you (I know not) telling you never more to write me. He

shall never know, I have suffered much. It can't be helped. Hope – we
may yet be happy.
Love your Mimi
[18th September 1855]

Yet within twenty-four hours she despatched another letter, this one
an uncompromising farewell letter. The pet names and effusive endearments were dispensed with and she signed off with a stark 'Madeleine'.

Farewell dear Emile a last fond farewell. My Papa shall not give his
consent. I have given my word of honour – I shall have no more
communication with you. Go to Lima. Forget your Mimi. Your once
loved Mimi. [...] Go, go to Lima. May God prosper you is my prayer.
As a parting favour may I ask that you will burn all my letters the day
your receive this do it. Adieu. I shall never see you more – no never ...
Madeleine
Mid-night

In the same post Madeleine sent a letter to Mary Perry confirming that
the affair was over:

Dearest Miss Perry,
Many kind thanks for all your kindnesses to me. Emile will tell you I
have bid him adieu. My Papa would not give his consent, so I am in duty
bound to obey him. Comfort dear Emile. It is a heavy blow to us both. I
had hoped some day to have been happy with him, but, alas, it was not
intended. We were doomed to be disappointed.
... I hope and trust he may prosper in the step he his about to take.
I am glad now that he is leaving this country, for it would have caused
me great pain to have met him.
Think my conduct not unkind. I have a father to please, and a kind
father, too.

These letters suggest that not only was she resigned to the relationship's ending, but that she had reached a truce with her father and was
content to return, metaphorically, to the bosom of her family and assume
the role of a dutiful and loving daughter. What are we to make of this
emotional see-saw and Madeleine's successive changes of heart? Mary
Hartman has suggested that the scenarios of Madeleine confronting her
father were entirely manufactured and designed to give her an excuse
to end the relationship.[22] It may have taken Madeleine some time to
pluck up the courage to confront her father and, given her penchant for
dissembling, she may very well have lied to L'Angelier about the timing
and details of her confession to her father. Certainly L'Angelier often
doubted her veracity and, in his draft letter in response to her breaking

off the relationship, he cryptically commented, 'I cannot put it out of my mind that yet you are at the bottom of all this'. However, there is no doubt that Madeleine did tell her father that she and L'Angelier were having a relationship. In his precognition statement James Smith admitted that in September 1855 he had been 'made aware by Madeleine that L'Angelier was paying some attention' and that he had advised her to discontinue the correspondence. He went on to say that he assumed that she had broken with L'Angelier, as he heard nothing more of him until March 1857.[23]

Thus, it would seem that at this stage in their relationship Madeleine was genuinely torn between the opposing pulls of her family and her romance with L'Angelier. Emile's response to Madeleine's farewell letter was full of self-righteous recriminations about her lack of honour, and deceit:

> Madeleine,
> In the first place, I did not deserve to be treated as you have done. How you astonish me by writing such a note without condescending to explain the reasons why your father refuses his consent. He must have reasons, and I am not allowed to clear myself of accusations [...] Never, dear Madeleine, could I have believed you were capable of such conduct. I thought and believed you unfit for such a step. I believed you true to your word and to your honour [...] What am I to think of you now? ...
>
> Madeleine, you have truly acted wrong. May this be a lesson to you: never trifle with anyone again.

Madeleine seemed to take these censures to heart and regretted her decision to end the relationship. Her letters to L'Angelier in the ensuing weeks are filled with self-admonishments:

> I have not known a moments happiness since I wrote that cruel note. I thought in that I had told you the whole proceedings. But I was mad that night, I knew not what I did. I had not been in bed for two nights, I wrote to Papa 'I have pledged my word to become the wife of Mr L'A' – that we had been engaged for some months. He would not hear of such a thing. He did not say a word against you. I was in a passion at the time. I have regretted it every moment since. It was cruel of him. It is a shame for a parent to dictate the affections of his child.
>
> You are my idol – your name I breathe to Heaven – your face is in my dreams ... It is my father's doing, not mine. If I could only break that promise made to him. I would escape with thee. I would do anything for thee dearest. I would work for thee. I would put up with anything for thy sake. I would leave friends who would never look at me more ... I hate myself. I have cursed the day of my birth. Send me not back my small gifts – keep them. I have grieved much I sent you back your likeness and

that lock of hair I wore next my heart. My conscience tells me I have not done my duty to Emile. [...] Could you love me once again?
I meditated self-destruction rather than break my word to you. But that would have incurred greater wickedness. [n.d. 1855]

In this and subsequent letters she does sound genuinely distraught at the prospect of losing L'Angelier and appears to have decided to disobey her father's wishes to end the relationship:

it was cruel of my father, I can never forgive him for the being whom I adored to say he would separate us – all because you are not rich [...] Write me, it is my only joy and comfort. Your likeness is my greatest sorrow, everything was done in such a hurry that night. Send me your lock of hair to beat against my broken heart [...] My love for you is past expression. I dote on you [...] I am truly wretched for my past conduct. [October 1855]

L'Angelier obviously took some persuading, given the numerous reassurances she made in her letters, 'My last letter was not filled with rash promises. But I cannot blame you if you will not believe any more of my promises ...' [19th October 1855]; 'How can I prove to you that I love you? I fear you doubt' [10th November 1855].

Despite the fact that Madeleine was kept under the watchful eye of her parents and forbidden to go out alone, their relationship resumed. In fact, once Madeleine and her family went back to Glasgow for the winter season, it took on a new dimension. Emile and she met more frequently, talked more of their impending marriage, and Madeleine expressed her increasing disenchantment with her parents, whom she portrayed as the obstacles to their love:

Can you blame me my own dear Emile when I confess to you that my love for my parents is cooling. Have they not given me cause to be cool, tried to prevent me loving you my ever dear Emile. [n.d. 1856]

It is true I owe some duty to my parents. I love them less and less each day. [3rd March 1856]

L'Angelier persisted in trying to persuade Madeleine to tell her parents that they intended to marry, but she did not have the stomach for further confrontations: 'I dread my Papa's second refusal. When he once says a thing no power on earth can change him' [16th November 1855]. Instead, she tried to convince Emile that they could marry without her parents' consent or blessing and that true love could overcome the 'want of riches':

I will never let [Papa] sell my affections. [December 1855]

I don't think what I am about to do is in the least wrong … It is not a sin to love a man though he is poor. [16th January 1856]

You may be poor but you are rich in love. [25th April 1856]

I have considered that we shall be poor but I know that happiness shall be found in our home and I don't care for any more outwards show. [31st May 1856]

[W]e shall be happy – and is it not that better a thousand times than wealth. [May 1856]

Although Madeleine was writing in a self-consciously romantic idiom and with her customary sense of melodrama and hyperbole, in this period of the relationship one has a sense that she was infatuated with Emile, despite the fact that he persisted in chiding and scolding her for any behaviour of which he disapproved. She referred frequently to their impending marriage, which was planned for September, and she indulged her romantic fantasies by imagining their life together:

To be your wife is my desire, to be the Mother to your child. [17th April 1856]

Some day darling we may have a cottage and a garden. [25th April 1856]

But humble as our home would be, we can be quite happy as if we were living in a large way, perhaps much more so, for we would only have ourselves to think of. To live quietly with you, seeing no-one but you … [18th May 1856]

I fear we shall spoil each other when we are married, we shall be so loving and kind. We shall be so happy, happy in our own little room. [14th June 1856]

Madeleine still balked at seeking her parents' consent and insisted that the marriage should be clandestine. However, she was more sanguine about her parents' recognising the marriage after the event. Such was her faith in their love for her that she was convinced that 'If we were married I don't think M and P would stand out. They must give in' [8th April 1856].

It was during this period that Madeleine and Emile's physical relationship began to develop. However, it was not long after they had first had sex that the tone of her letters began to change and one can detect a cooling in her affections. Her letters became more curt and sarcastic: 'If you wish to cut all the hair off your face, why then do it, but I am sure it won't improve your appearance in the least' [September 1856]. Even when her curtness was leavened with expressions of devotion, they were stilted and formulaic and read as though inserted merely for form. Her letter of 17th September was full of family gossip and desultory news in the midst of which she declared, 'I long to kiss you and lean on your bosom'. However, in the following sentence she immediately resumed her previous chit-chat:

> I must be in Glasgow soon. B will be with me, I must come as I want to get a new dress – but I don't wish to go up for a week or so – B. and some of them are at Loch Lomond – we have a lot of people in the house with us.

Given that Emile was based in Glasgow, he no doubt would have hoped for a little more enthusiasm from Madeleine for coming up to the city from Row. It is little wonder that he began to accuse her of being 'cool'. Her first response was to deny it and then to ask his forgiveness if she had been. Eventually she admitted, 'I have been very cool to you but you will forgive me I know you will sweet dear of heart'. Her defence was that she had been ill and 'indifferent to all things' [18th September 1856].

Despite Madeleine's frequent assertions that she valued love over riches, and her scathing comments about the bourgeois marriage market, '[In this cold unfeeling, thoughtless world] wealth is the ruling passion. Love is a second consideration, when it should be the first, the most important' [14th June 1856], she began to make allusions to Emile's lack of wealth: 'dear me dear Emile, have you only £50 from Huggins ... I thought you had £100 from H. How could I have made such a mistake? I wonder you stay for such a small sum. You should have much more' [11th September 1856]. She prodded him into thinking about leaving Huggins 'to get some situation with a larger income', and suggested that when he was visiting friends in England that he should try to get a position there. 'You dislike Glasgow and so do I' [September 1856]. She still referred to their impending marriage, but even as early as April 1856 she was discussing the housekeeping problems she would have when her maid left to be married in November, even though she and L'Angelier had planned to marry in September. September passed with no mention of a wedding, and by October she seemed to have abandoned any pretext of being on the point of marrying or eloping, when she wrote, 'I am to have a pony myself next summer.'

It was also during this period that the shadowy figure of William Minnoch assumed a more central role in Madeleine's letters. Minnoch was a junior partner in the firm of Houldsworth and Company, with whom the Smith family had social and business connections. He had first been mentioned in May 1856, when she had warned L'Angelier:

Darling there is an absurd report in Town at present, I have heard it from many. R. Anderson told it to Jack. That I am to be married to Mr Minnoch junior partner of the Houldsworths. He tried to get a house at Row but could not and he had taken the flat above us in Blythswood Square. I suppose it is these circumstances which have given rise to it. [18th May 1856]

Madeleine's speedy dismissal of the rumour before it came to L'Angelier's attention was designed to reassure him and she went on to mollify him with words of endearment and declarations of her undying love for him, 'My love for you has increased tenfold ... I shall love you as long as I live ... I am thine for life, only death shall separate us' [18th May 1856]. Although it might have seemed that she was protesting too much, at this stage Madeleine probably did not have any romantic interest in Minnoch. Her relationship with L'Angelier was at its most intense, physically and emotionally, and it is likely that she viewed Minnoch only as a family friend. Her father, however, almost certainly had other ideas.

The rumours persisted and by August 1856 L'Angelier was taking them seriously. Despite Madeleine's lofty denials that she and Minnoch were romantically involved, L'Angelier was not convinced and he forbade her to have any contact with Minnoch. Madeleine responded to his dictates by pointing out how unreasonable he was being:

I am truly sorry about the remarks regarding Minnoch – he is very pleasant to me and I cannot be rude to him – he is a great friend of P. I cannot promise not to go to his house as I know both of his sisters and I know very well he will be much with us during the winter, he will come often of an evening because both M and P asked to come downstairs to us whenever he pleased. Can I help this. It would look strange indeed if I were to leave the room when he came in or to ask P. to tell him not to come to the house. And if he should meet us in town this winter and walk by us, can I tell him to be off? No indeed I could not. [...] You must consider how I am placed. [31st August 1856]

Only a few days later she admitted that it was not merely politeness which prevented her from snubbing Minnoch and that she had changed her mind about him and thought he was 'so pleasant [that] he quite raised himself in my estimation'.

Although she and Emile continued their clandestine meetings at Row and Madeleine's letters continued to overflow with loving endearments to her 'sweet little husband', Emile's jealousy could not be assuaged and he continued to berate her for her lack of warmth and remonstrate with her for having broken off the relationship the previous year. Even their secret trysts at Row were marred by his carping and on one occasion he told her that he no longer loved her as he once did. This was probably designed to disconcert Madeleine, make her realise that his love was not unconditional, and that if she did not behave exactly as he wished her to, she might lose him. If this was so, it was a serious miscalculation. Madeleine wrote to him the following day, clearly weary of his constant reproaches, although she cloaked this in self-criticism. For the first time, she expressed doubts about their relationship and her ability to make him happy. She also confessed that she would not be able to meet him or write to him as often once she was back in Glasgow. The reasons she gave were logistical rather than related to any change in her feelings towards him. She still professed her undying love for him, but she was unsettled:

> Our meeting last night was peculiar. Emile you are not reasonable. I do not wonder at your not loving me as you once did. Emile I am not worthy of you. You deserve a better wife than I. I see misery before me this winter. I would to God we were not to be so near to Mr. M. You shall hear all stories and believe them. You will say I am indifferent because I shall not be able to see you much. I forgot to tell you last night that I shall not be able of an evening to let you in – my Room is next to B. and on the same floor as the front door. I shall never be able to spend the happy hours we did last winter. Our letters I don't see how I am to do. M. will watch every post. [...] I could not sleep all night. I thought of your unhappy appearance – you shed tears love – but I did not. Yes, you must think me cool – but it is my nature. I never did love any one till I loved you. – and I shall never love another. [...] I sometimes fancy that you are disappointed with me. I am not what you once thought I was. I am too much of a child to please you. I am too fond of amusements to please your fancy. I am too indifferent, and I do not mind what the world says, not in the least – I never did. [8th October 1856]

The relationship continued throughout the winter of 1856–57. Madeleine once again wrote of their impending marriage and even talked of eloping, suggesting February 1857 as a possible date. She informed L'Angelier that her maid, Christina Haggart, had agreed to send her possessions on to her [n.d. December 1856]. However, references to Minnoch cropped up with increasing frequency in her letters and, despite Madeleine's attempts to placate Emile, he was the source of repeated conflict between the pair. It was not just that Minnoch was mentioned more frequently in Madeleine's letters; he was also spending a good deal of time at the Smith household and escorting Madeleine to a number of social events that winter. She was very open about this, perhaps to forestall any objections on L'Angelier's part and ensure that he heard her version of the relationship before it came to his attention via the rumour mills. However, Madeleine's exasperation with Emile's constant rebukes erupted towards the end of December and she wrote:

> O why was I ever born to annoy you, best and dearest of men. Do you not wish you had never known me. I thought I was doing all I could to please you. But no. When shall I ever be what you wish me to be. Never! Never! Emile, will you never trust me – she who is to be your wife. You will not believe me. You say you heard 'I took M/ to the Concert against his inclination; I forced him to go.' I told you the right way when I wrote. But from your statement to-night you *did not believe my word.* Emile, I would not have done this to you. Every word you write or tell me I would believe. I *would not* believe every idle report. No, I would *not.* I would, my beloved Emile, believe my husband's word before any other. But you always listen to reports about me if they are *bad.* But you will think I am cross. I am not – but I feel hurted.

Madeleine's letters from January 1857 were sometimes rambling, often brief, and she seemed fretful and agitated. There were still the habitual endearments and references to their marriage, but she was finding excuses to postpone their wedding: 'I don't see the least chance for us, my dear love. Mama is not well enough to go from home – and I don't see how we could manage in Edinburgh, because I could not leave a friend's house without their knowing it. So, sweet pet, it must be put off till a better time' [23rd January 1857]. She also encouraged Emile to pursue a more active social life: 'Do, my dear Emile, go to the officers' Ball. It will do you good a little excitement' [16th January 1857].

Her letters became increasingly troubled and distraught:

> I never felt so restless and so unhappy as I have done for some time past [...] A dark spot is in the future. What can it be. Oh God keep it from us. [...] I weep, now, Emile, to think of our fate. If we could only get married and all would be well. But alas. Alas. I see no chance, no chance of happiness for me. [25th January 1857]

Madeleine knew only too well what the 'dark spot' was: the marriage proposal she was about to receive from William Minnoch. She also knew that her parents would never accept L'Angelier as her husband and that they had adroitly introduced Minnoch as a suitable match for her. In fact, Minnoch proposed on 28th January. Madeleine wrote to Emile soon after this, although she did not inform him that she was now engaged to another man. However, he either got wind of it or deduced it from her letter. In any case, something displeased him and he returned her letter. Madeleine seized the opportunity to break off the relationship:

I felt truly astonished to have my last letter returned to me. But it will be the last you shall have an opportunity of returning to me. When you are not pleased with the letters I send you, then our correspondence shall be at an end, and as there is coolness on both sides our engagement had better be broken. This may astonish you, but you have more than once returned my letters, and my mind was made up that I should not stand the same thing again. And you also annoyed me much on Saturday by your conduct in coming so near me. Altogether I think owing to coolness and indifference (nothing else) that we had better for the future consider ourselves as strangers. I trust to your honour as a Gentleman that you will not reveal any thing that may have passed between us. I shall feel obliged by your bring me [sic] my letters and Likeness on Thursday eveng. At 7 – be at the Area Gate, and C. H. will [take] the parcel from you. On Friday night I shall send you all your letters, Likeness etc. I trust you may yet be happy, and get one more worthy of you than I. On Thursday, at 7 o'C. [n.d. February 1857]

Madeleine softened the harsh tones of this letter in a postscript in which she told L'Angelier how much she had once loved him: 'I did at one time love you with heart and soul. It has cost me much to tell you this – sleepless nights, but it is necessary you should know.' She ended by wishing him well, but appealed to his sense of honour: 'I know you will never injure the character of one you so fondly loved. No, Emile, I know you have honour and are a Gentleman. What has passed you will not mention [...] Adieu.'

Madeleine was hoping that L'Angelier would act in accordance with the rules of etiquette for romantic relationships, which counselled that 'if a relationship is mutually broken off, all the love letters should be returned. To retain them is dishonourable.'[24] It was to prove a forlorn hope. L'Angelier did not respond to her letter and when she sent another curt, although polite, request for her letters to be returned he not only refused but issued a veiled threat to show them to her father. This drove Madeleine into a frenzy and she wrote him a long, hysterical letter begging him to return her letters:

Emile, for the love you once had for me, do nothing till I see you. For the love of God's sake, do not bring your once-loved Mimi to an open shame. [...] it would break my mother's heart. [...] Emile, for God's sake do not send my letters to Papa. It will be an open rupture. I will leave the house. I will die. Emile, do nothing until I see you. [...]

p.s. I am ill. God knows what I have suffered. My punishment is more than I can bear.

Do nothing till I see you. For the love of heaven, do nothing.

I am mad. I am ill

[9th February 1857]

Although L'Angelier immediately responded to this letter, he did not promise to return her letters, but asked to meet with her. Madeleine wrote back to him that same evening, once again throwing herself on his mercy and imploring him not to shame her:

> Emile, I have this night received your note. Oh, it is kind of you to write to me. Emile, no one can know the intense agony of mind I have suffered last night and today. Emile, my father's wrath would kill me; you little know his temper. Emile, for the love you once had for me do not denounce me to my P/. Emile if he should read my letters to you – he will put me from him, he will hate me as a guilty wretch. I loved you, and wrote to you in my first ardent love – it was with my deepest love I loved you. It was for your love I adored you. I put on paper what I should not. I was free, because I loved you with my heart […] If he or any other one saw those fond letters to you, what would not be said of me. On my bended knee I write you, and ask you as you hope for mercy at the Judgement [Day] do not inform on me – do not make me a public shame … for the love you once had to me do not bring down my father's wrath on me. […] But oh, will you not keep my secret from the world? Oh, will you not, for Christ's sake, denounce me? I shall be undone. I shall be ruined. […] I did love you, and it was my soul's ambition to be your wife. I asked you to tell me my faults. You did so, and it made me cool towards you gradually. When you have found fault with me, I have cooled – it was not love for another, for there is no one I love. My love has all been given to you. My heart is empty, cold – I am unloved. I am despised. I told you I had ceased to love you – it was true. I did not love you as I did – but oh, till within the time of our coming to Town I loved you fondly. I longed to be your wife. I had fixed Feb[ruar]y. I longed for it. The time I could not leave my father's house I grew discontented, then I ceased to love you … Oh, Emile, will you in God's name hear my prayer. […] Oh, for God's sake, for the love of heaven, hear me. I grow mad. I have been ill, all day. I have had what has given me a false spirit. I had to resort to what I should not have taken, but my brain is on fire. I feel as if death would indeed be sweet …

Madeleine added a postscript agreeing to meet with Emile and telling him that she would wait and watch for him at her window until one o'clock in the morning. The language of this letter may have been florid and she was no doubt indulging her characteristic flair for melodrama when she claimed that her father would kill her if the letters were discovered. However, her panic does seem to have been genuine and, by her own admission, enough to drive her to drink. There was an element of dissembling, since she omitted any mention of Minnoch, but her confession that Emile's incessant fault finding made her 'cool' towards him has a ring of truth.

In spurning L'Angelier and opting for the more socially acceptable Minnoch, either she allowed propriety to triumph over sentiment or else, weary of L'Angelier's exacting demands, she lost her appetite for the drama of their clandestine affair. It seemed as though her dalliance with L'Angelier and the allure of the forbidden ('Perhaps if you had been well off, I would not have loved you as I do') could not withstand the censure of her parents, the compelling demand to make a good marriage and L'Angelier's endless criticisms and controlling ways. Despite breaching social conventions throughout their relationship, Madeleine seemed eventually to succumb to the powerful canons of bourgeois society, that money and breeding were the *sine qua non* of a successful marriage. Had she prized love over money and social respectability, she could have risked her parents' wrath, defied the social codes of her class and married L'Angelier. However, she might have found some difficulty in persuading L'Angelier to follow this course. His insistence from the beginning of their relationship, that they should seek her parents' approval, was based not only, if at all, on propriety. Emile was only too aware that if they married against the wishes of Madeleine's parents they risked social exclusion as well as financial hardship. Neither of these outcomes would have appealed to the socially aspirant L'Angelier.

Much ink has been spilled in trying to work out whether Madeleine ever intended to marry L'Angelier or whether it was merely a game she was playing to add some excitement to what has been perceived by twentieth-century writers as her boring existence.[25] There is little doubt that much of her correspondence is suffused with artifice, and she admitted to L'Angelier that she had lied about many things, including the fact that her mother was aware of their relationship. What one must remember is that Madeleine was barely 20 when the relationship began; her experience of the world, let alone of romantic relationships, was limited. She was exploring identities which were fashioned from the cultural material to hand; romantic novels, prescriptive literature, the gendered codes of conduct of her class and so on. Some of these identities would have been self-consciously constructed and might be seen as mere performance, while others would have been the outcome of deeply ingrained meanings and practices which were embedded in the social relations of her world. It was not so much a game that she was playing, rather, she was composing a narrative of her life and her relationship with L'Angelier by drawing on a diverse set of culturally available identities and stories. Rather than seeing

Madeleine as a cynical manipulator who was indulging her fantasies for amusement, it is probably more accurate to see her as a young, infatuated woman, with no well-anchored sense of self, who could not break completely with the deeply ingrained codes and values of her class. The attentions of a more acceptable suitor, coupled with L'Angelier's unremitting complaints and admonishments, probably tipped the balance against him.

Yet, once again Madeleine was to demonstrate her inconsistency. We do not know what was said when Madeleine and L'Angelier next met up. But, despite all the *sturm und drang*, the crisis seemed to blow over and there was some kind of reconciliation. Only four days after sending her last hysterical letter she wrote to him:

> My dear Emile, I have got my finger cut, and cannot write, so, dear, I wish you would excuse me. I was glad to see you looking so well yesterday. I hope to see you very soon. Write for next Thursday, and then I shall tell you when I can see you. I want the first time we meet that you bring me all my cool letters back – the last 4 I have written – and I will give you others in their place. [14th February 1857]

The two resumed their relationship, although they met less frequently and corresponded less regularly. The question was, would Madeleine remain firm this time, or would there be another volte-face?

Notes

1 *Lancet*, quoted in the *Dumbarton Herald*, 16th July 1857.
2 Douglas MacGowan, *Murder in Victorian Scotland: the Trial of Madeleine Smith* (Praeger, 1999), prelude.
3 Ibid.
4 Ibid.
5 Ibid., p. 12.
6 Martin Lyons, 'Love Letters and Writing Practices: On Ecriture Intimes in the Nineteenth Century', *Journal of Family History*, 24, 2 (April 1999), pp. 232–9.
7 Quoted in MacGowan, *Murder in Victorian Scotland*, pp. 35–6.
8 Quoted in F. Tennyson Jesse, *The Trial of Madeleine Smith* (William Hodge and Co. Ltd., 1927), pp. 9–10.
9 Ibid., p. 9.
10 Ibid.
11 Ibid.
12 Sally Mitchell, 'Sentiment and Suffering: Women's Recreational Reading in the 1860s', *Victorian Studies* 21 (1977), pp. 29–45.
13 Ibid.
14 Ibid., p. 35.
15 Quoted in MacGowan, *Murder in Victorian Scotland*, p. 21.

16 Karen Lystra, *Searching the Heart: Women, Men and Romantic Love in Nineteenth-Century America* (Oxford University Press, 1989).

17 Quoted in MacGowan, *Murder in Victorian Scotland*, p. 22.

18 Draft of letter written by L'Angelier after they had first made love in June 1856.

19 NAS AD 4/57/255/3, Precognitions against Madeleine Smith, evidence of Christina Haggart.

20 Michael Mason, *The Making of Victorian Sexuality* (Oxford University Press, 1995); P. Jalland, *Women, Marriage and Politics 1860–1914* (Oxford University Press, 1986); M. Jeanne Peterson, *Family, Love, and Work in the Lives of Victorian Gentlewomen* (Indiana University Press, 1989); Peter Gay, *The Bourgeois Experience: Victoria to Freud*, vol. 1: *Education of the Senses* (Cambridge University Press, 1984).

21 Jimmy Campbell, *A Scottish Murder: Rewriting the Madeleine Smith Story* (Tempus, 2007), p. 21.

22 Mary S. Hartman, *Victorian Murderesses: A True History of Thirteen Respectable French and English Women Accused of Unspeakable Crimes* (Schocken Books, 1977).

23 NAS AD 14/57/255/3, Criminal precognitions of James Smith.

24 Quote from Thomas E. Hill, *Manual of Social and Business Forms: A Guide to Correct Writing* (Hill Standard Book Co., Chicago, 1882).

25 Mary S. Hartman, 'Crime and the Respectable Woman: Toward a Pattern of Middle-Class Female Criminality in Nineteenth-Century France and England', *Feminist Studies*, 2, 1 (1974), pp. 38–57. Hartman in particular sees Madeleine not as rebellious but as indulging in 'romantic play-acting', ibid., p. 44.

3

Too much waltzing

L'Angelier's obsessive jealousy and possessiveness were fuelled by the knowledge that Madeleine led an extremely full social life and she was not short of male company.

There is a common perception of young Victorian women that they lived in a gilded cage, shielded from the public gaze and cosseted in the bosom of their family and friends. Their few excursions into the public world are generally thought to have been closely regulated by the rigid etiquette which governed middle-class life.[1] Numerous fictional accounts of the lives of young middle-class women fuel this image. Even the novels of Jane Austen are often held to capture the quintessential life of these women, despite the fact that they are set in Georgian rather than Victorian Britain. Indeed, Madeleine Smith has been scrutinised from this perspective on more than one occasion. Professor Mary Hartman explored the case in 1970,[2] deconstructing Madeleine's letters and finding a flirtatious and mendacious minx who manipulated the poor, love-lorn L'Angelier. Whatever the veracity of this account, it is her explanation for Madeleine's behaviour which is worthy of comment. Hartman argues that 'the years of waiting for marriage, enclosed in the family with little use for one's time, produced a tedium which even contemporaries found disturbing'.[3] In other words, like the young women who were accused of being witches in the seventeenth century, Madeleine's behaviour is explained by the extent of her social and sexual repression. Hartman also assumed that Madeleine's contemporaries led restricted and confined lives which may not have driven them to murder but which, she claims, drove them in large numbers to the law courts, where they vicariously enjoyed the revelations of premarital sex and illicit love.

It is doubtful that Madeleine would have recognised this account of her life. On the contrary, such complaints as she had about her life, for example that she was 'feeling tired because of all the gaiety', suggest a robust social life which required considerable stamina. For days on end she was 'Never in bed a night before 2 or 3 o'clock and all day long going about' [18th March 1856]. The Glasgow that Madeleine inhabited was a thriving, confident city that rivalled many European capitals in the social and cultural fare it offered to its wealthier citizens. However, Madeleine did not even have to step out of her front door to experience a gay social whirl or to meet young men with little more on their minds than wooing and flirting with young women. There was a broad spectrum of entertainment available to the urban bourgeoisie which ranged from the domestic sociability of dinners and soirées to the balls, concert halls, theatres, exhibitions and galleries of the city.

As in most towns and cities, the middle-class year was neatly divided into two seasons: the winter season and the summer season.[4] The winter season began in November and was generally spent in the city, around domestic and public amusements which were mostly, although not exclusively, conducted indoors. Some time around April or May most middle-class families would decamp to their summer residences. For the Glasgow bourgeoisie these were often located on the Clyde coast, although a minority preferred the countryside. The Victorians also had a penchant for spas and health cures, which made towns such as Bridge of Allan, Strathpeffer and Moffat particularly popular. In this respect Madeleine's family were archetypal Victorians, regularly commuting between their summer residence on the Clyde coast at Row, their Glasgow town house and the spa resort of Bridge of Allan, where they took lodgings.

The summer season certainly did not signal a waning of social life. The dense, overlapping social, professional and economic networks which had been formed in the cities often regrouped in these locations and maintained their links through a continual exchange of visits. Summer activities replicated the social life of winter, but were supplemented by outdoor activities such as walking, climbing, bathing, sailing and riding. Far from the cocoon of a retreat, the summer season could prove even more convivial and socially exhausting than the winter one.

Some aspects of social life conformed to the familiar fare of Victorian novels. The rituals of 'at homes' and making calls were certainly present. However, there is little evidence of the ritual and formality usually associated with the Victorian era. Madeleine regularly paid calls to friends and acquaintances; some by were prior arrangement, but many were more casual affairs. Most calls tended to be fairly brief. Madeleine referred to having made 'a great many calls' one afternoon in St George's Road, where her aunts lived, and on another afternoon she made 'several calls' in Hillhead with her mother and sister Bessie. Most of these calls would have been made within walking distance from her home; however, depending on the distance and the weather, a carriage might sometimes be used, although she seems to have gone on foot even in inclement weather, since on a few occasions she complained that she had got thoroughly wet while out visiting. Occasionally calls might involve travelling some distance. On 20th November 1855 she informed L'Angelier that she was going into the country to make some calls. However, the country in 1850s Glasgow was barely a mile away from the Smith's town house. Therefore, when Madeleine referred to the 'country' she was probably alluding to the area just beyond Partick, a busy community where she regularly shopped.

Visiting was not only a town ritual. When in the summer home at Row, Madeleine and her family also spent some of their time paying and receiving calls. On more than one occasion she broke off her letter writing to L'Angelier in order to receive visitors. Typically, Madeleine took any opportunity to parade her popularity with the opposite sex and arouse his jealousy, as when she wrote: 'there are two gentlemen coming to call so I must go' [November 1856]. L'Angelier, no doubt, took the bait.

Some of Madeleine's comments reveal the façade and the polite insincerity which could cloak these rituals. The Tweedies – James Tweedie, his wife and their six children – were family friends who lived in Woodside Place, Glasgow and who also visited *Rowaleyn*. Madeleine clearly was not enamoured with them and did not regard visiting them as a pleasure, but as a chore to be endured or, more hopefully, avoided. In December 1856 she wrote, 'I called for the Tweedies today, but I knew they always go out at 2 o'clock, so we called at 3 o'clock, and as I expected, "they were not at home", for which I was very glad' [8th December 1856]. She had previously confessed to 'feeling very vexed with these horrid Tweedies – I wish that they had been any place but here' [27th October 1856]. However, etiquette required that she maintain a veneer of politeness, if not hospitality: 'I cannot cut them or I would.' Her parents may have shared her antipathy to them, for she added that 'They asked us 4 times last winter, we never went, and never did we ask them.' On another occasion she claimed that her father 'disliked Mr Tweedie' [17th October 1856]; and yet that summer the Tweedies had been guests at *Rowaleyn* for several days. The capaciousness of the house at Row, with its large gardens and grounds, presumably could make the visit of even unwelcome guests tolerable. One can only assume that the performance of these rituals, which maintained the appearance of conformity while manipulating them for one's own ends, was not unique to Madeleine or her family. Who knows how many of the Smiths' acquaintances adopted the same sorts of deception, upholding form while subverting the substance of social rituals?

Sometimes 'calling' did conform to the archetypal ritual of brief social visits which were prearranged and performed as a social duty by the ladies of the house. However, calling could also be a pleasurable and purely sociable affair, shorn of any social duty, and designed to cement friendships, exchange gossip or fulfil a spontaneous whim to drop in on a good friend. Nor was it the case that it was only women who engaged in the ritual of calling. Men were frequent callers at Madeleine's home, sometimes accompanying women, but just as often coming on their own or with other men. Miss Black – 'a great heiress' – and her brother visited the Smiths at *Rowaleyn* and, perhaps more pleasingly for Madeleine, officers of the 72nd Regiment stationed at nearby Dumbarton were regular callers there in the summer months of 1856. In the winter season, when the family were living in town, evening visits as well as the usual daytime ones were quite common. The Houldsworths regularly dropped in of an evening. When Madeleine's family had settled in their town house for the winter season in the middle of November 1856 they were inundated with visitors: 'We have had people with us every night since we came to Town. All our friends called of an evening whenever they heard we had come to Town' [28th November 1856].

In some respects Madeleine conformed to the image of the quintessential Victorian lady whose time was preoccupied with genteel activities. She took music lessons, played duets on the pianoforte with Bessie and spent some of her time drawing and reading. Despite the concern for young women to acquire all the 'accomplishments', her request for lessons in painting was refused by her mother on the basis that she did not need them. She also expressed a desire to learn the guitar, believing that this would please L'Angelier, and claimed that her father had promised to buy her one [11th September 1855]. Her reading matter, or at least that which she revealed to L'Angelier, leaned heavily towards classical histories and she had a typical Victorian penchant for biographies. Eager to please L'Angelier, she promised that she would 'read useful books. I shall not read Byron anymore. I shall do all I can to improve myself and shall not spend any time reading idly.' Not that she always found his recommended reading exactly to her taste, and she confessed that she struggled with Gibbon's *Decline and Fall* and Pollard's *Ancient History*, complaining that they 'are rather dry are they not?' [30th January 1856].

The church and religion occupied a central place in the lives of the Smiths. Like the majority of Victorians they were regular church attenders, although apparently not wedded to any one particular church or even denomination. And there was no shortage of places of worship. Since the Disruption of 1843, there had been a spate of church building in Glasgow, as rival denominations competed to meet the city's spiritual needs. By 1850 there were 121 churches, the vast majority of which belonged to the Church of Scotland (29), the Free Church (32) and the United Presbyter ians (27).[5] The remainder were scattered among other Secession churches, Roman Catholics, Episcopalians, Baptists and Methodists. In common with many wealthy Glaswegians, the Smiths gave their primary allegiance to the United Presbyterians and worshipped in the Gordon Street church. As with most subjects, Madeleine had decided views on places of worship, or more likely, their congregations: the United Presby- terian church she declared 'vulgar', while she was enthusiastic about St Mary's Episcopal church, which she 'liked best'. The attraction of St Mary's Episcopal church may well have been the social composition of the congregation, which tended to be drawn from Glasgow's social and business elite. On at least one occasion Madeleine spoke of attending the Roman Catholic church, and the family sometimes worshipped at her aunts' local church in St George's Road. However, there were limits to Madeleine's piety. She was not keen on going to church on weekdays, nor twice on Sundays, despite encouragement from her parents. She also resented lengthy sermons and complained sourly to L'Angelier about the communion she had attended one Sunday: 'Papa thinks it will make me good to stay so long. It makes me cross' [n.d. 1856].

The resident minister in part dictated the choice of church. When in Row the family preferred to attend the church in Helensburgh rather than the local church in Row, as they disliked the Row minister. Even the absence of the Helensburgh minister from the parish for four weeks was not enough to persuade her parents to worship at Row, and they opted not to attend church at all during these weeks [7th May 1855]. It is not clear whether the basis of this antagonism was theological, personal or social. It is certainly the case that the family counted their ministers among their friends and socialised with them. The two ministers of the Gordon Street church, the Reverend Beattie (who had baptised Madeleine) and the Reverend George Middleton, were old family friends. In fact, Madeleine and her sister dined with the Reverend Middleton two nights after L'Angelier's death.[6]

The role of religion and its centrality in the lives of Victorians would be difficult to overestimate.[7] For many women, religion not only defined the meanings of femininity, but also provided meaning and purpose to their lives.[8] Religious and imperial discourses provided a strong impetus for single women to travel abroad as missionaries. Some societies, such as the China Inland Mission, actively recruited single women missionaries, claiming that in some circumstances they could be more effective than men.[9] However, for the majority of middle-class women the salvation and rescue mission was pursued in their own localities. The Christian women's mission to save, convert and rescue those less privileged than themselves created an army of women who invaded the homes of the poor in order to dispense advice, food, clothing or whatever was deemed most needed. One can imagine that these privileged women would not always be welcomed warmly into the homes of the poor, particularly when any material comforts dispensed came laced with a hefty dose of upbraiding for lack of prudence. However, Madeleine, with the confidence of youth and her class, seemed in no doubt of her welcome by her social 'inferiors' or the 'Common People' as she grandly called them. Soon after the family moved back to Row for the summer season, Madeleine usually discharged her duty of *noblesse oblige* by visiting the local people near her father's estate in Row. It is unclear whether she actually gave them any material sustenance or whether her mere presence was deemed sufficient to uplift them. In any case, she wrote to L'Angelier that she had got 'such a welcome home again from all the poor people and workmen about here. They all profess such a great regard for me – one poor man has called his child after me which cost me a present.' Madeleine basked in their deference: 'I like visiting the Common People [...] All the work people I visit say they would do anything for Miss Smith' [17th and 25th April 1856].

Had Madeleine seen fit to deliver any homilies to 'the Common People' it would have qualified as unalloyed hypocrisy. She may have been no slouch in the ballroom, but her domestic skills could be found wanting, particularly in the handicraft department. In order to curry favour with L'Angelier, and no doubt prove her worth as an attentive wife, Madeleine had rashly promised to make some cuffs for him. Displaying a rare flash of self-knowledge and candour, she confessed to him that he might have to wait some time: 'I fear your cuffs won't be ready for this winter. I began a pair to send to the Crimea last winter and they are not done yet. My beloved you are getting a very idle wife' [21st December 1855]. One can only hope, for the sake of those fighting in the Crimea, that not all middle-class women were as dilatory as Madeleine when it came to fulfilling their patriotic duties.

Whatever significance religious faith had to Madeleine's personal beliefs, it was far from the case that her social life revolved around philanthropic or church activities, or was restricted to demure afternoon teas. Middle-class Glaswegians knew how to enjoy themselves and how to be hospitable. Within their homes they entertained on every scale: mornings or afternoons would see the arrival of casual or invited visitors; in the evenings they hosted dinner parties, dances, concerts and even balls in the grander households. The Victorian middle-class home was far from being a secluded enclave. Entertaining and being entertained lay at the heart of Victorian sociability, which gave the home an openness far removed from the tranquil haven that it has been portrayed as being.[10]

The Smiths belonged to a coterie of Glasgow families who formed a dense network of business, religious and political interests which provided a rich source of social contacts. James Smith's architectural business brought him into contact with a wide range of Glasgow's elite, from politicians and industrialists to professionals and bankers, with whom he formed friendships and social contacts. He designed houses for wealthy individuals such as Robert Dalglish, MP, of Kilmardenny House in Bearsden, who later came to stay at Row, while his design of the McLellan Galleries, which were opened in 1856, was commissioned by Archibald McLellan, a councillor, patron of the arts and friend. James Smith's Glasgow offices in St Vincent Street were adjacent to those of the Houldsworths, iron manufacturers, who were frequent visitors to the Smiths' home. The Houldsworths were very wealthy and probably the most socially elevated of the Smiths' friends, but the families were close. They wrote often to Bessie, brought Mrs Smith presents from trips abroad, and lent their yacht to the Smiths over the summer of 1856.

Families in the Smith social circle were frequently related to each other. The Smiths had regular contact with the Raits and the Griersons, whose families were partners in a Buchanan Street jeweller's. The latter, Madeleine said, were cousins of the Houldsworths. And so the social circle widened, one contact leading to others. James Smith's religious affiliations, which took in several churches in both Glasgow and Helensburgh, provided another layer of social contacts, as did his political activities. He sat briefly on Glasgow City Council and he regularly entertained some of his fellow councillors at *Rowaleyn*. This tight circle of Glasgow's social elite extended down to the next generation, with Madeleine's brother Jack having a friendship with William Moncrieff, whose father Hugh, a lawyer, was later to be part of Madeleine's defence team.

The Smiths' Row house was ideally suited for entertaining on a lavish scale. 'Tomorrow we shall have 15 young people to dinner from Arrochar' [July 1856]. The numerous bedrooms comfortably accommodated several overnight guests, while the large drawing room and dining room were perfectly proportioned to entertain large numbers of people. The commodious servants' quarters in the basement and the crew of servants whom they employed ensured that entertaining was conducted with all the precision and organisation of a military campaign. According to Madeleine, the more modest entertaining involved little effort on the part of the ladies of the household. When L'Angelier expressed surprise that they were able to have a dinner party for guests in the evening, having spent the entire day out walking and picnicking, Madeleine explained how it was managed: 'Dinner is at 7.30 that is our hour when we have friends. We have first rate servants – the night before a dinner party I write out the bill of fare and give it to the cook and that is all I require to do' [22nd August 1856].

As we have seen, the Smiths' town houses were more modest than *Rowaleyn*. However, this seemed to be no barrier to entertaining on a large scale. Although Madeleine complained to L'Angelier that at India Street for the winter season in 1855 'Papa is going to give no parties this winter' [5th December 1855], in fact they were far from being condemned to social isolation. Madeleine's next sentence reads, 'We seldom dine alone, someone is with us every day', and she added that Bessie and James were off to a dancing party the next evening. Madeleine's letters that winter are full of references to dinner parties, visitors and callers. They even interfered with her late-night rendezvous with L'Angelier. She complained to him that she would have difficulty meeting him at their usual time. In the same letter she wrote to him that 'We are to have a very quiet Christmas this year' [14th December 1855]. Yet the next few letters she penned were full of the 'diversions' which she and the family had been engaged in over the festive period and on Christmas day she wrote, 'We have a good many friends with us this afternoon.'

Perhaps Madeleine had a singular conception of what constituted a quiet social life. More likely, her letters expose the conflict between her desire to construct an image of herself as a subservient and obedient sweetheart whose dull life was cheered only by the presence of her lover, and her true nature as an inveterate flirt who enjoyed tormenting L'Angelier by flaunting her active social life. Madeleine's letters do not sound as though her social life had been seriously curtailed that season. However, perhaps the Smiths had decided to entertain on a relatively small scale rather than not at all, confining their entertaining to dinner parties and visitors, and eschewing the more extravagant parties which involved large numbers. If that was the case, normal social activities were resumed the following winter. Madeleine reported in October 1856 that they were 'quite full of company', and referred to numerous dinner parties, including one in December which she complained was 'all old people'. Throughout the winter months she also mentions dancing, card parties and the fact that their visitors 'never leave before midnight'. Fifty invitations were sent out to two large parties, one given by Madeleine's younger brothers and sister, the other by her parents. Madeleine professed to find New Year's Day 'a great bore', as they always had 'a host of people to call for us – all coming in, making such a fuss, wishing you happy returns etc' [28th December 1856].

Most of these occasions hosted by the Smiths were family affairs that catered for all generations. The dinner parties were attended by Madeleine and Bessie, while Janet, aged 13, danced so much at the party held by her parents on Christmas Eve 1856 that, exhausted, she retired to bed at 1 a.m. and that morning 'was very ill … She had danced so much (she is a very good dancer) last evening … that when she got up she fainted. I did get a fright with her. I thought the child was dead. She is not at all well tonight' [n.d. December 1856]. However, Janet clearly had a stronger constitution than Madeleine credited her with and was sufficiently revived to be able to go out, not only the next evening, but every evening the next week, apart from the Tuesday [ibid.]

By and large, home entertaining was not restricted to one genera- tion or one gender. The 'men only' affairs were few and far between. Madeleine mentioned one occasion only when her father went briefly to Row before Christmas 1855 with John Mackenzie and others for what seems to have been a 'gentlemen's dinner'. Parties for only young people were also the exception rather than the norm. More commonly, young people were in each other's company on a casual rather than a prear- ranged or formal basis. The Smith children routinely entertained friends of their own generation. This usually involved a few friends dropping round, chatting, gossiping or playing a game of billiards or cards. At the beginning of 1856 the Smiths had a billiard table made for their home and this proved to be very popular, not only with Jack's friends, but also with Madeleine. However, L'Angelier seemed to have disapproved of both cards and billiards, as Madeleine volunteered to stop playing both if they displeased him. Typical of Madeleine, this promise to please her lover was honoured more in the breach, for her subsequent letters continue to be littered with references to these pastimes. Of course, L'Angelier's objections may have been more to do with the fact that these amuse- ments brought her into contact with young men. But if this were the case, it would have been akin to stemming the flood with the finger in the proverbial dyke. Madeleine encountered young men at every turn, not only, as we shall see, at the dances, balls and concerts which she attended, but in her own home. Young men were frequent visitors to the house and flirting and kissing seemed to be standard practice. Madeleine was even prepared to tell L'Angelier that 'young gentlemen' had given her 'kisses, but no more' [May 1856]. She added that she had not kissed Mackenzie since becoming engaged to Emile. She excused her behaviour: 'I must dance with gentlemen and I must talk to them but then that is not flirting. What I call flirting is making desperate love. That I promise I shall not do. I never did flirt with any man I had the least regard for' [14th November 1855]. So a superficial flirtatiousness was an expected part of social interaction in her circles.

Madeleine and Bessie had a good deal of freedom to go out together with no chaperone, visit friends and even entertain young male visitors when their parents were not in the house. In February 1856 Madeleine and Bessie went to stay with friends in Edinburgh and enjoyed visiting and dining with the soldiers of the garrison at Edinburgh Castle, unchaperoned – 'without a Matron'. In Glasgow too, they were allowed to go alone to concerts and other public events. Although their parents seemed comfortable with this, L'Angelier was not. He complained vehemently to Madeleine about this lack of supervision, but she airily responded, 'M. and P. allow us without a Matron so I suppose it is a Glasgow fashion.' In January 1857 Madeleine and Bessie 'went for a long walk on Dumbarton Rd.' with 19-year-old Godfrey Pattison, but with no chaperone. Madeleine wrote excitedly to L'Angelier that Officers 'of the 72nd' had been sent to Dumbarton Castle and 'have taken a great fancy to visit our house'. Soldiers called before being sent to Gibraltar or the Crimea, sometimes when neither parent was present. At times it seemed as though the Smith household was entertaining the entire regiment of the Black Watch.

Playing billiards and cards, kissing and flirting with young men and using 'fast' language were not all that Madeleine confessed to. She seems to have enjoyed the occasional smoke, presumably of a cigar, as cigarette smoking had not yet become popular in Britain. Once again, L'Angelier disapproved and instructed her to break the habit. Madeleine professed to have complied: 'I am so glad you got me to give up smoking' [3rd November 1855]. However, she was practised at mollifying L'Angelier in word if not in deed, and it may well have been the case that she continued to indulge her habit regardless.

When the Smith family decamped to their summer residence at Row, they did their utmost to replicate the conviviality and hospitality of life in the city. Although Row was a small village on the Gareloch and situated at the gateway to Loch Lomond, it was well served by the steamer and was fairly accessible from the city. *Rowaleyn*, with its proximity to the coast, the country, the Highlands and lochs, was particularly popular with visitors, who descended on the Smith household in great numbers. Most were drawn from the Smith's city social circle, but some had travelled a considerable distance, and often they stayed for lengthy periods. During the summer of 1856 the Smiths entertained visitors from

Stirling, Greenock, Edinburgh, Liverpool, London, Manchester, Ireland and America. Madeleine, true to form, rarely missed a chance to rattle L'Angelier when recounting these visits. She disingenuously remarked to him of the Irish visitors that they included a 'very nice young fellow with large moustache' [n.d. September 1856], while she coquettishly referred to the fact that the 'great many friends' they were entertaining in August included '(four young men) (Englishmen)'.

The summer season's constant round of visitors was not always pleasing to Madeleine. In fact, she noted somewhat wearily in June 1856, 'Friends, friends staying with us.' One Saturday in June, she expressed relief that the house was to be empty for three hours. The Smiths had waved goodbye to one set of guests at eleven o'clock, only to greet another batch at two o'clock that afternoon [26th June 1856]. Entertaining house guests characterised the whole summer. In August of that year Madeleine wrote to L'Angelier, 'Our house has been quite a Hotel for the last ten days – any bed occupied ... We have too much company at home, it is dreadful expense but surely P or M will weary of it some day. Our house is more like an Hotel than any other thing, in fact it gets the name of Hotel from people about Row' [5th August 1856]. It was little wonder that the ordinary people of Row remarked on the ebb and flow of visitors to *Rowaleyn*. On 30th May 1856 Madeleine complained to L'Angelier, 'This has been a most tiresome day, so many visitors there were and a large dinner party.' Dinner parties seemed to be held on a daily basis that month: 'We had a large dinner party last night and one tonight. Also on Tuesday and Wednesday.' Nor was it only the Smiths who were entertaining. 'So many visitors there were and a large dinner party and we went up to the Wilsons in the evening to an evening party with Fireworks' [30th May 1856].

Visitors to *Rowaleyn* took advantage of its situation at the entrance to the Highlands of Scotland. Some came up for the shooting: 'We have had a great many sportsmen visiting us since the 12th. There are moors very near us' [24th August 1855]. Others, less bloodthirsty, took advantage of the beautiful scenery and were happy to be taken on sightseeing tours of the countryside: 'We went to the top of Loch Lomond, driving, and had luncheon in one of the beautiful glens, and returned to Arrochar in the afternoon' [n.d. July 1856]. The Smiths were fortunate to be able to borrow the Houldsworths' yacht, and took a party of eighteen to 'the Kyles of Bute and then to Inverary in the yacht. We shall take coach to Inverary' [23rd July 1856]. There were also local events to attend, such as a bazaar at Gourock, though Madeleine did not go; flower shows in Helensburgh; and a regatta at Dunoon. Picnics were popular – though not with Madeleine: 'I have a very great dislike of picknics. They are so stupid' [3rd July 1856].

When the family returned to the city for the winter season the rounds of visiting and visitors resumed. Madeleine's complaints about the constant company: 'I am so weary of this life. Company every day. Tonight the house is full. I have so little time to myself. I have to go here and there, do this thing and another and so on that my time is much occupied' [undated], must be understood in the context of L'Angelier chiding her for the amount of entertaining which went on in the Smith household. Rather than being genuinely 'tired of company', it is more likely that she was paying lip service to his reprimands, which were almost certainly motivated by his jealousy.

Of course, all this hospitality was reciprocated. The Smiths were entertained as well as entertaining. Invitations to dinner parties were frequent at both Row and Glasgow. From Row, the Smiths visited the Wilsons at Greenock and the Buchanans at Dumbarton for dinner or for 'parties'. Usually Madeleine would accompany her parents, but there were also occasions when she and Bessie were the guests, as when they went to a luncheon party at the Griersons' or to the famous dinner at the Reverend Middleton's just after L'Angelier's death.

In the 1840s and 1850s, the middle classes were as yet largely unrestrained by temperance censure. Not only was alcohol an accepted part of domestic life: it also featured prominently in entertaining. The Smiths' close friends, the Houldsworths, were generous hosts and their well-stocked cellar suggests that they were not among the city's temperance advocates. As well as 184 wine glasses, their cellar contained fifty-five dozen bottles of sherry and twenty-six dozen bottles of port and Madeira, whisky, champagne, claret and assorted other wines.[11] Madeleine makes very few references to alcohol, but it is likely that it was provided at these home entertainments. The only occasion when she explicitly refers to her own drinking is when, in response to L'Angelier's instructions that she should not drink toddy, she professed to have an intense dislike of the drink. However, on several occasions she complained of headaches after an evening of merriment and of the difficulty of getting up in the morning. They were, she wrote, 'Headaches from late hours so I feel ill in the morning' [14th December 1855] – conditions familiar to those who have overindulged in alcohol the previous evening, although Madeleine had different explanations: 'My head is aching, too much waltzing last night' [14th February 1855].

This domestic sociability was not of the claustrophobic and prim nature we tend to associate with the Victorians; it was not the all-embracing hospitality characteristic of the early modern period, but it was far from being exclusive to a select family group. Although conducted in the home, these 'private' gatherings, particularly the more lavish, often matched the sociability of many public dances and balls. Even if Madeleine had not put a foot over the threshold of her home, she would have had a lively and full social life.

Somewhere between the domestic sociability of the household and the public entertainment of the theatres, concert halls and galleries, lay the semi-public recreations which the bourgeoisie assiduously fostered as markers of middle-class identity and status. These were the dinners, lectures and balls which were usually referred to as 'public', but which in practice were limited to those who had social cachet and economic resources. Although many of these organisations had an exclusively male membership, the lectures and soirées which they organised were often open both to non-members and to women. Typical of these was the Athenaeum. On Wednesday 26th March 1856 it hosted a lecture on 'Light, Colour, Vision' which was illustrated 'by more than 30 disc movements'. Members gained free entry and were requested to 'bring a Lady', whose ticket was priced at sixpence. Gentlemen 'Strangers' had to pay one shilling.[12] The Victorians' appetite for education was insatiable, and newspapers regularly advertised 'improving' lectures which were designed to attract women as well as men. The week beginning 24th March was potentially a busy one for those bent on intellectual stimulation. On Monday the Architectural Association held a lecture in the Scottish Exhibition Galleries in Bath Street on 'The manners and customs of the Ancient Egyptians', which was preceded by a promenade with music. Again, members were urged to bring along a 'Lady' and the lecture was also open to members of the 'Public'.[13] At the Merchants' Hall in Hutcheson Street there was a reading from Macauley's *History*, with the best seats at the front advertised for one shilling and the back seats priced sixpence.

Although Madeleine makes no reference to having attended any of these particular lectures, we do know that she did attend lectures, and visited the Scottish Exhibition Rooms in Bath Street on more than one occasion [15th January 1856]. This was a venue which had been established in 1855 to provide a showcase for Arts and Manufactures. It exhibited paintings and inventions, held *conversaziones*, hosted lectures and had musical performances every evening. Opening times were from 11 a.m. to 10 p.m. and admission was one shilling during the day and sixpence for evenings. Although admission was reasonably priced, the Exhibition was probably designed to attract the more wealthy and fashionable elements of Glasgow society. The *Glasgow Daily Times* approvingly reported that 'a full dress conversazione was held in the Scottish Exhibition Rooms, Bath St ... There was a very numerous and fashionable company. The music was under the direction of Mr Agnew ... the principal novelty of the evening was a telegraph patented by Mr Walker.'[14]

Given Madeleine's character, it is likely that balls and dances were much more to her taste than public dinners and lectures. Balls were a regular feature of the bourgeois social calendar and figure prominently in Madeleine's letters to L'Angelier. Although there was no shortage of balls to attend in Glasgow, Madeleine and her family seemed prepared to travel to Edinburgh, Stirling and Ayr for the pleasure of dancing and socialising with their peers. Edinburgh was particularly popular with Madeleine's family. In February 1856 she and Bessie spent several days in Edinburgh, attending balls and luncheons and having a 'great deal of fun' [14th February 1856], waltzing often until 4 a.m.

Madeleine also attended a number of private balls, which were usually held in private homes to celebrate an occasion or by clubs and associations. Typical of the latter was the ball which followed the Annual Soirée of the Hutchesontown Horticultural Society, held in the Merchant's Hall and 'attended by a fair proportion of the fair sex upon whom we must look as the natural patrons of the floral kingdom'.[15] However, most balls were public affairs and open to anyone who had the ticket money. Tickets usually had to be obtained beforehand from the premises which were hosting the ball. The advert in the *Glasgow Herald* announcing a 'Grand Ball' in the McLellan Rooms on the 28th March 1856 contained the terse notice, 'no money taken at the door'.[16] This may have been designed to ensure social exclusivity, but the ticket prices at ten shillings for gentlemen and seven shillings for ladies was likely to be deterrent enough for those with limited resources.[17] Not all balls were so expensive, but it was unlikely that the denizens of working-class districts rubbed shoulders with the great and good of the city, even at the less grand occasions. However, balls were not confined solely to the upper reaches of the middle classes. L'Angelier, who was a clerk earning initially only £25 per year, attended many of the same balls as Madeleine, as did some of his friends and work colleagues.

Most balls followed a quite standard format. Fairly typical of this was d'Albert's Ball, which was held in the McLellan Rooms in March 1856. It was heralded as a 'Grand Ball' and was hosted by 'Monsieur Charles Albert composer and author of some of the most popular Dance music of the day', who had written new pieces 'expressly for the occasion'.[18] Although 'crowded with the elite of Glasgow', including 'James Smith esquire and party', it was typical of other balls of the period in other respects. Dancing began at ten o'clock, with reels, quadrilles, gallops, polkas and waltzes. The centre of the room was reserved for dancing and refreshments were 'provided most abundantly' at one end of the room. As was typical, patrons were instructed where to set down their carriages 'with the horses' heads up the Hill'. As with most recreational pursuits, balls were attended by young and old. The 12-year-old Janet was to dance at the d'Albert Ball [25th March 1856], while Madeleine's parents were seasoned ball goers. Indeed, Madeleine complained to L'Angelier that she thought her parents were too often out at balls: 'I think it is very foolish of M and P going about to Balls' [21st February 1856.] However, Madeleine seemed to be following in her parents' footsteps and clearly took some delight at the prospect of a ball. Usually she and Bessie went to these balls with their parents and family friends, although there seemed to be occasions when she and Bessie were allowed to go to dances unaccompanied, provided that both sisters went: 'B has been invited to Edinburgh Castle.' But because Madeleine would not go 'P. won't allow her by herself' [July 1856].

There was certainly plenty of freedom and opportunity for young people to flirt and dance with each other and to fix up dances before-hand. On their visits to 'Town' in the days before Thomson's Ball on 8th December 1856, Madeleine and Bessie had met up with 'several Gentlemen who asked for the pleasure of dancing with us' [8th December 1856]. It was customary for gentlemen to send one or more flowers to those ladies whom they wished to court. If these discreet advances were welcomed, the young lady would take the flower to the ball to signal encouragement to her admirer. Bessie and Madeleine proved to be particularly popular for one ball where, if Madeleine is to be believed, they were each sent three large flowers [n.d. 1856]. Madeleine, of course made sure that L'Angelier knew that she had been sent flowers, but promised him, 'I shall take no bouquet to the Ball so no one shall be encouraged by my taking a flower if any should be sent' [3rd March 1856].

The relative social exclusivity of the semi-public entertainment of balls, lectures and dinners was to some extent diluted by the range of public entertainment available in the city. The Theatre Regulation Act of 1843 had swept away the monopoly of the patented or Royal theatres over spoken drama and allowed any licensed theatre to perform plays.[19] Consequently the number of theatres in Glasgow swelled in the following decade. The Adelphi opened in 1842, the City theatre in 1845, the Queen's in 1849 and the Prince's Theatre Royal in 1850.[20] Some of these theatres were vast buildings which seated thousands; the Adelphi was a substantial building and very spacious, seating almost two thousand people, while the City theatre, which had been the dream of John Henry Alexander, 'The Wizard of the North', who wanted to make his theatre the largest and most magnificent in Glasgow, seated five thousand. By contrast, the 'penny theatres', the music halls and singing saloons in the city could be cramped and relatively small. However, theatres were extremely vulnerable to fire in this period, particularly if they were timber constructions like the Adelphi. The Adelphi, which had been the first theatre to open after the new Licensing Act, burned down in November 1848 – somewhat ironically during rehearsals for a new piece, *The Ship of Fire*. The City theatre had an even briefer existence and burned down only five months after opening. After its demise, its owner, in a remarkable display of resourcefulness and imagination, constructed a temporary theatre in fake granite, a replica of the recently constructed Balmoral Castle, complete with rhododendron bushes. However, it would be difficult to match the optimism of the owners of the Theatre Royal which was rebuilt within the year after it burned down in January 1863.[21]

By the 1850s, when Madeleine was a young woman, there were probably only about two theatres which she would have considered visiting: the Theatre Royal, Dunlop Street and the Prince's Theatre Royal in West Nile Street.[22] There were numerous other establishments but, like Mumford's Geggie and the Queen's Theatre, they were located in the less fashionable districts of the city around Glasgow Green and tended to attract a working-class clientele. Glaswegians' appetite for theatrical entertainment was omnivorous, embracing all genres, including pantomime, variety shows, equestrian shows, musical entertainment, Shakespeare, melodrama and adaptations of Walter Scott novels. In the first half of the nineteenth century Glasgow companies mounted their own productions, usually under the auspices of actor-managers. However, by the middle of the century, with the rise of the railways, touring companies became more common. Glasgow was able to attract good companies and quality productions, but even so, productions and performances could be of uneven quality. Perhaps for this reason Madeleine claimed that 'Unless there is some Star in the theatre we do not go' [16th November 1855].

To a limited extent, theatres specialised in different genres. The most prestigious theatre, the Theatre Royal, mounted productions mainly of Shakespeare and melodrama and in the 1850s favoured lavish productions of plays based on Walter Scott novels. A few weeks after Madeleine and L'Angelier had begun their affair, the Theatre Royal presented *Julius Caesar* for five evenings, followed by six performances of the comedy *Masks and Faces*.[23] The Prince's Theatre Royal presented a mixture of drama and opera and a sprinkling of 'improving' productions like the 'Diorama of the overland mail to India'.[24] Although the theatres located around Glasgow Green were more likely to present variety entertainments, they also staged Shakespeare and melodramas. Mumford's, for example, specialised in rough-and-ready versions of melodramas and

Shakespeare, with the actors willing to repeat particular scenes which proved particularly popular with the audience.[25] However, productions at the more prestigious Theatre Royal could display similar lack of regard for the authorial text. The actor-manager until 1851, John Henry Alexander, was a colourful figure whose eccentricities included arguing with the audience, and stopping the show to dance a 'jig', at the request of the gallery audience.[26]

The Theatre Royal's reputation as Glasgow's premier theatrical venue did not mean that its audience was drawn exclusively from the middle classes. It competed with the 'penny theatres' for the same audiences and often staged the same plays.[27] The 'half-price' night offered by the theatre on Saturday 8th December 1855 for 'the bride of Lammermoor and several other plays' may have signalled the fact that the theatre was struggling for audiences, but it probably was cheap enough to entice the working class along.[28] The Prince's Theatre Royal's Diorama production the same week was also likely to have attracted the 'respectable' working class, with gallery seats reasonably priced at sixpence.[29] So while these two theatres probably did not have a socially exclusive audience, the fine distinctions of the Victorian class system were carefully preserved by the gradation of seat prices. The disaster which struck the Theatre Royal in 1849 provides clear evidence that its audiences were socially diverse as well as socially segregated. During the second act of *The Surrender at Calais* somebody in the gallery raised a false cry of alarm. Everyone rushed for the doors and sixty-five largely young, working-class people who had been attracted by the low prices in the gallery were killed.[30]

Madeleine often mentioned having been to the theatre – once in a party of sixteen – but never seems to have felt moved to comment on the play [n.d. 1856]. She also frequently attended the opera. When she and Jack went to the Italian opera in spring 1856 they had seats in a box, but initially Madeleine 'did not like it at all' [21st March 1856]. However, by the autumn season of 1856 she went 'several times to the opera' in one week. Although her fellow theatre goers would probably have included some of the inhabitants of the Saltmarket and the Gallowgate, it is unlikely that she would have encountered them. They would have been consigned to the cheapest seats in the gallery, while Madeleine opted for the social exclusivity of the 'box', costing £30 for the season.[31]

The socially diverse clientele of two premier theatres contrasted with the music halls, singing saloons, and 'penny theatres', which attracted an almost exclusively working-class audience. These establishments would have been *terra incognito* to Madeleine, although perhaps not to some of her young gentlemen friends in the army. Madeleine did, however, go to the pantomime several times during the winter season of 1856, although she declared of one, 'I did not much like the Pantomime. It was stupid, but I suppose it is as good as a Pantomime can be' [28th December 1856].

The variety of theatrical entertainment extended to musical perform-ances. Newspapers are full of adverts for musical events to cater to every taste. A flavour of what was on offer can be gained from an article in the *Glasgow Punch* of 15th October 1856. In the course of a week the English Opera Company was performing at the Theatre Royal, the London Orches-tral Union was in Merchants' Hall, Dr Mark and 'a band of juveniles' were performing in the Minerva Rooms, there was a 'superior concert' in the City Hall and another in the Minerva Rooms, both on Saturday, and a host of musical societies and instrumental bands practising for future performances.[32] The variety of music on offer prompted the author of the article to complain that 'music is dinned into ears in every quarter of the city'.

As with the theatre, there was a degree of social segregation of musical events. The *Punch* article referred to a performance given by 'Piccolomini, and other accomplished artistes, charming the fashionables, who mustered in large numbers'.[33] Similarly, a report in the *Glasgow Herald* on the first concert of the Glasgow Orchestral Union in the McLellan Galleries, which may well have been attended by the Smith entourage, approvingly noted that 'the rooms are to be filled from the most fashionable circles of the city and neighbourhood'.[34] On another occasion, in September 1855, Madeleine had 'spent a very pleasant evening at the MacLelland Rooms, met a great many friends', and had been introduced to Lucien Bonaparte, the nephew of Napoleon. The *Glasgow Times* was less impressed by the 'fashionables' and commented of the audience at a festival of Scottish music in the City Hall that their response 'contrasted pleasantly with the modern transports of the opera and the fashionable concert room'.[35] To be sure, some musical events were designed to display the 'fashionable': to see and to be seen. Several of the concerts Madeleine mentioned were 'Full Dress' affairs [n.d. 1856]. This was part of the middle-class project of defining the boundaries of their class, who belonged to it and who did not.[36] The concerts which Madeleine attended with family or friends in the McLellan Galleries and the Scottish Exhibition Rooms may well have been exclusive events whose primary function was to mark the bounda-ries of the middle class and be a marker of middle-class identity. However, other musical events would have attracted a socially mixed audience and provided a variety of musical genres.[37] This was increasingly the case from the 1840s, when temperance, evangelical and municipal authorities became actively involved in promoting musical entertainment as a means of weaning people from the public houses and music halls. Although these 'moral' amusements were directed at the working class, it is likely that some of this entertainment also attracted middle-class audiences. Perhaps typical of this kind of musical evening were those held in the Royal Polytechnic Institution. Advertised as 'intellectual entertainment of vocal and instrumental music', with an entrance fee of sixpence, and offering eight different performances in one week, it is likely that they attracted the 'respectable' working class as well as the usual consumers of 'intellectual' entertainment.[38]

The Saturday night concerts in the City Hall, promoted by the Glasgow Abstainers' Union and inaugurated in 1854, were one of the most popular forms of this kind of entertainment and attracted huge audiences. We do not know whether Madeleine attended any of these, but she certainly was no stranger to the City Hall. On Friday 18th April 1856 she went there to hear Jenny Goldschmidt (née Lind), one of the leading opera singers of the period, give a concert at which she sang tunes from Mozart and various operatic pieces. Whether or not the audience were drawn from Glasgow's 'fashionable', we do know that they were not the best-mannered. The *Glasgow Herald* reviewer complained that when the singer's husband began to play his piano solo 'the buzz of the conversation around the hall made it impossible to hear him distinctly'.[39]

Like most of her class, Madeleine regularly 'promenaded', often in the Botanic Gardens or in the newly created West End Park, both of which were nominally public but which were accessed almost exclusively by the privileged middle classes. Madeleine also engaged in more robust forms of walking, particularly when at Row. These walks could be long and energetic: 'I walked eight miles yesterday (Sunday), and did not feel tired.' Sometimes these were organised walks with companions or family members. She and Jack regularly went out walking together, and not only for a leisurely stroll: 'Jack and I had a walk of four miles.' On other occasions they were impromptu or for the purpose of exercising her dog. She wrote of 'running and jumping with my large Newfoundland dog "Major"' [20th October 1856]. Riding and rowing are other pursuits she mentions, although she professed to be poor at rowing: 'I have been out in the Boat all night with the Boys. My hands are so sore, I had one of the oars. I am not a very good sailor. I mean I cannot pull very well' [24th July 1856]. These were activities which she enjoyed in the company of young men, as she repeatedly told L'Angelier: 'After luncheon, two gentlemen, my little brother James and myself went and had a walk of 7 miles – over the hill to Loch Lomond' 24th [July 1856]. Madeleine leaves unexplained the identity of these two gentlemen.

Madeleine's horizons extended far beyond Glasgow, and indeed Scotland. She travelled with her family to take advantage of the cultural life of the Continent. She dropped hints that she had travelled quite widely in Europe. She had once 'Seen a young girl take the veil' in France [22nd August 1856]. She had seen Paris, so 'did not care' to go again. When L'Angelier was in Louvain in Belgium, she casually mused that 'I think I must have passed through Louvain on my way from Antwerp to Aix La Chapelle, did I not? There was no place I liked so much as Antwerp. I also liked Heidelburg' [24th August 1855].

The social life which Madeleine enjoyed was fairly typical of her class. It was certainly circumscribed to some extent by her age, her gender and her class, but within these restrictions she had a good deal of freedom to meet and flirt with young men; she could walk alone in the city, albeit within a well-defined area; she sampled the music and theatre enjoyed in the metropolis; she danced until her head ached. Some weeks she was out most evenings, often till after midnight. Her social circle was extensive, although limited to her social peers. She travelled extensively and saw more of the world and probably of her own country than young women not of her class. However, it was the extent of her social contact with young men, often unchaperoned, which nettled L'Angelier and was the source of so much tension in their relationship.

Notes

1 See the Introduction for a discussion of the debate about the influence of the separate spheres ideology.
2 Mary S. Hartman, 'Crime and the Respectable Woman: Towards a Pattern of Middle-Class Female Criminality in Nineteenth-Century France and England', *Feminist Studies*, 2, 1 (1974), pp. 38–57.
3 Ibid., p. 44.
4 See Leonore Davidoff, *The Best Circles: Society, Etiquette and the Season* (Croom Helm, 1973).
5 Carol Foreman, *Lost Glasgow* (Cromwell Publishing, 2002), p.163.
6 NAS AD14/57/255/3, Precognition of James Smith.
7 See Callum G. Brown, *The Death of Christian Britain* (Routledge, 2001).
8 Jenny Daggers, 'The Victorian Female Civilising Mission and Women's Aspirations towards Priesthood in the Church of England', *Women's History Review*, 10, 4 (2001), pp. 651–70.
9 Delia Davin, 'British Women Missionaries in Nineteenth-Century China', *Women's History Review*, 1, 2 (1992), pp. 257–71.
10 See Eleanor Gordon and Gwyneth Nair, *Public Lives: Women, Family and Society in Victorian Britain* (Yale University Press, 2003), chapter 4.
11 GCA TD 862/70, Inventory of valuation of William Houldsworth.

12 Ibid.
13 Ibid.
14 *Glasgow Daily Times*, 18th April 1855.
15 *Tartar*, 22nd March 1855.
16 *Glasgow Herald*, 24th March 1856.
17 Ibid.
18 *Glasgow Herlald*, 24th March 1856.
19 Alistair Cameron, *See Glasgow See Theatre: A Guide to Glasgow Theatre Past and Present* (The Glasgow File, c. 1990).
20 Ibid.
21 Carol Foreman, *Lost Glasgow*, p. 155.
22 Alistair Cameron, *See Glasgow See Theatre*.
23 *Glasgow Daily Times*, 18th April 1855.
24 *Scottish Daily News*, 3rd December 1855.
25 Alistair Cameron, *See Glasgow See Theatre*.
26 Ibid.
27 Elspeth King, 'Popular Culture in Glasgow', in R. Cage (ed.), *The Working Class in Glasgow 1750–1914* (Croom Helm, 1987).
28 *Scottish Daily News*, 3rd December 1855
29 Ibid.
30 Carol Foreman, *Lost Glasgow*, p. 155.
31 *Glasgow Times*, 16th January 1856.
32 *Glasgow Punch*, 15th October 1856.
33 Ibid.
34 *Glasgow Herald*, 24th March 1856.
35 *Glasgow Times*, 16th January 1856.
36 Simon Gunn, 'The Public Sphere, Modernity and Consumption: New Perspectives on the History of the English Middle Class', in Alan Kidd and David Nicholls (eds), *Gender, Civic Culture and Consumerism: Middle-Class Identity in Britain 1800–1940* (Manchester University Press, 1999), pp. 12–29.
37 Paul Maloney, *Scotland and the Music Hall* (Manchester University Press, 2003).
38 *Glasgow Times*, 16th January 1856.
39 *Glasgow Herald*, 21st April 1856.

4

A great many things

Not only were middle-class women like Madeleine immersed in the social life of the city, they also engaged with its commercial life. From Madeleine's letters we can identify a tension between her professed readiness to live frugally with L'Angelier and her obvious delight in shopping, fashion and simply being out and about in town. L'Angelier understood this; hence his many injunctions to dress plainly, to save money, not to promenade the city streets and so on. He presented this as a moral concern – and he was indeed priggish, but behind this may well have lurked the knowledge that he could not provide such a life. 'Don't be frightened at my allowance,' Madeleine wrote to him. 'I shall not want money as I do now. That is I shall not want the dresses I do now – I shall want little money, not more than you do yourself' [31st May 1856]. But L'Angelier probably *was* frightened at her allowance: we don't know how large it was, but Mr Smith was an indulgent and wealthy father, and Madeleine loved spending his money. 'I shall tell you I have no pin money saved. I paid all I had away before I left Glasgow. I got so many things this last winter, it took all I had to pay before I left. I have a great many things, many more than I need' [17th June 1856].

During her lifetime Madeleine witnessed a transformation in the ways that this spending was carried out. Historians of nineteenth-century retailing often describe the changes in shopping in terms of a move from necessity to pleasure. Middle-class women of the later nineteenth century were expected to take pleasure in the act of shopping rather than to view it as a necessary chore. The enjoyment lay as much in the shopping as in the goods bought. The epitome of this new style of shopping was, it is argued, the department store. Aimed particularly at women, the department store allowed – indeed encouraged – browsing and strolling without the necessity to buy.[1] It offered a huge range of goods, and eventually provided refreshment, rest and toilet facilities too.

Another way of seeing the change is in terms of a shift from 'personal' to 'public'.[2] There was an anonymity about shopping in the new stores: the intimacy and personal service of the old, smaller shop was gone. In these 'traditional' shops, with small window panes, it wasn't really possible to see into the interior.[3] The threshold was distinct, and the customer entered the shop only to buy. The department store, with its huge, plate-glass windows and gas lighting, not only displayed goods to the customer but also displayed *itself* and its luxurious interior. It drew the customer in, entertained her and even overwhelmed her with the vast array of goods on offer.

Chambers Journal, one of Madeleine's favourites, a few years later described London shops as like a glittering stage setting: 'Enormous plate-glass windows, gilded or polished brass frames, expensive mirrors … iron Venetian blinds which roll up and down … like a stage curtain displaying or concealing the gorgeous scenery within.'[4] When Glasgow shops began to look like this, Madeleine and other middle-class women must have found the change striking and exciting.

The department store had its origins in Paris and London.[5] Erika Rappaport charts the rise of Whiteley's, London's first department store, in the 1870s.[6] Only as a married mother of teenagers would Madeleine Smith have known the true department store in the capital. Yet some of the shops she knew and used as a young woman in Glasgow were much closer to this model than is usually acknowledged. Whiteley's was unique in the way in which it offered disparate goods under the same roof – drapery, meat and greengrocery in the early days. But in other respects the warehouses and arcades of Glasgow of the 1850s were startlingly like department stores in their architecture, their ambience and their appeal.

Other shops of the same period, however, followed the older model – small, intimate, personal. The Smith family knew and used both kinds of shop; and shopping – both for pleasure and out of necessity – played a large part in the lives of all its members.

As a young woman in Glasgow in the 1850s, Madeleine was well aware of this distinction. She implied that 'old style' instrumental shopping was unavoidable, and thus less suspect, even to a jealous and censorious lover, than strolling through the principal shopping streets of the city and shopping for pleasure:

> I did promise not to go on S[auchiehall], R[enfield?] and B[uchanan] Sts but it was necessity that took me there on Saturday. I went to town at 12 o'clock to make some purchases. I do promise I shall not walk for pleasure. [21st February 1856]

She also implied that shopping for the family household, rather than for personal items, was above reproach: 'I was on S. Road *necessity* caused me to go to do *household shopping.*'

It is alleged (albeit for a slightly later period) that there was a sexual element to the way female shoppers were regarded. Women were victims, 'seduced' by retailers and the bewildering array of goods that they offered, perhaps into profligacy with their husbands' or fathers' money. In the city centre, a site of 'public pleasure', women were themselves on display, and men could ogle them.[7] In an inchoate way, L'Angelier seems already to have been aware of this. He was concerned about what time of day Madeleine walked on Sauchiehall and Buchanan streets, about how long she spent there and whom she met. He might well have been, of course, having himself contrived to be introduced to Madeleine while she was shopping on Sauchiehall Street.

Not everyone, though, shared his view. Madeleine's Mama positively encouraged her daughters to go shopping: 'Everyone is asking why B and I are not walking on S St in the afternoon. M was quite annoyed we did not go out several times this week in the afternoon' [17th December 1856]. Even the family doctor, visiting the India Street house to see Mrs Smith, remarked in passing to the girls that they should go out every day. Neither he nor Mama seems to have expected them to be chaperoned, which is at odds with the argument that women strolling and shopping in the city had to have a male chaperon if they were not to be mistaken for prostitutes.[8] Madeleine and Bessie had been accustomed to walk out together every winter, she says, and Madeleine often went shopping alone, sometimes quite late in the evening. 'Then this evening about half past seven I had to go out to get a lot of things' [7th April 1856]. She doesn't say at what time she got home, but it cannot have been before 8 p.m/, by which time it would have been dark. Naturally, Emile would not approve of this, especially as he was astonished to see her 'so late' on the same street another day, at twenty past three, and wanted her not to be out after 1 p.m. On this last occasion she was alone, waiting for her mother, who did not turn up. Of course, Madeleine, especially shopping alone, did not stay out as late as some shops allowed. B. Hyams, National Tailor and Clothier (admittedly, specialising in men's clothes) stayed open until 11 p.m. on Saturday evenings.[9] However, we know that Madeleine came up to Glasgow from Row on her own to do some shopping in May 1855.

Although a male chaperon was clearly not a necessity, Madeleine did sometimes go shopping with men. She went with her father to Rait the jewellers in the Argyle Arcade, for instance; and Jack accompanied Madeleine and Bessie to shops on Sauchiehall Street in December 1855.

Later, William Minnoch went with the sisters on at least one occasion. This kind of outing was a mixture of shopping and promenading. It took Madeleine to the 'best' shopping streets of the city and allowed her to bow to acquaintances, note what they were wearing, to see and be seen as well as making purchases. Similarly, during the summer months Madeleine and others of the family were shopping in Helensburgh every Saturday morning between about eleven and twelve. It was very definitely shopping for pleasure.

Shops were starting to recognise this aspect of middle-class social life, and the arcades and warehouses already catered to it long before the advent of the department store proper. Clothes shops and furniture shops, in particular, developed into warehouses that foreshadowed many of the features of the department store. These had two or three floors, and their goods were arranged into 'departments'. Messrs John Little and Co's Furnishing and Ironmongery Emporium in Buchanan Street advertised in 1855 that its 'bewildering array' of goods was in departments 'each ... being so extensive as to form a shop in itself.'[10] But a telling feature of the warehouse was its gallery on the upper floor, which formed 'a magnificent promenade'. Here it was possible to enjoy all the pleasures of strolling on the city streets, but *inside* the shop. The proprietors were keen to stress that 'free access' was allowed to the public during business hours and that the warehouse had thus 'become a great resort to the Glasgow public'. As early as 1855, then, customers were being offered the chance to promenade and browse without obligation to purchase – another key attribute of department stores. John Little had arranged for a 'magnificent organ' to be played daily until eight in the evening to underline the 'shopping as entertainment' aspect of his establishment.

William Whiteley and other London department store proprietors of the 1870s and later claimed that they drew their inspiration from the plethora of items displayed at the London and Paris Exhibitions of 1851 and 1855. John Little of Glasgow was quicker off the mark: in 1855 his Emporium was 'lighted entirely by means of a glass roof, galleried and painted in the same way as the Crystal Palace in London.'[11] By January 1856, its name had been changed to The Crystal Palace Furnishing and Ironmongery Establishment, in case the similarities had escaped anyone.[12] Madeleine had visited the 1851 Exhibition, though we do not know whether she patronised Glasgow's Crystal Palace.

Little's was not the only store to use an iron frame and plate glass to produce a spectacular new style of shop. Gardner's, built in 1855–56 in Jamaica Street, epitomised this glamorous style.[13] An admiring observer of the Glasgow scene in 1856 commented on the way 'iron as a material in architecture is giving a new character to the construction of shops ... they are becoming universal window-palaces of crystal'.[14]

To a large degree, it was the potential of women as shoppers that influenced the design of new stores and ultimately helped to shape the centres of British cities. Another forerunner of the department store was the shopping arcade. The arcades of Paris have attracted much scholarly attention: they are an ambiguous urban space, 'neither inside nor outside, a passageway which is also a space of consumption'. [15] They perfectly balanced the twin pleasures of strolling and buying. Glasgow's foremost arcade was the Argyle Arcade, built in 1827.[16] It too had a glass roof to shield its promenading window-shoppers from the weather. The separate shops offered mainly luxury goods and appealed almost exclusively to the middle class. But its appeal was also directed particularly at women. If we take an imaginary stroll through the arcade in 1857, we can see how almost every shop would have had something to interest Madeleine and Bessie. Here is a complete list of the businesses in the arcade:

A. Harris	jeweller
Geo. Barker	shoemaker
C. Campbell	jeweller
D. McGrigor	bootmaker
A. McMillan	watchmaker
D. Buchanan	jeweller
P. Macfarlane	hardware merchant
T. Boston	seal engraver
J. Kerr	bootmaker
Lorimer & Moyes	perfumers
E. Scott	muslin printing
Mrs J. Scott	lace printing
D. Robertson	jewellers
Stewart & Donald	perfumers
Miss Gilmour	milliner
J. Galetti	optician
J. Russell	jeweller
Mrs Smith	milliner
J. Adams	Berlin wool
D. Tod	watchmaker
Miss Scott	baby-linens
D. Douglas	watchmaker
J. Robertson	cutler
Brown & Austin	seedsmen
J. Begg	bookseller
F. Reid	engraver
A. Watson	hosier and glover

J. Robertson	toy warehouse
G. Johnston	toy warehouse
G.I. Wardle	lace warehouse
D. Greenshields	music seller
W. Macintyre	umbrellas
F. Pritty	engraver
M. Morrison	milliner
R. Taylor	lace warehouse
Miss M. Elson	Berlin wool
Mrs J. Alexander	confectioner
Misses Waddell	milliners
M. Martin	milliner
Mrs J. Arnold	toy merchant
Miss E. Moffatt	stay maker
Miss A. Walker	milliner
W. Macintyre	umbrellas
G. Hinmers	lace man
Blackhall & Scott	combs etc.

None of these shops sold women's clothes as such, but a majority catered for female interests and sold female accessories. The lace, the combs, the hats and the stays were for *women* customers. The two Berlin wool shops were catering to a fairly new craze – Berlin work or needlepoint, where charts could be followed to produce decorative embroideries for cushions, chair seats, fire screens and the like. The toy shops were for mothers (or nursemaids) and their children.

In fact, a considerable number of the shopkeepers here were women, too. The arcade was a place where respectable middle-class women like Madeleine and Bessie could wander from window to window, seeing and being seen, out of the rain but in the public eye.

Clothiers were also beginning to recognise the influence of the female shopper. James Webster, shirt fitters, announced the opening of a 'ladies' department', specifically for marriage outfits and underclothes, and 'exclusively conducted by females'.[17] In fact, bridal outfits seem to have been big business. Dawson & MacNicol, ladies' outfitters, 50 Buchanan Street, specialised in 'Ladies' marriage outfits in all the various articles of underclothing, linens, flannels, hosiery, stays, dressing gowns, breakfast robes, caps, jackets, jupes, crinolines etc.'[18]

Madeleine had thought about the question of her trousseau, though of course there were complications caused by the necessary secrecy in assembling it. She felt that she could get everything together which she needed in ten days, if she was eloping. The way she proposed to do it harked back to an earlier, more traditional way of shopping. She would, she said, 'send an order to the house we deal with'. The same place would also furnish all the linen – presumably household linen. This would be made easier because she got 'all [her] under dress ready made' [14th December 1855]. Indeed Mama had already bought her a new set of underclothes ready for a trip to Edinburgh. It seems that the Smiths were quite up to date in this, for Fraser tells us that underclothes were only widely bought ready made from the 1870s.[19]

If they were in the forefront of changing practice in that matter, however, they were traditional in dealing with one 'house' and ordering goods from it. Of course, the older ways of shopping, based on small, intimate shops and a personal relationship between shopkeeper and customer, were not totally superseded by the new 'superstores'. We don't know which 'house' it was that enjoyed such patronage from the Smiths, but it may be significant that Madeleine was allegedly first introduced to Emile as she went into a draper's shop on Sauchiehall Street. Morland names this as Paterson's.[20] In fact, John Paterson had two shops: draper's at 277 Sauchiehall Street and clothier's at 263 Sauchiehall Street. This could well have been the business that could provide both underclothing and household linen.

Whichever shop it was, it is certain that the Smiths would have had a personal account there. Mr Smith certainly had an account with Alexander McRead, grocer, who testified that he knew Madeleine from her having been in his shop in Sarah Street on several occasions. There was even an account at the druggist's (Murdoch Brothers, 143 Sauchiehall Street) where Madeleine bought sixpence worth of arsenic and charged it to the family account.[21] When shopkeepers tendered these accounts, they did so by personal letter, thanking the recipient for their custom and politely – almost incidentally – suggesting that the account might be settled. Short-term credit like this was a feature of traditional shopping. L' Angelier had a 'pass book' with a butcher's and another with a grocer's, both on St George's Road near his lodgings.

Such small purchases were obviously at a fixed price: but it seems that the old practice of haggling over larger items might still linger. The changeover from one method of pricing to the other has been cited as a key feature of the modernising of shopping from the mid-nineteenth century.[22] It also made it more acceptable (because less vulgar) for women to shop via fixed-price tickets rather than haggling over prices. Hyams, National Tailor found it necessary to inform customers that 'All goods [are] marked in plain figures, the lowest selling price from which no abatement can be made.'[23] Other shops advertised 'fixed tickets' and 'cash prices'.

The main shopping streets where Madeleine walked and shopped remained a mixture of large and small shops, old and new style shopping. The Argyle Arcade is just off Buchanan Street, which from the 1830s constituted, with Sauchiehall Street, the most chic and upmarket shopping area of the city. The streets – and her shopping habits – were so well known to L'Angelier that Madeleine consistently had only to refer to them as 'S and B streets', although there are several central streets beginning with these letters. In the recent past, early Victorian ladies had waited in their carriages for retailers to bring goods out to them.[24] By the mid 1850s, Madeleine and her circle strolled the shopping streets, popping in and out of small shops as well as browsing in larger shops and arcades. She and Mary Jane Buchanan famously called in at Currie's on Sauchiehall Street to buy arsenic while out walking. There is no sign that Madeleine stayed outside shops, even when using transport. Occasionally, when the weather was bad, she used a cab: 'I was in Buchanan St on Monday but I was in a cab. I only walked from one shop to the next' [20th November 1855]. She means merely that she took a cab to get to Buchanan Street: even so, she was walking between shops.

Most of these were more intimate than the new warehouses and large stores. Before the advent of plate glass, shop window panes were some twelve by sixteen inches in size: by about 1830 that had grown to seven feet by three feet, and when Madeleine was shopping in the 1850s, to perhaps fourteen feet by eight.[25] But many Glasgow shops still had the old-style shop front, where windows were small and thresholds marked. It was difficult to see the goods inside – or, indeed, the customer. 'I was so much disappointed at not seeing you today. I was in a shop in S. St when you passed. I was at the door but you dearest did not see me' [30th March 1856]. Shops were too small to chat with other customers, it seems – or perhaps it was not acceptable to do so. Madeleine had to step outside to be introduced.

Middle-class women, then, even young, single, unaccompanied ones, could 'shop for pleasure' in the centre of the city with what, to the eyes of everyone except a jealous lover, was seen as perfect propriety. But what did they shop *for*? We pointed out that Madeleine discounted 'household shopping' because it was a necessity. Elsewhere she speaks of 'making markets'. This is usually taken to mean shopping for foodstuffs and the like – consumables for the home, rather than items for adorning either the home or the shopper. Davis points out that, at this period, much food was still bought at markets to which it had been brought by its producers – even in cities such as Glasgow. Here there were permanent 'bazaars' that seem to have been covered markets. The large one at Candleriggs, for instance, had fruit and vegetable dealers, ham merchants, egg merchants, butter sellers, poultry dealers, shoemakers and booksellers. This is clearly 'provision' shopping, and different from the kind of shopping in the Argyle Arcade. But it seems that Madeleine and other middle-class women 'housekeepers' did do at least some of their own provision shopping. When in Row over the summer, Madeleine went to nearby Helensburgh for this kind of shopping: in August 1856 she was there early, 'making markets'. 'I often wonder what they would do if I were not here. Mama never goes to a shop herself.' Presumably they would not have starved, for it seems unlikely that Madeleine was responsible for buying (or even ordering) all the provisions for the large household. Nevertheless, it seems that middle-class women were 'hands-on' shoppers for at least some of the household's food.

We know little about the kinds of food Madeleine and her circle were buying. Madeleine (who seems not to have been very interested in food, or not to have felt it a fit subject for romantic letters) was more likely to mention missing meals than to describe eating them. In fact, more is known about L'Angelier's provision shopping, which, given his frequently problematic digestion, sounds provocative to say the least. The very fact of his having a pass book at the butcher's suggests that he was a regular meat eater – and indeed he had bought a nice piece of beef to celebrate getting over an earlier illness. His pass book records two or three meat purchases a week, mostly chops and steak or a roast, although he did occasionally enjoy kidneys or sausages.[26] On another occasion he convalesced from a bilious attack by enjoying pickled herrings. But this was not what most alarmed his good Glaswegian landlady. What worried her was the quantity of vegetables that he consumed – although he assured her that he had been used to doing so in France with no terrible effect.[27] At the grocer's, Chalmers of St George's Road, he regularly bought his staples of bread, butter, eggs and sugar. In a curiously modern touch, he also bought salad oil and vinegar to make his own – suitably French – dressing.[28]

Emile sent Madeleine grapes, though we don't know where he bought either them or his shocking amounts of vegetables. Apart from the Bazaar, Glasgow in the 1850s was not awash with greengrocers that he might have used. The 1856–57 Directory lists fifty-six, as compared to some 676 grocers. Perhaps the landlady's suspicion was widely shared. Most grocers and greengrocers were situated just outside the inner core of what Madeleine called 'S., B and R. Sts'. The 'household shopping' that Madeleine explained in February 1856 was done only out of necessity was in fact done somewhat further out, in Partick, which was technically a separate burgh, although only a mile or so to the west. 'Necessity' shopping, then, could be done almost anywhere, not necessarily in the city centre.

However, most of the shopping that Madeleine and other middle-class women did was more personal. It was important for women to show good taste, whether in choosing furnishings and ornaments for the home or in their personal dress. Achieving the right fashionable look – a tasteful home, clothes that were stylish but not 'fast' – was one of the responsibilities of the middle-class woman.[29]

The new proto-department stores did not destroy the older style of smaller shop. The two could coexist because the new stores did not simply take all their custom from existing shops.[30] They created a new, often female-led market for an increased range of goods. 'Choice' and 'fashion' were, together with taste, the key words of shopping in mid century; and the market that was aimed at was both female and middle class. S. Woolfield, importer of continental novelties, 61 Buchanan Street, offered 'The new patent fans – a decided improvement. With many other novelties in hair pins, bouquet holders, dress combs, and more particularly bracelets which this season surpass any hitherto produced.'[31] Next door, at number 59, Simpson, Hunter & Young were 'at present showing a choice variety of evening dresses in every new and fashionable material – A magnificent assortment of rich silks for dinner dresses. Opera mantles, headdresses, flowers, laces, ribbons etc'.[32] The social standing of the target audience is clear, and the repetition of 'new', 'novelties' and so on appealed to their sense of fashion.

When Madeleine came up from Row to Glasgow 'for some things I want – gloves' [28th March 1856], she felt it necessary to travel all the way up to the city to get them. It was important to be at the forefront of fashion, and although Madeleine played down her concern with fashion to Emile, it is clear that she did dress in considerable style. The only known photograph of Madeleine, taken in 1856, shows her wearing a tight-fitting, waisted jacket of mid-thigh length, virtually identical to those on French fashion plates of 1855 (see Figure 6).

Good taste and the latest fashions came from Paris or, at a pinch, London. Dougall and Mathie advertised 'the new tissue bonnet, so much admired and patronised in the fashionable circles in Paris and London', and now available in Glasgow (Figure 8).[33] Metropolitan glamour inspired both the advertising and the naming of the 'new and elegant' London Bonnet Saloons, where 'the splendid array of millinery now exhibited to admiring crowds has never been excelled at the saloons of Paris or London'.[34] Bonnets were indeed still fashionable: but the really avant-garde were adopting hats. Madeleine and Bessie had new bonnets

8 Adverts from *Punch*, 1856, including for Parisian bonnets and a Crimean outfit

in November 1856 – Bessie's was pink but Madeleine chose fawn, as she thought L'Angelier would find pink vulgar. In the same month, 'I was in Town today with B. only fancy she wanted me to get a hat to wear – but I won't. You would not like me to wear one I am sure so dear sweet pet I won't have one a mile' [18th November 1856]. Hats were clearly rather racy. However, the photograph of Madeleine submitted at the trial was also taken in November 1856, and clearly shows her holding a dark-coloured straw hat with a wide brim. Her sister Janet described this as 'a brown straw or wideawake hat'.[35] Mama 'went out today and got hats velvet for B. and I. But I sent them back and told her I would not wear them' [n.d. 1856]. Hats were replacing caps and bonnets slowly from the mid 1850s, so once again the Smiths, including Mama, who was after all only 45, were in the vanguard of fashion.[36] It is interesting that she went out and bought hats for her girls without consulting them. Another way of ensuring fashion and individuality was to customise ready-made bonnets: 'I have got a blue bonnet to dress' [24th November 1855]. Unfortunately, we don't know at which of the very many milliners in the city Madeleine and Mama had bought her headgear.

One thing is certain: there was plenty of choice. Another crucial characteristic of 'new-style' shopping was the vast array of goods from which the customer could choose. This, together with high fashion, was the key selling point for advertisers. The London Bonnet Saloon offered 'a vast and fairy-like melange … bonnets, head-dresses, caps, flowers and ribbons, illimitable in variety and number'.[37]

One way in which Madeleine and Bessie kept up to date in terms of fashion was to have new clothes for each season. The stylish jacket that Madeleine wears in her photo was almost certainly made for her by a dressmaker. Although she never mentions going for fittings, it was standard practice still to buy fabric and have clothes made up; and here the jacket is so tight fitting that it probably was made to measure. Janet later explained that it was 'got last summer' (1856) and that her sister wore it in autumn in town, but not over winter. Perhaps it wasn't warm enough, although it appears quite substantial – and indeed Madeleine recognised this when she wrote in October 1856, 'I shall have on the jacket. I cannot help it. I have nothing warm but it.' This is probably the new jacket which she says Mama and Papa like but she does not, as it makes her look a fright [n.d. 1856]. In another undated letter in 1856, Madeleine reports that 'Papa has got jackets for us.' This does sound more like the purchase of ready-made garments, and may refer to a different jacket altogether. However, the image of Mr Smith – who did seem to take an interest in his daughters' clothes – going out and actually choosing and purchasing jackets for his girls is an unlikely one.

It is similarly unclear how the garment was actually obtained when L'Angelier bought a dress for the maid, Christina Haggart. We first hear of this bribe in March 1856, when Madeline writes, 'CH tells me her dress is so pretty. I have not seen it yet.' Shortly afterwards: 'I have not seen CH dress it has been sent out to be done up.' Presumably it had gone to a dressmaker: but what does 'done up' mean? Was it a ready-made dress, gone to be altered? Or perhaps 'dress' meant a dress length, and what L'Angelier had bought was simply the material, now gone to be made up. The latter seems the more likely.[38] Beveridge Brothers of Sauchiehall Street sold 'Shawls, mantles, millinery, ribbons, flowers, dress stuffs, lace goods, tweed goods, gloves and hosiery' as well as haberdashery and other fabrics – all for making up by a dressmaker, it seems.[39]

Singer's newly invented sewing machine arrived in Glasgow in this same year, 1856, though it clearly took a while for its use to reach a wide domestic market.[40] Machine-made clothes, at least for men, were already being offered in 1856. Hyams National Tailor informed the public that 'Garments produced by the aid of machines, both in the cutting and sewing, possess uniformity in style, elegance in appearance, and durable workmanship unattainable by ordinary hand labour.'[41] A kind of hybrid solution was open to women: they could buy a ready-made skirt and have the more fitted bodice hand made. In September 1856 Madeleine, still in Row, said that she would have to go up to Glasgow soon 'as I want to get a new dress'. This could also be taken to mean a ready-made garment, but could just as well refer to a length of dress fabric. It is also significant that Madeleine had to go up to Glasgow to get it, as she did for the new gloves. In the same way, when Mama bought the girls new bonnets in the summer of 1856, they came from Glasgow: 'M. made me the present today of a very pretty thin white bonnet. She sent to Glasgow for one for B and I' [17th June 1856]. Glasgow was the Mecca for fashionable purchases, but in any case Mrs Smith seems to have preferred others to do her shopping. Even when in Glasgow 'Mama this winter cannot go out much so I am obliged to do both her messages and my own' [24th January 1856].[42]

The advent of mass production and the emergence of a clothing industry from the 1850s brought fashion to an ever-widening social stratum. So it is not a coincidence that 'couture' and 'designer fashion' began to appear in reaction to this development, notably with the work of Charles Worth in Paris, in this same decade.[43] After Paris and London, the great provincial cities like Glasgow were first to adopt new fashions.

Madeleine had also had experience of shopping in London and Paris, the two places frequently invoked by Glasgow advertisers as epitomising glamour. Nevertheless, in London in the early 1850s she might have been made to feel more at home by the increasing presence in shops there of 'Scotch' garments, tweeds and plaids. Scotch Tweed Warehouses and Scotch Tartan Warehouses existed by the end of the 1840s to cater for the royal-instigated craze for all things Scottish. Because of their appeal in France, they also printed their advertising in French: so Scotland set the style for some things in London and Paris, as well as the other way round.[44]

Clothes, by their cut and their colour, gave off signals (then as now) about the wearer. Madeleine was constantly trying to reassure Emile as to the propriety of her dress. Her new white bonnet she later described as 'very plain'. Earlier in the year she had stressed how she planned to wear only simple bonnets: 'Don't fear I shall never again put *pink flowers* to my bonnet. I have a plain straw bonnet with a white ribbon. I shall wear a white bonnet all summer' [27th April 1856]. Pink seems to have been a particularly suspect colour for bonnets: Madeleine's new aversion to it extended even to her mother's wearing the colour, and she found an effective way of dissuading her: 'I have got Mama to put off that pink bonnet by telling her it made her look old' [n.d., probably 12th April 1856]. L'Angelier constantly, it seems, remonstrated with Madeleine about was and was not proper for her to wear. To what extent was this simple jealousy on his part, not wanting her to look attractive to other suitors? To what extent was it realism, knowing that she would not be able to wear such expensive and fashionable clothes if she became his wife? Or maybe his petty bourgeois ideas of propriety were at odds with those not only of Madeleine but also of her family and her social circle.

In order to please him, Madeleine frequently presents herself as negotiating with her parents to wear plainer dress, adopting more sober colours and more demure accessories. She says her favourite colours are white and grey, the same as his [16th November 1855]. Her new dress for the winter season of 1856 was of dark grey tweed – 'You will like that, I am sure' [October 1856]. The 'bright blues and greens' of current fashion Madeleine professed to see as 'vulgar'. (Although Mary Perry had 'green ribbons to her bonnet', which seems to have been acceptable.) Black was always suitable, of course, and lace seems to have been preferable to silk on the grounds of being less shiny.

> I did not buy a silk dress on Monday but I got a black lace one. I remember you saying to me you liked me in black so I thought I would please you by getting it. I knew you would be horrified by my blue dress on Monday. I hate it. The red trimming is all out some time ago. [n.d., probably November 1856]

L'Angelier may also have wanted Madeleine to dress like a married woman, which in his eyes she was. So perhaps some of his strictures, however petty they seem, reflect the difference in dress expected of married and single women. Nevertheless, some of his objections are hard to fathom: what was wrong with a white handkerchief? 'I shall not carry a white handkerchief again' [n.d. 1856]. Others are perhaps more understandable. Already at the very beginning of their relationship, Emile was issuing injunctions about Madeleine's evening dresses. As early as 7th May 1855 she was agreeing to 'wear her dresses higher' as he had obviously complained about her décolletage – though she honestly said she couldn't promise always to wear them high. For balls and dinners, the dictates of fashion could not be totally disregarded.

The latest and most extreme fashion of the day, of course, was the crinoline. Skirts had been growing more voluminous and the number of petticoats required to support them burdensome, so the natural development was a lightweight frame to carry the skirt. The crinoline or 'hoops' allowed ever-wider skirts, and afforded great potential for caricature in publications such as *Punch*. The first real crinolines were adopted in 1856 and the first British patent for a metal-framed crinoline was taken out in July of that year.[45] Madeleine first mentions the new fashion in August 1856: 'I shall not wear "crinoline" as you don't like it.' She continues: 'It is off today' [14th August 1856]. This sounds as if she has got a crinoline but has given it up because – predictably – L'Angelier objected. However, presenting herself as the dutiful daughter, Madeleine reported some months later: 'Mama does not like hoops or crinoline so we will not have them' [late November/early December 1856].

The crinoline is often cited as the epitome of restrictive and impractical dress for the confined Victorian woman. Although it had its inconveniences, in fact the crinoline was lighter, cooler and more liberating than the petticoats that preceded it. Furthermore, it swayed and tilted provocatively, revealing ankles or more. The crinoline was, for its day, sexy. No wonder Mama had her doubts about it and L'Angelier had expressed disapproval. We can guess that Madeleine did have a crinoline and did wear it, but wished her priggish lover to think otherwise.

In fact, closer inspection of Madeleine's 'sacrifices' in this respect reveals a pattern. Where she could present a decision to dress plainly (or 'neatly' as Emile had exhorted her in a letter of November 1855) as her own choice, she did so. Where this was not possible, then parents or current custom were blamed. Indeed she went so far as to allege that she had no interest in clothes and did not choose her own: 'I have no idea of dress myself. M. and B. do all that for me' [October 1856]. Because Papa had bought her jacket, she 'had to wear it'. She 'could not' wear high-necked dresses in the evening.[46] In other cases, she disguised her own preference as a concession to Emile's sensibilities. She presented the black lace dress she had chosen as being preferable *to him*: he had thus governed her choice. Yet this was at the end of 1856, and apparently 1857 saw a craze for black lace dresses.[47] Once again, Madeleine was in the vanguard of fashion: as with the crinoline, she adopted a new fad as soon as it appeared, and then glossed over it to her lover. To him, she portrayed herself as 'above' such frivolous concerns and wishing only to appear plainly and soberly dressed.

The most sober dress of all was mourning. It has long been accepted that Queen Victoria's lengthy and conspicuous adoption of mourning for the Prince Consort led to the development of a retail industry based around mourning dress.[48] Yet although the rules of mourning reached their apogee rather later in the century, they were already rigid and would have applied to Madeleine had she suffered a family bereavement during this period. She made her priorities plain: 'Uncle is not yet dead so I may not be in mourning for some time to come' [21st March 1856]. No doubt it was galling to have to adopt mourning wear – though since Madeleine had already professed to prefer black, grey and white to other colours she might have spared a thought for Uncle's health too. She fails to mention this again, so presumably Uncle surprised her by living at least another year. If he had died, not only Madeleine but the rest of the household, including the servants, would have had to go into mourning.[49] The provision of mourning clothes was already a lucrative and reliable business, well before the death of Prince Albert. In the 1850s some shops and warehouses existed to sell only mourning attire and were not, as has been alleged, a product of royal bereavement. L'Angelier had been spotted wearing mourning, and Madeleine asked who it was for. However, men's mourning dress – perhaps a black hat, armband or cravat – was less all-encompassing than women's.

In the same way, men's costume was less susceptible to rapid changes in fashion than was women's. Nevertheless, acquaintances of L'Angelier agreed that he was something of a dandy – a smart dresser, proud of his appearance. He too seems to have been up to the minute in adopting such changes of fashion as there were for men. Men's trousers became wider from the mid 1850s;[50] and already in 1855, as we have seen, Madeleine was telling him that she thought his trousers too wide. Unfortunately we do not know his reaction; but he seems not to have been pleased that she failed to notice, when seeing him in the street in the same month, that he was wearing a new top coat, even though he had already told her about it in a letter. We also know that he favoured a Balmoral bonnet, now most frequently seen as part of the uniform of Scottish regiments – a particularly Scottish accessory, so he had tempered his exotic 'foreignness' at least to this extent.

There were numerous shops in the city centre where men's ready-made clothes could be bought, and their prices were coming down, thanks to the introduction of mechanised production methods. The National Tailor who lauded new machine-made goods pointed out the advantages:

> The introduction of machinery renders necessary a complete division of labour, and effects great saving in production, which fully warrants me in stating that for real service, beauty and cheapness, these machine-produced garments are not to be equalled by any other house in the kingdom.[51]

The garments were, in the main, men's trousers.

It was fortunate for Emile that cheapness was one of the benefits of machine-made clothes, for it must have been quite difficult being a dandy on ten shillings a week. Nevertheless, poorly paid clerks like him were recognised as assiduous followers of the latest fashions: 'These are the dashing young parties who purchase the pea-green gloves, the crimson braces, the kaleidoscopic shirt-studs … these are the glasses of city fashion for whom the legions of fourteen, of fifteen, of sixteen shilling trousers, all unrivalled, patented and warranted, are made.'[52] But of course Madeleine, with the resources of a wealthy family behind her, did not have to make the kinds of sacrifices that must have been involved in L'Angelier's pursuit of the latest fashions.

Although Madeleine was able to charge purchases to the family account, it is clear that she did also carry money. In April 1856, having been shopping in town, she thought she must have dropped money or had her pocket picked. That she felt the latter a possibility is interesting, as it suggests that even middle-class women could be subjected to the jostling and crowding that a pick-pocket needs. Perhaps one of the unsung benefits of the crinoline would be to keep such thieves at bay! We have seen that Madeleine urged L'Angelier not to be alarmed by the generosity of her personal allowance because 'I shall not want the dresses I do now' [31st May 1856]. So she expected to dress less lavishly when married to him. This also suggests that she bought at least some of her dresses out of this personal allowance; and she asked how this was to work when she and Emile were married. 'I shall save as much of my money as I can. Would you wish me to buy things for myself – clothes etc? I could do it quite easily – as you like love' [15th July 1856].

Since money for shopping was not a problem, how did Madeleine decide what to buy with cash and what to charge to the family account? She could have bought her arsenic more secretly by paying for it out of her own pocket. If the arsenic really was for cosmetic purposes, as was alleged, there was also reason for secrecy. The use of any aids to beauty was regarded as morally ambiguous in the 1850s.[53] At the trial, several Glasgow chemists were called to testify that numerous young women had tried to buy arsenic from them as a means of improving their complexions, but this seems to have been done in a rather furtive way. About half of the entries in Murdoch's poison register were of sales of arsenic to women, all of whom said that it was to kill rats.[54] Also at the trial, the idea that Miss Giubelei, a pupil-teacher at Madeleine's school, might have used any cosmetics was rapidly dismissed by Mary Jane Buchanan, as if such use threw her character into disrepute.

At this period, using creams and lotions to improve the skin was more common than using actual cosmetics like rouge or powder.[55] Madeleine certainly used preparations on her skin, though whether or not they included arsenic remains debated. Janet and Papa had both noticed 'a whiteish powder' left on her skin. Bessie acerbically remarked that she was 'always working away' at her complexion with a great many 'tinctures', although Bessie professed not to know where she bought them. The utmost secrecy was needed for any more drastic cosmetic action. For those with grey or (interestingly) red hair, Rosalie Coupelle's hair dye was obtainable from all chemists, but it could also be sent 'secure from observation' to one's home.[56]

Perfume, though, was quite respectable. Its popularity is underlined by the presence of twenty-four perfumers in the city centre. Some doubled up as hairdressers, others as chemists (or 'druggists'), of whom there were sixty-four. The latter sold soap and 'pomade', the only toiletries Janet had seen on Madeleine's washstand. But their main function was to sell remedies for minor ailments. Bessie and James had also visited Murdoch's, where Madeleine had bought arsenic, to buy mixture for toothache. L'Angelier had a considerable stock of such remedies at his lodgings. Madeleine had urged him to visit his doctor rather than 'doctoring yourself' with potions from the chemist. If it was L'Angelier whom witnesses described walking through the outskirts of the city from Coatbridge the day before his death, he seems to have been unable to pass a chemist's without popping in for some medicine or other.

Emile wasn't Madeleine's only correspondent: like many Victorian women of her class she was a prodigious letter writer, and she once told him that his was the sixteenth letter she had written that day. She kept a writing slope in her room, and assumed that others of her family would be similarly assiduous in writing. When James went away to school in autumn 1856 she reported: 'I am just going to Helensburgh to buy him a present. I intend to get him a tourists writing case' [n.d., probably

August, 1856]. Helensburgh, although too limited for fashion shopping, could supply essentials such as this. Madeleine bought writing paper from Robert Oliphant of Argyle Square, Helensburgh, although she complained about its poor quality. She had ordered a hundred envelopes for herself from Oliphant's, and another hundred for Bessie. She preferred to get her paper and ink in Glasgow, from Walter Ogilvie in St Vincent Street. For added feminine delicacy, she got perfumed ink (Emile complained about the perfumed paper, but she replied that it was the ink rather than the paper that was scented). Madeleine had her own seal with her initials, MHS, for sealing her own letters, although she could also use the Smith family crest, which, perhaps not inappropriately, was a shark. The use of seals was sufficiently widespread to keep the Smiths' seal engraver, David Crawford of Argyle Street, in business.

Ogilvie's was not only a stationer's, but a bookshop and 'reading club' too. If Blyth is right in saying that Madeleine and Emile used to meet there in the early days of their courtship, then the establishment was not an all-male preserve. In fact a lending library or reading club would have been an excellent place to meet: the only problem is that there is no mention of these meetings anywhere in the letters. Robert Oliphant, the Helensburgh stationer, also ran the 'Athenaeum' – a reading room 'amply supplied with London, Glasgow and other provincial newspapers, maps, reviews etc'.[57] Oliphant's establishment, and probably Ogilvie's too, were definitely aimed at the middle class. The Helensburgh Athenaeum cost a guinea a year in membership. However, it does seem as if they were intended for a male clientele, notwithstanding Madeleine's purchases of stationery in Ogilvie's.

Like other middle-class families, the Smiths regularly bought books, newspapers and magazines. The popularity of reading was immense: there were scores of booksellers and thirty-three libraries in the city in 1857. Madeleine got *Chambers Journal* and *Blackwood's Magazine* each month, the latter, 'the best conducted monthly publication', being her favourite. Not all magazines met with her approval. She '… caused M. to stop the London Journal, a most blackguard publication, not fit for the likes of James to read' [25th April 1856]. On the other hand, she got a copy of 'a paper called The Waverley written by ladies' but did not like it because 'it was milk and water writing, you know the style' [6th August 1856]. As for newspapers – 'We do not take the Glasgow Herald. The Daily Mail comes every morning that is our paper' [26th June 1856]. Newspapers were obviously delivered to the house, at least at Row.

Madeleine and Emile were pretty much the first generation of lovers for whom keeping in constant touch by letter (even on a clerk's meagre salary) was not financially demanding. The penny post was younger than Madeleine, yet already its use, together with stamps, postmarks and frequent deliveries, had become taken for granted. Madeleine visited the Glasgow Post Office in George Square frequently, both to send and collect letters, though she sent Christina to collect her letters from Row Post Office. Perhaps Christina also posted some letters in Glasgow, although Madeleine implied that she did this herself when she explained that 'It is not easy for me to post letters – I cannot do so every day' [21st November 1856]. Someone was out and about, posting her letters in Sauchiehall Street and nearby, two or three times a week, and often late in the day: postmarks were recorded 'after 6.20 pm'; 7 p.m.; 'during the night' – as well as mid-morning and mid-afternoon. All were to be delivered within a few hours.

Even more novel was the couple's ability to exchange 'likenesses', in the form of photographs rather than miniatures or silhouettes, which of course, being more costly, would be less easy to pass on secretly. The invention of the wet collodion process in 1851 enabled multiple copies to be made from the same negative, and boosted the photographic industry.[58] By 1855 there were several photographers' studios in Glasgow, and even one in Helensburgh. In August 1855 Madeleine said that she had had five photographs done but they were 'horrid' and that the photographer (not a good businessman) had said she 'will never take a good likeness'. These were most likely ambrotypes,[59] and were still not cheap, with the smallest size of 'likeness' costing 2s 6d and the largest, or fourth size 7s 6d.[60]

Nevertheless, Madeleine had more photographs taken in September 1856 by William Young, photographer of Helensburgh. These too were 'horrid' because she looked cross. She had been in the studio from twelve until four, had not eaten since the night before, and was 'furious'. As well she might be, if the process were as long drawn out as that. L'Angelier had also had his likeness taken, and Madeleine had one by summer 1855. She returned it when the engagement was first broken off in September that year, but seems to have acquired another one later. Photography and Emile were made for each other, and he probably had several.

Finally, Madeleine shopped for services as well as goods, at least to a limited extent. The end of her formal education at 18 did not mean the end of all lessons. She continued to have music lessons: Morland tells us, citing a letter from L'Angelier to his sister, that these were with Robert, Richard and Edith Adams in Hill Street. This was probably in spring 1855, for a year later, while writing about music lessons (which she was still taking), Madeleine suddenly referred to receiving her first note from Emile 'in

Hill Street'. In fact, the Adamses of 102 Hill Street in Garnethill taught piano, harmonium, violin, flute, cornopean and concertina. Madeleine was having piano lessons, at least in 1855, when she reported going 'to music' on Fridays from ten till one and playing duets with Bessie [5th December 1855]. These, though, seem not to have been with the Adamses: 'Mama has picked up some old man to give us lessons. I do not know his name yet. B. goes with me to take them, he lives on Bath St' [29th November 1855].

Later that December, she was confident that Papa would buy her a guitar, as she wished to learn that too, no doubt to please Emile, who also played the guitar. He was also inexplicably keen that she should take lessons in watercolour painting, and the topic cropped up repeatedly. 'Did I tell you I have got consent to take water colours this winter rather than music lessons?' [13th October 1856]. It isn't clear, though, whether she ever did take these lessons.

Perhaps she lacked the time. Shopping, whether 'making markets' or 'walking for pleasure', took up a lot of Madeleine's time. When in Row, she walked into Helensburgh every day, once it had become too cold for driving; otherwise she took the carriage [13th October 1856]. In Glasgow, mentions of shopping and walking in the city centre, sometimes with others, sometimes alone, are very frequent. Whether by cab, family carriage or (more often) on foot, Madeleine's movements around the city were not restricted. There was no apparent need for a chaperon – certainly not a male one. At least once she came up from Row to shop in Glasgow and met up with Emile in town. At other times she went shopping accompanied by her sister, her visiting cousin or her friend Mary Buchanan – that is, a couple of young women going shopping on their own.

However much she tried to present herself to L'Angelier as rising above an interest in the material (unlike the other 'vulgar and mercenary' Glasgow folk), it is obvious that Madeleine loved to shop. She delighted in strolling through the bustling streets, with their bright and tempting shops; she loved the latest fashions; she enjoyed spending the money and receiving the presents given to her by indulgent parents. No doubt there were scores of other young, middle-class women who felt exactly the same.

As an architect, James Smith contributed directly to the shaping of Glasgow city centre as it developed in the mid nineteenth century. Some of the buildings he designed remain important features of the cityscape. Yet indirectly, his wife and daughters were contributing too, together with others of their sex and class. By influencing the way that goods were bought and sold, they too helped to shape the city. The new-style shops (and later the department stores that they foreshadowed) were directed towards an expanding middle class. Bourgeois culture and bourgeois ambitions were laid out for display there.[61] But the way that women, in particular, engaged with retail trade was instrumental from mid century in determining how the city *looked* – bright, inviting, luxurious. It was in order to cater for a specifically female market that many innovations in retailing were adopted. The role of the 'new' middle class in these developments has long been recognised. The role of women, though, has been seen as largely a passive one: shops were built for them, they were lured into the city centre and its 'halls of temptation'.[62] The view of women as actively shaping the city by their presence, their desires and their purchasing is a much newer one.[63] It is a view that is fully supported by Madeleine's experience in mid-century Glasgow.

L'Angelier was right to be suspicious, then. He tried to prevent Madeleine 'walking' on Sauchiehall Street not only because she might meet someone else, just as she had met him, but also because she was enjoying consumerism of a kind that would for ever be denied to her as his wife. They both knew that the wife of a warehouse clerk would shop for necessities much more than she shopped for pleasure; that there would be far fewer new dresses and few luxuries. Madeleine's protestations that she could live happily and frugally on his salary were constantly undermined by her artless recounting of her shopping trips and the careless pleasure she took in the world of fashion.

Madeleine's best-documented purchases were those of sixpence worth of arsenic, one bought from Murdoch's and two from Currie's, both 'chemists and druggists' on Sauchiehall Street.[64] These purchases offer telling detail about the nature of shopping in mid-century Glasgow. There was a family account at Murdoch's, to which Madeleine happily charged her 'secret' purchase. Two young women, Madeleine and her friend Mary Jane Buchanan, strolling and chatting on Sauchiehall Street, could pop in to Currie's and buy arsenic without anyone thinking it odd. Madeleine scrawled her name in the poisons register, airily saying that she would 'sign anything you like' at Currie's. The first purchase, at Murdoch's, she said was 'for garden at country house'.[65] Other purchasers recorded in his poisons register, who said the arsenic was for 'rats', were Miss Pagan, Miss Ewing, Miss Orr, Miss Taylor and so on – all with very middle-class addresses. No one queried why these young women were doing shopping that one would expect to be delegated to servants or gardeners: presumably chemists were happy to go along with the fiction. It was an era of deference in retailing: the customer – or at least the middle-class customer – was always right.

Madeleine's three purchases of arsenic were made on 21st February 1857 at Murdoch's, and at Currie's on 6th March and 18th March. This became of vital importance when, on 23rd March, Emile L'Angelier's health, often problematic, worsened dramatically.

Notes

1 William Lancaster, *The Department Store: A Social History* (Leicester University Press, 1995).
2 Cynthia Wall, 'Window Shopping', University of Virginia, online publications, 2001.
3 Bill Evans and Andrew Lawson, *A Nation of Shopkeepers* (Plexus, 1981).
4 *Chambers Journal* 1864, quoted in Wilfred Whitaker, *Victorian and Edwardian Shopworkers* (David and Charles, 1973), p. 32.
5 Michael B. Miller, *The Bon Marche: Bourgeois Culture and the Department Store, 1869–1920* (George Allen & Unwin, 1981).
6 Erika Diane Rappaport, *Shopping for Pleasure: Women in the Making of London's West End* (Princeton University Press, 2000).
7 Ibid., p. 13.
8 Judith Walkowitz, *City of Dreadful Delight* (University of Chicago Press, 1992).
9 *Glasgow Herald*, 7th March 1856.
10 *Morning Bulletin*, April 1855.
11 Ibid.
12 *Glasgow Herald*, 11th January 1856.
13 Rudolph Kenna, *Old Glasgow Shops* (Glasgow City Archives, 1996), p. 5.
14 *Hamilton Advertiser*, 13th September 1856.
15 Sherry Simon, 'The Paris Arcades, the Ponte Vecchio and the Comma of Translation', *Meta*, XLV, 1 (2000), p. 75 (summarising the arguments of Walter Benjamin).
16 Kenna, *Old Glasgow Shops*.
17 Female shop assistants were in fact a rarity at this date: it was the 1880s and 1890s before they became widespread. Dorothy Davis, *A History of Shopping* (Routledge & Kegan Paul, 1966), p. 260.
18 *Glasgow Herald*, 21st March 1856.
19 W. Hamish Fraser, *The Coming of the Mass Market* (Archon Books, 1981), p. 63.
20 Nigel Morland, *That Nice Miss Smith* (Frederick Muller Ltd, 1957), p. 39.
21 NAS JC 126/1031/1/152, Madeline Smith trial papers: Murdoch's poison register.
22 Davis, *History of Shopping*.
23 *Glasgow Herald*, 7th March 1856.
24 Rappaport, *Shopping for Pleasure*, p. 10.
25 Evans and Lawson, *A Nation of Shopkeepers*, pp. 120–1. Cited in Wall, 'Window Shopping'.
26 NAS JC 126/1031/1/157, L'Angelier's pass book with John Stewart, butcher.
27 F. Tennyson Jesse, *The Trial of Madeleine Smith* (William Hodge & Co., 1927).
28 NAS JC 126/1031/1/156, L'Angelier's pass book with J. Chalmers, provision dealer.
29 Eleanor Gordon and Gwyneth Nair, *Public Lives: Women, Family and Society in Victorian Britain* (Yale University Press, 2003), pp. 213–14.
30 Davis, *History of Shopping*, p. 259.
31 *Glasgow Herald*, 28th January 1856.

32   *Glasgow Herald*, 2nd January 1856.
33   *Glasgow Daily Times*, 9th May 1855.
34   *Dumbarton Herald*, 24th May 1855.
35   NAS AD 57/255/49, Precognition of Janet Hamilton Smith.
36   Hamish Fraser, *Mass Market*, p. 63.
37   *Dumbarton Herald*, 24th May 1855.
38   *Hood's Magazine and Comic Miscellany*, 1844, quoted in Alison Adburgham, *Shops and Shopping, 1800–1914* (Barrie and Jenkins, 1989), p. 68 has a shopkeeper asking his customer 'Would you allow me, Ma'am, to cut off a dress?' This clearly means a length of material.
39   Glasgow Post Office Directory 1856/7, p. 188.
40   Ibid., p. 159.
41   *Glasgow Herald*, 7th March 1856.
42   'Messages' is Scots for errands or items to be bought: in this case personal items, it seems, rather than domestic marketing.
43   Elizabeth Wilson, *Adorned in Dreams: Fashion and Modernity* (Virago, 1985), p. 32.
44   Adburgham, *Shops and Shopping*, p. 73.
45   Alison Gernsheim, *Victorian and Edwardian Fashion: A Photographic Survey* (Dover Publications, 1981), p. 45.
46   In fact evening dresses of the 1850s were low necked and worn off the shoulder, and so were quite revealing, and as Madeleine says in another letter, 'rather cold' [January 1857].
47   Gernsheim, *Victorian and Edwardian Fashion*, p. 43.
48   J. Anderson Black and Madge Garland, *A History of Fashion* (Orbis Publishing, 1975) p. 291.
49   Adburgham, *Shops and Shopping*, pp. 58–66.
50   Gernsheim, *Victorian and Edwardian Fashion*, p. 36.
51   *Glasgow Herald*, 7th March 1856.
52   George Augustus Sala, *Twice Round the Clock; or, the Hours of the Day and Night in London* (Houston & Wright, 1859), quoted in Judith Flanders, *Consuming Passions: Leisure and Pleasure in Victorian Britain* (Harper Press, 2006), pp. 87–8.
53   Wilson, *Adorned in Dreams*, p. 107.
54   NAS JC 126/1031/1/152, Madeleine Smith trial papers: Murdoch's poison register.
55   Wilson, *Adorned in Dreams*, p. 109.
56   *Glasgow Daily Times*, 8th August 1855.
57   *Dumbarton Herald*, 7th June, 1855.
58   Avril Lansdell, *Fashion a la Carte, 1860–1900* (Shire Publication, 1985).
59   Robert Pols, *Family Photographs 1860–1940* (Public Record Office, 2002).
60   *Glasgow Time and Daily Advertiser*, 15th May 1855.
61   Miller, *Bon Marche*, p. 3, refers particularly to Parisian department stores: but the arcades and warehouses of Glasgow shared the same characteristic.
62   Rappaport, *Shopping for Pleasure*.
63   Rappaport, ibid.; Rappaport, '"A New Era of Shopping": The Promotion of Women's Pleasure in London's West End, 19091914', in Leo Charney and Vanessa R. Schwartz (eds), *Cinema and the Invention of Modern Life* (University of California Press, 1995).
64   *Glasgow Post Office Directory*, 1857. Madeleine used the older term, calling them both 'apothecaries'.
65   NAS JC126/1031/1/152, Madeleine Smith trial papers: Murdoch's poison register.

5

This unparalleled case

At 2.30 a.m. on Monday 23rd March Mrs Jenkins, L'Angelier's landlady, was wakened by the insistent ringing of her doorbell. Alarmed, she rushed to answer it, to be greeted by L'Angelier, bent in agony, on the doorstep. He had left his lodgings at nine o'clock the previous evening and taken his pass key, as he expected to be late. However, he was in such pain that he was unable to use it. Mrs Jenkins helped him into bed and tended to him, but as L'Angelier continued vomiting violently and writhing in pain she was forced to call a doctor, who prescribed some medication but did not visit. Dr Steven was called again at 7 a.m., and this time did visit but, despite his medical attentions, L'Angelier died about eleven o'clock on Monday morning.

A post-mortem was carried out at the request of L'Angelier's employers. The preliminary report by Drs Thomson and Steven was given on Tuesday 24th March and, although they were guarded about their findings, their examination showed that L'Angelier had almost certainly died of arsenic poisoning. Rumours began to circulate when one of L'Angelier's supervisors, William Stevenson, found Madeleine's letters in his office desk drawer and handed them over to the Procurator Fiscal. The next day Madeleine mysteriously disappeared from the family home in Blythswood Square. Her brother and William Minnoch went in pursuit, guessing that she had gone to *Rowaleyn*. They managed to intercept her on board the steamer for Helensburgh and brought her back to Glasgow. Minnoch faithfully continued to visit the house during these strained days in the Smith household, despite the increasing gossip and speculation, and Madeleine's confession to him that she had written a number of letters to a 'Frenchman'. On Tuesday 31st March Minnoch again called at the Smiths', to pay a call on Mrs Smith, who he had heard was ill. He had a brief conversation with Madeleine during which she alluded to L'Angelier's death and said it was rumoured that he had died of poisoning. She also felt compelled to tell Minnoch that she had on occasion bought arsenic for cosmetic purposes. That was to be their last conversation. Later that day, James Hart, the Procurator Fiscal of Glasgow, issued a warrant for the arrest of Madeleine Hamilton Smith for the murder of Emile Pierre L'Angelier.

The few weeks before L'Angelier's death are shrouded in confusion, supposition, speculation and, perhaps, lies. While Madeleine and L'Angelier appeared to have a reconciliation, her letters, although affectionate, lacked the passion of her earlier ones and she no longer referred to him as 'husband' or herself as 'wife'. L'Angelier continued to press Madeleine about her relationship with Minnoch and on several occasions asked her directly if she was engaged to anyone else but him. Madeleine, for her part, was evasive. They continued to see each other, although much less frequently, and her letters suggest that she was not overly enthusiastic about meeting up with him. The Smiths were planning a family holiday in the Bridge of Allan from 6th to 17th March. Madeleine's letter to Emile just before her departure provides a flavour of the tone of her communications with him in the last weeks of his life and their relationship:

> My Dearest Emile,
> I hope by this time you are quite well and able to be out. I saw you at your window, but I could not tell how you looked – well, I hope … On Friday we go to Stirling for a fortnight. I am so sorry, my dearest pet, I cannot see you ere we go – but I cannot. Will you write me for Thursday, at eight o'clock, and I shall get before I go – which will be a comfort to me – as I shall not hear from you till I come home again. I will write you – but, sweet pet, it may only be once a week – as I have so many friends in that quarter … I have not seen you all this week – have you been passing? … You won't get a letter from me this Saturday, as I shall be off – but I shall write the beginning of the week. Write me for Thursday, sweet love.
> With love and affection,
> Mimi
> [5th March]

Madeleine omitted to mention that William Minnoch would be staying with the family for a few days at their Bridge of Allan lodgings. When she did write an anodyne letter to L'Angelier from the spa town, she conveniently omitted to tell him that she and Minnoch had set their wedding date for 18th June 1857. Although there is no indication of panic in her letters, one can only assume that Madeleine was frantic with worry about how she was going to resolve the situation. L'Angelier was piling on pressure for her to commit to their marriage, while at the same time she

VIEW OF THE HOUSE AND MADELEINE SMITH HANDING A CUP OF CHOCOLATE FROM HER BED-ROOM WINDOW TO L'ANGELIER

9 View of 7 Blythswood Square and Madeline Smith handing a cup of chocolate to L'Angelier from her bedroom window

had become officially engaged to Minnoch. Moreover, L'Angelier still had not returned her letters, and had made it perfectly clear that if she broke off the relationship he would show them to her father.

On the basis of the results of the post-mortem and the clutch of her letters found among L'Angelier's possession, Madeleine was arrested. She was taken into custody by Archibald Smith, Sheriff-Substitute of Lanarkshire, and made a lengthy statement in which she freely admitted having a relationship with Emile L'Angelier, giving him cocoa through the bars of her bedroom window (Figure 9), and buying arsenic on three separate occasions. However, she denied having administered arsenic to L'Angelier and claimed not to have seen him in the three weeks before he died. This statement or 'Declaration' was to be Madeleine's only contribution to the evidence heard during her trial. Under Scottish law defendants were not allowed to enter the witness box to give evidence on their behalf.

There was an uncharacteristic silence from the press in the first two days after her arrest. It was not until 3rd April that the public were to read accounts of her arrest in the local newspapers. We can gain some understanding of this reluctance from the *Glasgow Herald*'s account, which refused to name Madeleine and reported that:

> For the last few days the recital of an event of the most painful character has been passing from mouth to mouth and has become the subject

of almost universal excitement and inquiry ... we fervently trust that the cloud which at present obscures a most estimable and respectable household may be speedily most effectively removed ... and though she should be found pure and guiltless, as we trust may be the case, the family will have suffered deeply by having had one of their household even suspected of a crime so odious.[1]

Although the *Manchester Guardian* was not so squeamish about naming Madeleine, its concern for middle-class sensibilities was also evident. While reassuring its readers that justice would be blind, regardless of the status of Madeleine's family, somewhat contradictorily it also made a plea that 'some consideration might be made for the lady's former position as imprisonment even under the mildest circumstances, must be bitter as death'.[2] Most newspapers' accounts referred to the 'painful' nature of the episode and were clearly sympathetic to the plight of a young woman and her family who were drawn from the same social class as the bulk of its readership.

Not everyone took the same view as the *Herald* and other newspapers. The city throbbed with rumour, speculation and allegations about the case and the gossip in the pubs, if not the clubs, of the city was rife with claims that Madeleine's respectable status and fashionable address would ensure that she would escape punishment. The city's working classes may not have developed the class-consciousness predicted by Karl Marx in his recently published *Communist Manifesto*. However, the denizens of the wynds had enough awareness of the inequalities of life not to share the angst of the middle-class press over the plight of an extremely wealthy member of the middle classes, even if she were an attractive young woman. The insistent references in the papers to the impartiality of the law were perhaps a response to the strength of allegations among the working-class citizens of Glasgow that Madeleine would get preferential treatment from the legal establishment.

Although the papers framed the story in terms which were broadly sympathetic to both Madeleine and her family, for the most part, the press concentrated on providing factual details of the case and, in some instances, detailed reconstructions of L'Angelier's last hours. Meanwhile the legal proceedings trundled on. The voluminous evidence gathered by the Procurator Fiscal was despatched to the Lord Advocate, in order to decide whether there was a case to answer. By mid April he deemed that there was, and Madeleine's case was set to be tried in the High Court of Justiciary in Edinburgh as soon as the arrangements could be made. It was not until 13th June that she was formally indicted and her trial set for 30th June. The specific charges which she faced were: 1) having on two separate occasions in February 1857 administered arsenic, or other poison, to Pierre Emile L'Angelier, with intent to murder him; and 2) on an occasion in March 1857, by means of poison, murdered L'Angelier.

Madeleine had been refused bail and so remained in custody in the North Prison of Glasgow from the time of her arrest until her trial some three months later, when she was transferred to Edinburgh's East prison. She spent these months reading, corresponding and receiving visitors. In these unfamiliar and bleak surroundings she apparently tried to recreate some of the normality of her life outside by requesting access to a piano. The authorities could or would not oblige, although by all accounts she was treated with great consideration by the prison authorities.[3] Her family kept its distance in these months, and only her father made his way to Duke Street, in Glasgow's insalubrious east end, to visit her in prison. This was part of a deliberate strategy to remain as aloof as possible from the scandal, although Douglas MacGowan claims that, 'in true Victorian fashion', the family continued their active business and social life throughout Madeleine's incarceration.[4] It is likely that, out of necessity, Madeleine's father continued with his business affairs, but one doubts the appetite that the rest of the family had for the usual round of balls, concerts and dinner parties, given the notoriety gained by the case the length and breadth of the country. In fact, the initial reaction of both her parents to the news that Madeleine might be implicated in L'Angelier's death was to take to their bed. Perhaps they had rallied and were stoically continuing with 'business as usual'.

It seems to be the case that there was collusion within the legal establishment to protect the Smith family from becoming embroiled in the legal proceedings. Although every member of the family had been interviewed (precognosced) as part of the preparations for the trial, the only member of the family who was called as a witness by the defence during the actual trial was Madeleine's young sister Janet. The prosecution, unusually, called no family members as witnesses. The family's resolve to distance itself from the scandal was so firm that not one of them made an appearance in court during the nine-day trial. However, they did not completely desert Madeleine and spared no expense in mounting her defence. A leading firm of Glasgow solicitors was hired to prepare the case and they retained the services of the Dean of Faculty, John Inglis, to plead her case in court. Inglis later wrote a letter of appreciation thanking them for their 'very large share of the work of the defence' in 'this unparalleled case'.[5]

The steady stream of reports in local and national newspapers in the weeks leading up to the trial whetted the public's appetite for more revelations. Therefore, unsurprisingly, on Tuesday 30th June, the first day of the trial, thousands gathered in the late June sun outside the High Court building and the surrounding streets to see Madeleine arrive at the court. The majority of the crowd were there to catch a glimpse of the young woman who had been the object of so much prurient gossip, but there were those who had arrived in the optimistic hope of gaining admission to the court. However, their hopes were to be dashed. The doors of the court had been opened at eight o'clock and the public gallery was filled almost immediately. This did not deter a huge crowd from hanging around outside the court the whole day, eagerly seizing on anyone leaving the building for any titbit about the progress of the trial.

Although there was not such a great commotion or chaos inside the High Court building, the corridors or 'lobbies' were brimming with people, who had to be kept in order by policemen, charged with keeping the passages clear. The courtroom itself was jam packed (Figure 10), and there was a buzz of anticipation as the crowded court waited for the trial to begin. Members of the general public were mainly seated in the upper gallery, although some sat at the back of the courtroom. A number of newspapers focused on the small number of women or 'ladies' who were present in the room. It was noted that they had brought along their embroidery and sewing, suggesting that they intended to be there for the duration. However, these would-be Madame Defarges were vastly outnumbered by men, who constituted the majority of those in court and included a fair sprinkling of clergymen. Whether these men of the cloth were present in their role as guardians of the nation's morals or for baser reasons is not entirely clear. Reporters sat in the body of the hall,

10 All observers commented on Madeleine's remarkable composure in the crowded Edinburgh courtroom

right behind the dock, and immediately behind them was a phalanx of legal men, almost the entire membership of the Faculty of Advocates, according to the *Glasgow Herald*. Bewigged and bedecked in their legal finery, they listened with rapt attention to the court proceedings. No doubt their interest was sparked by a desire to hear the luminaries of the Scottish legal world debate the intricacies of a fascinating and unprecedented legal case. However, one might suppose that they were also drawn by less lofty concerns and, like for those in the public galleries, the potent mix of illicit sex, poison and scandal proved irresistible. Like the 'few ladies' present, the members of the Faculty came prepared for a lengthy sitting, many of them having brought pocket flasks, biscuits and sandwiches.[6]

The all-male jury of fifteen was seated to the left of the dock. In contrast to the impressive spectacle presented by the ranks of lawyers in their official robes, the members of the jury were plainly dressed and, according to one observer, were 'the least imposing aspect' of the spectacle. The majority of them were ordinary working men, although artisans: boot makers, cabinet makers, clerks. There were one merchant and one teacher among them, and two who had no listed occupation. As one report commented, 'we say nothing in disparagement of their acumen or sagacity ... [but] the majority of them looked what they actually were, working men who had more to do with hand than head work'.[7] The number of jurors drawn from agricultural work was a reminder that Edinburgh was surrounded by a large rural hinterland.

The courtroom was teeming with legal heavyweights. The trial was presided over by the Right Honourable John Hope, Lord Justice-Clerk. Hope was from a well-connected family of noble descent. His influence and ability ensured that he quickly rose through the ranks. However, he was not particularly popular as a judge. Contrary to his jovial appearance, he had an arrogant manner and was ill tempered and given to badgering counsel appearing before him. After one encounter with him Sir Walter Scott commented that 'he is hot, though, and rather hasty'.[8] He was assisted in overseeing the case by Lord Handyside and Lord Ivory. By the standards of the legal profession, John Inglis, Madeleine's chief defender, was from a fairly lowly background. He was the youngest son of the Rev. Dr John Inglis and had been born and brought up in Edinburgh. Called to the Bar at the age of 25, he was highly regarded in his profession, and in the course of his life occupied most of the high offices in the legal hierarchy. He also harboured political ambitions and had stood, unsuccessfully, as a Conservative candidate for Orkney and Shetland. He cut a striking figure in the courtroom, being tall and elegant, with a dignified manner. Such was the significance of this trial that Madeleine had the privilege of being the only client he ever visited within prison walls.[9] Inglis was supported in the defence by George Young and Alexander Moncrieff. The case for the prosecution was conducted by Lord Advocate James Moncrieff, assisted by the Solicitor-General, Edward Maitland, and Advocate Depute, Donald Mackenzie.

For almost two and half hours the courtroom audience chattered in eager anticipation of the opening of the proceedings. At half-past ten, when the judges and lawyers took their seats, the noise abated. However, only when Madeleine entered the courtroom did silence descend. She entered the court by a trapdoor from the cell beneath the courtroom and, accompanied by a female turnkey, took her place in the dock. Several of the newspapers had a detailed account of her appearance – to meet the interest of its female readership, it was claimed. The *Courier's* version read:

> She is elegant without show. A rich brown silk gown, with a large brooch low-set on the breast; a white straw bonnet simply trimmed with white ribbon; a white cambric handkerchief and a bottle of smelling salts in her kid-gloved hand. Her hair, of which she has a rich profusion, is quietly arranged in the fashion prevalent before the Eugenie style, although the smallness of the bonnet, which is of the most fashionable make, necessitates the leading of two ebony braids across the crown of her head. Miss Smith is about 5 feet 2 inches in height. She has an elegant figure and can neither be called stout nor slim. She looks older than her years, which are 21. I should have guessed her age to be 24. Her eyes are deep-set, large and some think beautiful by they certainly do not look prepossessing. Her brow is of the ordinary size, and the face inclined to the oval. Her nose is prominent, but is too long to be taken as a type of the Roman, and too irregular to remind one of the Greek. Her complexion, in spite of prison life, is clear and fresh. Her cheeks are well-coloured, and the insinuation that a rosy hue is imparted by artificial means, made by some portions of the press, does not seem well founded.[10]

There was little disagreement among the newspapers in terms of describing the bare essentials of her dress. Most accounts also agreed that she was 'elegantly but simply' dressed. However, the consensus broke down when it came to assessing her appearance. The *Times* wrote of her figure as 'girlish and slight', while the *Glasgow Courier* thought it neither 'stout nor slim'. The *Spectator* thought her complexion suggested 'artificial colour', while the *Glasgow Herald* thought it 'soft and fair'. Her dark eyes were either admired or dismissed as 'unprepossessing', and her features were described variously as 'striking', 'prominent', 'cast in a delicate mould' and 'irregular'. While the 'eye witness' account in the *Glasgow Courier* remarked that she 'looks older than her years ... I should have thought 24', the *Dumbarton Herald*'s correspondent thought that she looked 'younger than her reputed age of 21'. (She was in fact 22.) Beauty is indeed in the eye of the beholder. Madeleine certainly did not conform to the stereotypical image of a mid-Victorian beauty, which favoured regular and delicate features, blue eyes over brown and fair, curled hair over dark, straight hair. However, these contradictory descriptions would have reflected the different journalists' particular predilections, or possibly even their views on the question of her guilt.

On one issue there was complete unanimity among the press, and that was the question of Madeleine's composure. This perception pervaded all accounts of her, from her initial arrest to her courtroom appearance. F. Tennyson Jesse, in her edition of the *Great Trials* series, claimed that when Madeleine made her declaration to the Procurator Fiscal she was 'calm and unruffled, her gaze candid'.[11] Similarly, an observer of her entrance to the court amid the crowds swarming outside wrote: 'she was the only unmoved, cool, serene, personage to be seen ... She passes from the cab to the court room – or rather to the cell beneath the dock – with the air of a belle entering the ball-room. She ascends the narrow staircase leading to the dock with a cool jaunty air'.[12] There were numerous allusions in the newspapers to Madeleine's calm and unruffled demeanour. The *Glasgow Courier* noted that 'when she is called upon to plead, she says in a clear, sweet treble – no trace of huskiness or emotion perceptible in her voice, no trembling on her tongue – "Not guilty"'. The *Glasgow Herald* also mentioned her 'composure' and 'good spirits', while the *Glasgow Sentinel* not only alluded to her 'wonderful calmness and self-possession', but with a hint of criticism claimed that she exhibited the utmost 'cheerfulness and apparent unconcern' as she chatted with various officials.

It is doubtful that the press was constructing this image of Madeleine, which was too universally shared to have been manufactured for the purposes of creating a good story. In all likelihood the depiction of her as composed can be taken at face value. No matter how she had presented herself, it was probable that her behaviour and appearance would have come under close scrutiny, with every gesture and expression analysed to see what it revealed of her character. However, Madeleine's apparent calmness and serenity confounded all the expectations one would have of a young, middle-class Victorian woman who stood accused of a heinous crime. Hence, the newspapers were understandably perplexed and fixated with this aspect of her demeanour; some seemed to admire her coolness, others were bewildered by it, and at least one was censorious.

When the trial opened it was not Madeleine's role as a transgressor which shocked – many of the details which were later to scandalise the public had not yet been revealed – it was the stark incongruity of a young woman of her class appearing in the dock. In the lead-up to the trial the press had made extensive reference to the respectability of the family and had largely been sympathetic to what was portrayed as their 'ordeal', 'suffering' and 'pain'. Therefore it might have been expected that in court Madeleine's manner would have reflected the wretchedness and distress she and her family were assumed to be suffering. Perhaps she might also have been expected to conform to the gender stereotypes of the period, particularly as found in the melodramas so popular in Victorian fiction. Madeleine did not oblige. Not only was she self-possessed in her manner, she never once made use of her veil to conceal her face, and she seemed comfortable enough casting her eye around the courtroom, on occasion turning round to observe the journalists who sat right behind her, and 'returning every stare with compound interest'.[13] In struggling to convey to their readership how anomalous her behaviour was, journalists represented it as conforming to the more common public context of her class: the drawing room, the theatre and the ballroom, rather than the courtroom. We will never know whether Madeleine's behaviour was feigned or real. We do know that, whatever inner turmoil she may have been enduring, it was not openly displayed.

The trial opened with the Advocate Depute, Donald Mackenzie, reading out the indictment against Madeleine. Her 'clear and distinct' reply, of 'Not guilty' was cited by many of the papers as evidence of the composure which she was to maintain throughout the first days of her trial. Once the jury had been selected, Moncrieff opened the case for the prosecution. He called fifty-seven witnesses to give evidence against Madeleine, beginning with L'Angelier's landlady, Ann Jenkins, whose testimony was lengthy and detailed. She made some comments about his working, social and eating habits, but in the main her testimony centred around the three separate occasions on which L'Angelier had experienced severe bouts of illness characterised by vomiting, diarrhoea and stomach pain.

Lengthy cross-examination of its witnesses was a feature of the prosecution's case and only a few would escape with a brief time in the witness box. The essence of the prosecution's case was to demonstrate that Madeleine had both motive and opportunity to kill L'Angelier. Moncrieff called witnesses who would provide evidence that L'Angelier and Madeleine had a romantic relationship unknown to her parents. Madeleine's maid, Christina Haggart, provided damaging testimony not only that L'Angelier had been invited by Madeleine inside the family homes, but that she could easily have done so without anyone knowing. There was undisputed evidence of Madeleine's three purchases of arsenic 'to kill rats'. Augusta Giubelei, one of the pupil teachers at Madeleine's London finishing school, flatly contradicted Madeleine's statement that she had been recommended arsenic for her complexion by the teacher. However, the attempts by the prosecution to prove that Madeleine's purchase of arsenic coincided with L'Angelier's bouts of illness, and that he had met with her before each of his attacks, were only partially successful. His landlady, Ann Jenkins, and his friend Mary Perry gave contradictory evidence about the date of his first bout of illness. Crucially, there was no evidence that Madeleine had bought arsenic before 21st February, when, by all accounts, L'Angelier's first attack had occurred before that date; nor was there conclusive evidence that they had met on the Sunday of his last illness.

Medical men gave copious amounts of scientific information about the properties of arsenic, including its ability to remain undetected in a drink, and various witnesses provided evidence of L'Angelier's general health, character and temperament. All of the prosecution witnesses gave positive accounts of his character, claiming he was industrious, religious and temperate. Auguste De Mean, who worked for the French Consul and had been friendly with Emile for three years, introduced a mildly critical note about him when he said he was excitable and given to vanity and boastfulness.[14] Emile's immediate superior at Huggins and Co., William Stevenson, who had been responsible for removing the letters from Emile's lodgings, also claimed he was vain and 'mercurial'.[15]

The newspapers reported daily on the events taking place in court; mostly they provided verbatim accounts of the evidence, which occupied acres of column space. At this stage in the trial opinion and comment continued to revolve around the paradox of Madeleine's calm and relaxed manner. The *Glasgow Herald* remarked of the third day of the trial that 'the prisoner on this as upon the previous days remained at the bar from the commencement of the proceedings till the close without partaking of any refreshment, although on more than one occasion invited to do so'.[16] The *Glasgow Sentinel* reported that on the fourth day of the trial Madeleine 'appeared as composed as ever, and on coming into the dock she smiled and shook hands with one of her agents with an almost nonchalant air. Indeed she seemed in no way impressed with the awful position in which she is placed'.[17] The *Glasgow Courier*'s 'eye witness' singled out a number of witnesses whose testimony had seemingly failed to penetrate Madeleine's sangfroid:

Dr Penny describes his analytical investigations of her old sweetheart's body, and the ribbons on her bonnet are so still that you clearly perceive there is not even a hidden shudder passing through her frame. Dr Steven narrates how L'Angelier's body was exhumed, and she only leans forward on the railing before the dock to study the doctor's face and hear his words more easily. The poor Frenchman's landlady relates with pathetic simplicity how L'Angelier died, and Madeleine meets the eye of the honest matron without blinking for a moment. She sees her old school companion and friend Mary Buchanan in tears; but the smirk does not desert her, and she cannot shed a responsive tear to those of the girl who was to have been bridesmaid. Even Mr Minnoch in the witness box ... fails to steal from her a single particle of her equanimity, and she looks steadily at that deeply injured merchant, who has too keen a sense of his own humiliation to direct even a solitary glance in the direction of the dock![18]

These first four days of the trial passed fairly unremarkably; there were few juicy revelations to titillate the public, or at least, none which had not previously been known. However, the evidence of the fifth day was seismic in its effects both inside and outside the courtroom. At the end of the previous day Moncrieff had proposed that Madeleine's letters to L'Angelier should be read. However, the defence team objected to the admission of the letters on the grounds that there had been procedural irregularities in the way the letters had been recovered and stored. Unhappily for Madeleine, the Lord Justice-Clerk overruled the objection and deemed that seventy-seven letters of the letters she had written to Emile should be read aloud in court the next day. The recitation of the letters took most of the fifth day, Saturday 4th July, being preceded and followed by evidence from the prosecution's two final witnesses. The scandalous content of the letters made a bizarre contrast to the colourless and unanimated tone in which they were read out by the Clerk of Court. Madeleine had written over 250 letters to her lover, but only a fraction were presented as evidence by the prosecution. Clearly, some selection had been involved and obviously those letters which added weight to the prosecution's case were ones which those in the courtroom, and ultimately the world at large, were to hear. The courtroom audience listened, enthralled by letters which confirmed an illicit relationship, secret lovers' trysts, L'Angelier's visits to the Smith household, assignations in the large grounds of *Rowaleyn*, plans of elopement, and which charted Madeleine's disenchantment with the affair and her attempts to retrieve her missives from a reluctant L'Angelier. And of course, most scandalous of all, they heard confirmation that their relationship had not only violated one of the most sacred sexual codes of Victorian society, but that it was at Madeleine's instigation as much as L'Angelier's. The Lord Justice-Clerk even refused to read out sections of her letters because they were written in terms 'perhaps ... never previously committed to paper as having passed between a man and a woman'.[19] His distaste was shared by the correspondent of the *Durham Advertiser*, who claimed to have read complete and unexpurgated copies of the letters and wrote, 'I have seen [completed] copies of these epistles ... and I pray God I may never see such again. Ugh!'[20]

Madeleine's preternatural calm was not completely shattered by the public disclosure of the lurid details of her affair, but for the first time the newspapers noted a change in her manner:

> There was a marked change in the appearance and demeanour of the unfortunate prisoner today. On coming up to the dock she had a more saddened and less elastic gait than formerly and during the course of the day while the reading of the letters was in progress her colour went and came, sometimes her cheeks were flushed and at others they were pale while there was a frequent compression and quivering of the lip. Altogether at times she seemed to be much distressed.[21]

A number of newspapers remarked on the fact that, since the reading out of her letters to L'Angelier, Madeleine had seemed to struggle to retain her composure. The *Times* reported that 'the prisoner scarcely maintained her jaunty, indifferent air during today's proceedings, but appeared to feel the exposure which her letters made'.[22] Not every newspaper chose to note the change in Madeleine's demeanour. The *Glasgow Sentinel*, a best-selling weekly paper whose front page proclaimed that it was 'sympathetic' to the causes of the labour movement and the working man, had always had a more critical edge to its reports on the trial. It did not appear to share the concern of many of the other newspapers for the predicament of a respectable middle-class family, at least not in print. More than most papers, it focused on Madeleine's 'nonchalant air' and 'self-possession', but the register of its reports – 'one almost expects to hear her laugh' – implied criticism of her behaviour, rather than bewilderment or admiration. Having represented Madeleine as a cold, rather arrogant, young middle-class woman, it was reluctant to abandon this carefully constructed image, even when the facts seemed to contradict it. This led to a rather ambiguous account of the revelatory fifth day of the trial, when the *Glasgow Sentinel* reported that 'Miss Smith continues to exhibit that wonderful calmness and self-possession which has characterised her demeanour. While some letters were being read today, she leaned forward in the dock, and covered her face with her hands.'[23] In a later report it claimed that 'On Saturday evening after the reading of the letters, her spirits were as good as ever, and she has more than once expressed her confidence in a verdict in her favour.'[24] The coded message to its readers was the suggestion that the law was not impartial, and that the class which it favoured knew it.

On that Saturday evening newspaper offices and booksellers' shops were besieged by members of the public rushing to get hold of the latest editions of the newspapers. Glasgow could not read enough about the young, respectable woman who had acted so contrary to the codes of her class and gender. The printing presses went in to overdrive for the duration of the trial, producing several editions each day in an effort to sate the public's craving for every nugget of information about the case. But it was not only Glasgow which indulged in this feeding frenzy; reports of Madeleine's words and deeds circulated throughout Britain and beyond. There was scarcely a household in the country which had not heard about the 'Glasgow Poisoning Case' and did not have some view on it. A short piece from the *Glasgow Herald*'s Paris correspondent commented that 'I will trouble you with a few lines only [as] your columns are no doubt filled with the cause célèbre now going on in Edinburgh and which is creating so great an interest even in Paris.'[25]

Opinions about her guilt or innocence were freely given. After her letters had been read out in court and published in many of the newspapers, opinion swung over to the belief that she was most probably guilty, although many continued to insist on her complete innocence.[26] Excitement and interest were most intense in Glasgow. The Sunday following the revelations, hundreds of people gathered outside the Smith house in Blythswood Square, peering into the windows and showing particular interest in Madeleine's bedroom, perhaps voyeuristically hoping for a re-enactment of some of the scenes they had read about in the evening newspapers. Many went round the back of the house to see the door through which L'Angelier had been sneaked inside.[27] By nightfall the crowds had begun to disperse, no doubt hoping that the next day would see the unfolding of more sensational tales of sexual transgression.

Although the prosecution had successfully exposed Madeleine's sexual misdemeanours, there was still a question mark over her role in Emile's death. On Monday, the sixth day of the trial, Moncrieff and his team hoped to produce a piece of evidence which they believed would seal Madeleine's fate and resolve the case in favour of the prosecution. On the Saturday they had asked the judges for permission to read out the entries in L'Angelier's pocket book. However, the defence objected on the grounds that the contents were unreliable and uncorroborated, and that there was no legal precedent for such a book being used as evidence. The three judges deliberated over the weekend and at the opening of session on Monday gave their judgment. The defence team must have heaved a collective sigh of relief when the majority verdict was that the pocket book was inadmissible – for it contained entries in L'Angelier's handwriting which seemed to confirm that he had seen Madeleine on the first two evenings that he had taken ill, despite her denials.

The evidence for the defence began early on the Monday morning. In contrast to the lengthy sessions in the witness box that the prosecution witnesses had to endure, the defence witnesses followed each other in quick succession. The case which the defence was set on making was that L'Angelier had committed suicide. Witnesses were called to testify to the fact that he was unstable, excitable and easily depressed, that he was vain about his personal appearance and often boasted of his conquests over women. Medical witnesses were examined to prove that people who committed suicide by taking poison usually died without confessing that they had done so. Other witnesses testified that L'Angelier had bought drugs, including laudanum, and several witnesses provided evidence that arsenic could be acquired easily without necessarily buying it. A number of 'ladies' were called to prove that many women believed that arsenic was good for the complexion (which was the reason Madeleine had given for buying it). Contrary to the evidence given by medical witnesses for the prosecution, two medical men argued that there was no evidence that arsenic could be dangerous if applied to the skin. The defence rested its case after less than a day of evidence. All that remained now was for the prosecution and the defence, in their address to the jury, to exercise their legal and debating skill and attempt to persuade the jury that the weight of the evidence was in their respective favours.

On the seventh day of the trial James Moncrieff, the chief prosecutor, expressed clearly in the opening words of his final address to the jury where his heart lay, if not his head.

> I have now to discharge perhaps the most painful public duty that ever fell to my lot. Gentlemen, I could have rejoiced if the result of the inquiry which it was our duty to make and of the laborious collection of every element of proof which we could find, would have justified us on the part of the Crown in resting content, with the investigation into the facts, and withdrawing our charge against the prisoner … [but] I fear … you will arrive at the conclusion that every link is so firmly fastened – that every loophole is so completely stopped – that there does not remain the possibility of escape for the unhappy prisoner from the net that she has woven for herself.[28]

Most of his lengthy address to the jury consisted of laying out in minute detail the disjointed pieces of evidence in order to demonstrate that there was an unbroken chain of evidence which pointed to Madeleine's guilt. In a forensic but prosaic address to the jury Moncrieff tried to persuade them that L'Angelier had met with Madeleine on each occasion that he had taken ill and that she had previously bought arsenic. Most of the time was spent trying to prove, contrary to Madeleine's denials, that the evidence contained in her last letter, as well as L'Angelier's actions, suggested that they had met on the evening before his death. He chose to avoid the route of dwelling on the moral and sexual aspects of the letters and using them as proof of Madeleine's moral depravity; rather, he suggested that her age, sex and 'condition' would induce people to feel commiseration as well as horror for her predicament. Although he did allude to 'the disgrace, and sin, and degradation'[29] which the letters had revealed, his decision not to dwell on them suggests that the Victorian discursive universe of gendered relations struggled to conceive of a young, respectable woman behaving in this way and thus preferred to draw a veil over it. Moncrieff attempted to put a moral gloss on the situation by suggesting that the couple were in fact married, having spoken of their intention to marry and having had sexual intercourse. In Scots law this form of irregular marriage, by promise *subsequente copula*, was still recognised by the church and the state so long as a regular marriage followed soon after. Therefore Moncrieff was able to depict L'Angelier as acting honourably when he threatened to hand over Madeleine's letters to her father. He argued that, as the relationship had been consummated or, to use his words, 'repeatedly acts of improper connection took place', L'Angelier had every right to think of Madeleine as his wife: 'she belonged to him, and could with honour belong to no one else'.[30]

Moncrieff did not shy away from denouncing the behaviour which the letters revealed, but he refrained from making any direct criticism of Madeleine or impugning her character, and he expressed commiseration for the plight in which she found herself. However, he was less considerate of L'Angelier's character. He drew the jury's attention to the fact that L'Angelier had been a hard and industrious worker and he tried to demonstrate his respectability by reference to the evidence of the French Consulate and a number of landladies who had spoken of him 'in the highest terms'. On the other hand, he accepted many of the derogatory points which the defence had made about L'Angelier and admitted that his 'conduct from first to last [was] not always that of a "man of honour"' and that it was 'impossible to speak of him in terms other than the strongest condemnation'.[31] Moncrieff read out a censored version of Madeleine's letter which indicated 'the commencement of their criminal intimacy', in order to illustrate 'the moral and mental state to which she had reduced herself'. He commented sorrowfully: 'where the prisoner learned this depraved moral state is not for me to say. I shall not much dispute that L'Angelier had his own share in corrupting her moral sense.' Madeleine was accorded some agency but, in line with prevailing views on respectable female sexuality, it was assumed that she had been corrupted and seduced rather than being the temptress. Even when alluding to Madeleine's affections towards L'Angelier having cooled, Moncrieff could not conceal his dislike of L'Angelier: 'the reason … it is not necessary that we discern. He seems to have been rather exacting.'[32]

The defence had carefully built a case arguing that L'Angelier's temperament was volatile and unstable and that he had suicidal tendencies. Moncrieff's riposte to this was not to deny that L'Angelier was excitable and unpredictable but to claim that this kind of temperament was the reverse of suicidal and that 'It is more characteristic of our neighbours on the other side of the Channel.'[33] National characteristics were again invoked as a defence, when Moncrieff presented more evidence to persuade the jury that L'Angelier was not suicidal. He described him as 'a kind of gasconading, boasting man, such as a Jersey man might be.'[34] In both portrayals, foreigners were depicted as 'the other' and, by implication, not only different, but of lower moral standards.

Moncrieff's prosecution of the case and his final address to the jury were scrupulously and carefully argued. Indeed his speeches have been described as brilliant. However, he extended more latitude and consideration to the defendant than is usually considered normal. In fact, in his summing up the judge observed that the Lord Advocate had acted 'with a degree of anxiety for the interests of the defender which he had never known before'.[35] It is obvious, from Moncrieff's repeated allusions to the 'painful' nature of the case, that he did not relish the role of prosecutor in this case and that Madeleine's youth, sex and class made him more sympathetic to her case than he might normally be. He made his feelings transparent and explicit in his final words to the jury:

> As I said before, I have nothing but a public duty to perform. I have no desire to plead this cause as an advocate. My duty is to bring the case before you, as the ends of truth and justice require. If I had thought that there were any elements of doubt or of disproof in the case that would have justified me in retiring from the painful task which I have now to discharge, believe me, gentlemen, there is not a man in this Court who would have rejoiced more at that result than myself; for of all the persons engaged in this trial, apart from the unfortunate object of it, I believe the task laid upon me is at once the most difficult and the most painful.[36]

When the Dean of Faculty rose to give his address to the jury on behalf of the defendant on the eighth day of the trial, he immediately acknowledged the 'great moderation' of the Lord Advocate's address, which 'must have convinced you that he could hardly expect a verdict at your hands'.[37] Inglis may have been taking some licence in drawing this conclusion, but there is no doubt that the prosecution, while making a sound legal case against Madeleine, had been sympathetically disposed to her and was reluctant to go for the jugular, knowing that a guilty verdict would result in her being sent to the gallows.

Inglis began his address by launching an assault on L'Angelier's character. He described him as an 'unknown adventurer', conceited, vain and pretentious, with 'a very silly expectation of admiration from the other sex'. He denounced him as a fortune hunter and claimed that he had a history of becoming engaged to 'women of some station'.[38] Madeleine, on the other hand, was portrayed as an innocent, passionate and trusting young woman who fell prey to his charms. Inglis read out excerpts from her letters which expressed her love and devotion to L'Angelier and held these up as examples of her innate gentleness and goodness. He argued that it stretched credulity to believe, as the prosecution claimed, that she could make the transition from devoted amoureuse to cold, deliberate murderer the moment that she became engaged to Minnoch. Of course, in keeping with this picture he had painted of an ingénue, he laid the blame for Madeleine's 'fall' squarely on L'Angelier's shoulders:

> She had lost not her virtue merely, but ... her sense of decency. Gentle-men, whose fault was that? – whose doing was that? Think you that, without temptation, without evil teaching, a poor girl falls into such depths of degradation? No. Influence from without – most corrupting influence – can alone account for such a fall.[39]

Unlike, the Lord Advocate, Inglis did not draw explicit parallels between L'Angelier's character traits and his 'foreignness'. It might be said that Moncrieff had done that job for him. However, his first task when he rose to make his speech for the defence was to lay out the details of L'Angelier's early life, his origins, his arrival in England and his return to Jersey. Inglis's implicit purpose was to show that L'Angelier was an outsider, a foreigner with no pedigree, who had to contrive an introduction to Madeleine in the street because he 'could not procure an introduction otherwise or elsewhere'. He returned to this theme of the outsider on several occasions: when he spoke of L'Angelier 'clandestinely' introducing himself into the Smith household, or referring to him as a corrupting influence from 'without', or indeed in his persistent reference to him as a Frenchman, despite the fact that he was from Jersey and therefore a British subject. Inglis repeated the evidence of several witnesses, that L'Angelier was mercurial and temperamental, but did not spend much time dwelling on the alternative theory of suicide which he had constructed in his cross examinations. As Inglis correctly pointed out, it was not the task of the defence to provide an explanation for L'Angelier's death, but to point out the flaws in the prosecution case.

Once the Dean of Faculty had condemned L'Angelier's character and presented Madeleine as an innocent who had been corrupted, he turned to the legal basis of his case. His main argument was that all the evidence implicating Madeleine in L'Angelier's death was circumstantial. He set about demonstrating how each of the charges against Madeleine could be disproved by carefully reconstructing the details and pattern of their meetings. He pointed out that although there was a conflict between Mary Perry's evidence and Ann Jenkins's as to the date of L'Angelier's first illness, the key point was that either date fell before Madeleine's first purchase of arsenic.

He went on to show that the prosecution were unable to provide conclusive evidence that L'Angelier and Madeleine had met on the day of L'Angelier's second illness, or indeed on the night of his death. In fact, Inglis's argument was that there was no evidence to support the contention that Madeleine and L'Angelier had met at all between her first purchase of arsenic on 21st February and L'Angelier's death one month later.

Madeleine's unnatural calm in the midst of such dire circumstances had elicited so much comment from the press that Inglis obviously felt compelled to address the issue. Indeed, the prosecutor had also alluded to it, but was ambivalent about the meaning which could be ascribed to it. In his final address to the jury Moncrieff noted that the prisoner had exhibited great courage since she had been charged with the crime, but warned the jury that 'such a demeanour was not inconsistent with the theory of her guilt'. However, in his peroration to the jury Inglis launched into a passionate plea for them to see Madeleine as a courageous and innocent young woman. He argued that such courage as she had displayed was more consonant with someone who was innocent rather than guilty, and reminded the jury of a case of a young servant girl in the city of London who was tried for poisoning her employer. Like Madeleine, she had remained calm and serene throughout the course of her long trial and it was only many years later that the real murderer had confessed on his deathbed. In flamboyant and extravagant language, Inglis drew parallels with Madeleine's case and warned the jury of repeating this miscarriage of justice by quoting Shakespeare's *Measure for Measure*: 'When, after execution, Judgement hath repented o'er his doom'.[40]

Evidently, Inglis was not entirely convinced that the evidence and legal arguments alone were sufficient to save his client from the gallows, for he urged the jury to use their hearts as well as their heads when arriving at a verdict: 'I beseech you, not only to [bring] your clear heads, but your warm hearts – your fine moral instincts, and your guiding and regulating conscience ... To determine guilt or innocence by the light of intellect alone is the exclusive prerogative of infallibility.'[41] He stopped short of asking them to ignore the evidence, but his appeal to their consciences and 'warm hearts' was exploiting the dominant Victorian models of masculinity and femininity, which deemed men to be responsible, self-controlled and to protect and provide for women. L'Angelier had clearly breached each of these codes. Since women, particularly of Madeleine's class, were deemed to be morally pure, her fall from grace could only be attributed to her having been corrupted by L'Angelier. The inference was clear: Madeleine's legal guilt might be ambiguous, but L'Angelier's moral guilt was unequivocal. The fact that L'Angelier was of French extraction, although a British subject, compounded his sins and was evidence of the inferior moral standards of foreigners. Despite having effectively deployed his legal brain to meticulously deconstruct the prosecution's case and expose the circumstantial nature of its evidence, Inglis ended his four-hour address to the jury with a plea to their consciences rather than their intellects: 'no verdict will be either honest, or just, or true, unless it at once satisfies the reasonable scruples of the severest judgement, and yet leaves undisturbed and unvexed the tenderest conscience among you'.[42] Inglis's impassioned speech to the court had the desired effect, judging from the applause which broke out when he ended his address.[43]

After a fifteen-minute break the Lord Justice-Clerk began his charge to the jury. He was quick to remind them that the evidence, and only the evidence, should be considered. He delivered a mild rebuke to both counsels for allowing their personal opinions to intrude into their addresses to the jury. Predictably, his summing up was shorn of any of the passion, special pleading and appeals to the conscience and hearts of the jurors which had marked the speeches of the two counsels. His address was precise and judicious, and not particularly favourable to Madeleine. He rejected her reasons for buying arsenic and was equally dismissive of the defence's case that L'Angelier had committed suicide. It was to be expected that Madeleine's situation would be represented in different ways in court. Given the adversarial nature of the legal system, one would have predicted that the prosecution and the defence would have taken different views and drawn different conclusions from the indisputable fact that she had engaged in 'criminal connection' with L'Angelier. And yet it was from the judge and not the prosecution that the most damning remarks came. Lord Justice-Clerk launched into a blistering attack on Madeleine's character, arguing that the 'letters show as extraordinary a frame of mind and as unhallowed a passion as perhaps ever appeared in a Court of Justice'.[44] Unlike the prosecution, he was damning of Madeleine's behaviour and pointed out that she had invited and provoked sexual intercourse, rather than being an innocent victim of a sexual predator. He condemned the licentious detail of her letters and compared her behaviour to that of 'a common prostitute'.[45]

On the other hand Lord Justice-Clerk warned the jury that they should not engage in any conjecture about what had happened, even if they were unconvinced by some of the points made in her defence. He stated that there was no evidence to indicate that Madeleine had arsenic in her possession on the occasion of L'Angelier's first bout of illness, and was unambiguous in instructing the jury that the first charge against Madeleine was not founded. With regard to the other two charges, crucially, the murder charge, he argued that though it might be probable that L'Angelier and Madeleine had met on the night of his death, the jury could only deduce this on the basis of 'just and satisfactory inference' based on evidence, not suspicion. In other words, if there was no clear proof that they had met, then there was no unbroken chain of evidence linking Madeleine to L'Angelier's death. Lord Justice-Clerk had been hard headed in his assessment of Madeleine's character and her moral culpability but, fortunately for her, he was equally hard headed in his assessment of the weight of evidence against her. In his summary he advised the jury that, 'however heavy the weight and load of suspicion is against her, and however you may have to struggle to get rid of it, you perform the best and bounden duty as a jury to separate suspicion from truth and to proceed upon nothing that you do not find established in evidence against her'.[46]

The jury took barely half an hour to consider their verdict: not guilty on the first charge and not proven on the second and third charges. Despite the judge's warning to the court that there should be no exhibition of emotion when the verdict was announced, the pent-up feelings which had been reined in by the rigid codes of the court erupted into loud cheers, shouting and applause. The court officials tried without great success to silence the crowd, but it was only when Lord Justice-Clerk instructed the police to arrest a particularly disorderly young man that some semblance of order was restored to the courtroom. When Madeleine descended the courtroom stairs to the cells below, she was roundly cheered. Outside, the scenes were even more uproarious. Thousands had gathered in the streets surrounding the court, and when news of the verdict reached them, they went wild, shouting and cheering. They remained for some time, anxious to catch a glimpse of the infamous Madeleine Smith. When she finally appeared and quickly boarded a waiting cab, the crowd began to disperse, convinced that they had finally seen Madeleine. They would have been disappointed to learn that the woman who had made a hasty exit from the court was not Madeleine but another woman, dressed in Madeleine's clothes, who had been used by her defence team as a decoy. Meanwhile, Madeleine had slipped out of the rear entrance of the court, accompanied by her brother Jack and another young male, undetected by the throngs outside. Her cab took her to Slateford, a small village to the south-west of Edinburgh, where she caught the train to Glasgow but alighted at Stepps, a few miles outside Glasgow, in order to elude the scores of people who were waiting for her at the station in Glasgow.

The sensational nature of the case guaranteed that for the duration of the trial it had loomed large in the pages of newspapers throughout the land. For nine days it had been a topic of conversation in households all over the country as people read the lurid details of a tale of passion and mystery which surpassed anything they might read in popular fiction. The draconian laws which normally tightly regulated what could appear in print forbade any references to sexual matters, so the 'Glasgow Poisoning Case' filled a void which otherwise was filled by the lucrative underground market for pornography which flourished in Victorian Britain. The public fascination with the case was fed by the press: in their eagerness to supply an avid public with as much detail as they could, and to outdo their rivals, papers often resorted to embellishment or outright fabrication. Some reporters purported to know not only what Madeleine ate for breakfast, dinner and supper, but how much she had enjoyed it, what she had said to her jailers and, despite her calm appearance, that her pulse was one hundred beats per minute. Comments from the bizarre to the mundane were attributed to her, and after the trial she was alleged to have fled variously to Orkney via Aberdeen, to New York accompanied by Minnoch, and to Liverpool. In fact she retreated to the family home, *Rowaleyn* in Row.[47] There was a good deal of self-referential comment in the reports as the rival publications sought to discredit the information supplied by competitors with some deprecating comment about the provenance of that information. There were even conflicting interpretations of Madeleine's reaction to the verdict. The *Glasgow Herald* reported that, amid the chaotic scenes in court, Madeleine chatted calmly with her agent, while the *Daily Telegraph* noted that there was little discernible effect on Madeleine when the verdict was announced and that she merely rearranged her cloak around her shoulders and 'settled herself more comfortably in her seat'.[48] In contrast, other newspapers commented on the fact that she broke into an 'agitated' smile and was demonstrably moved when her agent and the prison matron grasped her hands to express their sympathy and congratulations.[49]

The close of the 'Glasgow Poisoning Case' brought forth a flood of editorials, comments and correspondence debating and deliberating the import of the trial and the lessons to be drawn from it. In popular mythology the verdict of 'Not Proven' in the Madeleine Smith case has been attributed to moral rather than legal reasons. Madeleine's youth, sex and class are often thought to have influenced the jury's decision, which otherwise would have brought in a guilty verdict. However, the verdict was not necessarily an indication that moral issues clouded the jury's judgement, nor that there was a moral vacuum or that dominant discourses could not make sense of the whole story.[50] It is impossible to know what the jury's thoughts were, how influenced the members were by their own reading of the case, and how much they were influenced by the character assassination of L'Angelier which had taken place in the courtroom. We do know that it was a verdict towards which the judge had guided the jury because the evidence was almost entirely circumstantial. In fact, it had been the verdict which had been widely expected by the Scottish public. As the *Glasgow Sentinel* commented, 'She has left the dock ... legally released ... because an important link in the chain of evidence was wanting.'[51] It was almost certainly on this legal basis that Madeleine was not convicted of the murder of L'Angelier.

The conclusion of a criminal trial in Victorian Britain was routinely the occasion for newspapers to mull over the lessons, moral and otherwise, to be drawn from the case. However, the open nature of the verdict and the clear evidence of an illicit affair between Madeleine and L'Angelier provided the press with even more scope to speculate, theorise and moralise. Yet there was almost complete unanimity that there could have been no other verdict. Both conservative and liberal papers alike applauded the verdict; some commentators may have strongly suspected Madeleine's guilt, but were persuaded by the legal arguments that the prosecution case was based largely on circumstantial evidence, while others, influenced by sentiment and moral rather than legal concerns, could not conceive of Madeleine being anything other than innocent. Some English newspapers made complimentary comments about the uniquely Scottish verdict of 'Not Proven', which they thought 'considerate' and 'just', while the *Saturday Review* argued that 'even to those most convinced of the guilt of the accused, we say that things are best as they are.'[52]

For many papers, not only the verdict but also the way the trial was conducted were evidence of the impartial nature of the law, which was of course taken as a mark of the superiority of British society and culture. The *Glasgow Courier* observed that 'it is satisfactory to know that in a case of such magnitude the rules of law were adhered to as if the accused had belonged to the humblest class of life'.[53] Only the radical *Glasgow Sentinel* struck a discordant note by viewing the case through the lens of class: 'Had Madeleine Smith been Peggy Smith of the Old Wynd or Goosedubs, without worth or influence at her back to defend her and make the worse appear the better cause, she might … have been waiting in jail for the last finisher of the law to do his work.'[54] The key issue for the *Glasgow Sentinel* was not the flawed and biased nature of the judicial process, but social inequalities which saw a great chasm between the few, who had money and position, and the vast majority, who had neither. Money enabled those who had it to buy justice by employing the ablest legal minds. The *Glasgow Sentinel* did not dispute the verdict of 'Not Proven', nor question the legal processes; but for the *Glasgow Sentinel*, access to justice was unequal. Yet even the *Glasgow Sentinel* observed that the jury 'came to the only conclusion which could satisfy their consciences and fulfil the obligations of the oaths they had taken'.[55]

The consensus among the press about the legal issues of the case fragmented when it came to discussing the moral and social questions. The trial became a crucible for the discussion of issues such as class, gender, national identity and the British way of life. The furore surrounding the case and the extensive debate which took place in the press indicate the multiplicity of discourses in Victorian society and the ways in which core beliefs and values were the product of a continual process of negotiation and debate, rather than being fixed and uncontested.

The almost universal support for the verdict in the press can be relatively easily explained. What is more puzzling is the degree of sympathy extended to Madeleine in many quarters of the press and in Scottish society: a young woman whose transgression of the morals of her gender, class and position had been publicly paraded. Her legal guilt had not been proved, but there could be no doubting her moral guilt. Why was she not universally vilified when she had so clearly breached the fundamental principles of the Victorian social and gender order? How did those who presented a picture of a young, innocent girl – and for some, even a heroine – manage to reconcile this with the incontrovertible knowledge that she had trespassed, not only willingly but with apparent relish? Indeed, when she was one whose actions the judge had branded those of 'a common prostitute'.

Some who rushed to defend Madeleine's character were motivated by chivalrous concern at the plight of a young woman whose fall from grace and honour was precipitated by a manipulative and untrustworthy lover. In this scenario, one which was replicated in diverse artistic genres from poetry to painting, Madeleine was represented as a fallen woman, but one who should receive sympathy rather than condemnation because her love was pure. One might imagine that this idealised and romantic image of Madeleine found most favour among young middle-class men who envisaged themselves rushing to be the agent of her redemption and to restore her faith in honourable masculinity. It was even reported that some of the merchants and bankers of Glasgow had set up a subscription with the aim of collecting £10,000 for Madeleine.[56] However, there were those who saw this ideal of pure and innocent womanhood bound up with the Victorian way of life. They were motivated by a desire to show that the fundamental moral codes of Victorian society and the probity of the private sphere were robust and intact. To do so, they had to construct a narrative which portrayed Madeleine as an innocent who had been corrupted by a sexual predator. Crucially, L'Angelier had to be depicted as an 'outsider' and an 'interloper' who had insinuated his way into respectable society. This view was neatly encapsulated in the *Glasgow Courier*'s editorial which argued that:

> such mental pollution as they [her letters] indicate could not have been natural to any young woman of decent parentage in this country, and must have resulted from the contamination of a thoroughly corrupted associate. That associate could only be the obscure foreign adventurer whose acquaintance the unhappy girl made upon the street, and of whose antecedents the little that is known is not favourable; and it is but true that, having succeeded in uprooting every principle of honour and virtue, and in reducing her to the degraded condition in which we found her at her trial – the bond slave of his lust [*sic*].[57]

A number of strands in this editorial were taken up by other sections of the press. The image of Madeleine as a defiled innocent who was worthy of 'Christian sympathy' found expression in a number of newspapers. Edinburgh newspapers were even more effusive in their defence of Madeleine than were their Glasgow counterparts. The *Edinburgh Evening Post and Scottish Record* was 'touched' by the 'age, sex, and social position of the accused'. It could scarcely contain its admiration for the 'young gentle nature not altogether devoid of heroism', who was 'endowed with a firmness of character that would have been reverenced among the maidens of Sparta or Rome',[58] while the *Edinburgh Evening Courant* lamented that 'never, perhaps was there one in which deeper consideration should be felt for the accused'.[59] Madeleine also had her supporters south of the border, not least the London *Morning Post*, which reminded its readers that 'it was when a thoughtless girl and witless of the ways of the world, that she took the first step in her downward career'.[60]

The representation of Madeleine as a virtuous and wholesome innocent who had been defiled found its antithesis in the representations of L'Angelier as a villainous and wily seducer of low morals. The image of L'Angelier as an alien predator who had corrupted a young innocent, the scion of respectable society, was one which found echoes in a number of publications. The *Glasgow Citizen* descended into melodramatic prose in its condemnation of one whom it viewed as having defiled respectable society. 'A wolf had indeed stolen into the fold and entrapped one of its precious lambs: but what family might not suffer from such a disaster?'[61] Irrespective of its views on Madeleine, the press was virtually unanimous in its condemnation of L'Angelier. The *Saturday Review*, which remained agnostic about Madeleine's culpability and regarded the sympathy she had garnered in sections of the press as rather unhealthy, nonetheless sought to lay the blame for her debasement at L'Angelier's feet:

> A meaner and more contemptible scoundrel it would be difficult to conceive; ... a profligate, vain adventurer, boasting, as it seems, of his *bonnes fortunes*, and trafficking with this liaison, as perhaps with others, as a means of advancement – this is what L'Angelier was.[62]

He was portrayed as a cynical manipulator whose mission was to 'assail ... the purity and peace of households', 'a vile scoundrel', and 'dishonourable, mean and villainous'.[63] Those who were at pains to underscore that all was well in the private haven of the British home found ammunition in the portrayal of L'Angelier as an outsider who sought to taint the purity of British maidenhood. The fault lay not within British society but in dangerous external forces. The *Glasgow Courier* warned against consorting with foreigners of unknown provenance:

> How such a man could have found access to respectable society in this city and been received into the houses of people as a favoured guest, we cannot even imagine; but the fact is so, and as M. L'Angelier's vanity and wickedness have brought discredit upon the society of Glasgow and impressed an indelible stain upon the national morality, we may venture to express a hope that the lesson will not be thrown away upon us, and that if foreigners are to be introduced to our sons and daughters, care will be taken to learn something about their history and character.[64]

The demonisation of L'Angelier involved not simply parading his character flaws, but also coupling these with his low rank in society and, crucially, his status as a foreigner. Rather than presenting L'Angelier as a Jersey man and therefore a British subject, he was portrayed as a foreigner, of French origins. This, of course, fitted the narrative which was being shaped of malign influences outside society. His 'vanity', 'selfishness' and all other character weaknesses were often located in his nationality rather than in his psychology. The *Spectator*, whose political philosophy in the 1850s was 'educated radicalism', nonetheless exhibited as much xenophobia as the conservative press:

> L'Angelier is the designing seducer. His object is the indulgence of vanity: then probably the employment of profligacy; then finally a provision for his own life by a compulsory marriage ... his character is French ... French in its faults and perhaps in its unlucky attractions ...[65]

L'Angelier's behaviour was frequently referred to in the press as 'unmanly' and dishonourable. The traits which were usually cited as evidence of this were his seduction of Madeleine, his threats to reveal her letters to her father, his conceit and his foppishness. Usually by implication, but sometimes explicitly, this behaviour was equated with 'foreignness' rather than 'Britishness'. The Edinburgh-based *Witness* clumsily punned that 'one result of the late trial will be to strengthen society in her suspicions of fragrant fops or unfragrant foreigners, who may possibly be Counts or what not at home, but do not count much with us'.[66] The British standard of manliness was regarded as a model which foreigners were not expected to meet; hence the prosecution could excuse L'Angelier's volatile temperament by claiming it was typical of 'our neighbours across the channel'.

Judging by the qualities which were reviled as 'foreign', those qualities which were central to British masculinity or 'manly honour' were self-restraint, mastering of passion and, crucially, man as the protector of woman. Therefore John Inglis's eloquent and impassioned plea to the jury, to see Madeleine as an innocent corrupted by a low scoundrel, was described by one newspaper as full of 'rich, manly feeling' and contrasted with L'Angelier's 'unmanly' seduction and betrayal of Madeleine. To underscore L'Angelier's failure to behave as an 'honourable man' his behaviour, character traits and even his corporeality were sometimes described in feminine language. The *Lancet* did not mince its words and dismissed him as a 'miserable little fop, possessed of a pretty face', while the *Spectator* described him as, 'prepossessing in appearance, delicate and even "pretty" ... exacting as a woman, but had a selfishness more frequently found in the other sex'.[67] The *Witness* was more circumspect, but its sardonic reference to ' gasconading "swells" that perambulate the streets and parade under windows, with the charitable intention of gratifying their enthusiastic admirers by a glimpse of their dainty moustache, delicate feet, and darling curls', was obviously a thinly veiled reference to L'Angelier.[68]

The representation of Madeleine as victim and L'Angelier as a foreign predator, while at the same time vaunting the superiority of British values of restraint and probity, could be interpreted as a defensive response to an episode which, subject to another reading, might lead to serious questioning of the shibboleth of the moral sanctity of the private sphere. Certainly the *Witness* mounted a robust defence of the British way of life:

> Foreigners may cry out upon the insular conventions of society with us and its inexorable formalities, complaining of our want of freedom, and our limiting ideas of propriety. But we suspect that shrewd old society knows well what she is about in clinging to her old-fashioned notions of what is a fitting environment for the social gathering of friends and the inviolate circle of home.[69]

On the other hand, this response might be interpreted as a display of supreme confidence in the superiority of British values in the face of recent threats to the British Empire, such as the equivocal outcome of the Crimean war and the challenge to British rule in India. Either way, by plotting the 'Glasgow Poisoning Case' as a story of innocence defiled by a libidinous interloper who had inveigled his way into respectable society, the middle classes could sleep easily in the knowledge that nothing untoward lurked underneath the calm surface of respectable society. As the editorial in the *Glasgow Citizen* almost triumphantly observed, 'Suddenly the curtain has been lifted, and nothing has been descried but a pious and well-ordered household'.[70]

This satisfaction with the moral state of 'respectable' society was shared by a small number of those who found nothing in Madeleine to arouse sympathy and who condemned her as 'depraved' and morally guilty. The *Glasgow Chronicle* did not shy away from pointing out that Madeleine had been as much the seducer as the seduced and decried those who sought to make a martyr or heroine of her. Unlike those who saw Madeleine as a young, passionate woman who loved not wisely but too well, the *Chronicle* dismissed her love as 'not the sterling metal but a base and spurious thing heavily alloyed with impurity, deceit and treachery'.[71] Like the *Glasgow Sentinel*, it subscribed to the view that Madeleine was 'one of those abnormal spirits that now and then rise up in society to startle and appal us'.[72] Therefore it saw no need for critical reflection on the state of the nation's morals: 'We feel not one whit more inclined than before to suspect the prevalence of moral rottenness in our social and private life'.[73] The correspondent in *The Era*, a weekly periodical for professionals in the theatre, perhaps voiced the response one might have expected to be more widespread regarding someone who had violated so many of the tenets of respectable middle-class society: unreserved condemnation of Madeleine as 'unchaste, unwomanly, and immoral in the highest degree'. It railed against those (particularly the 'Scotch') who indulged in 'maudlin sympathy' for her, claiming that she was 'out of the pale of deserved commiseration'. It was Madeleine's breach of the moral codes of her gender which particularly exercised the paper: 'so long as virtue hold its place as the basis of all our moral worth, so long will society repudiate those women who outrage the domestic obligations of daughter, lover, and affianced bride'.[74]

For others, the conclusion of the trial was an occasion for critical reflection on the state of British society, and the lessons to be drawn transcended questions of individual morality. Some saw it as an opportunity to ventilate generalised anxieties about social and private life; to others, it was about more specific concerns and the need for some degree of reform or change. For these commentators the trial was appropriated to prop up their political and social critiques of contemporary society. The *Spectator* was quick to point the finger at family life and the nature of relations between parents and children 'of even the most "regular" of families'. It bemoaned the social distance between parents and children, the fact that their knowledge of each other was 'very slight', and recommended 'a better reciprocal knowledge' in the home. There were familiar contemporary resonances in the claims that parental influence was weak and that young people sought companionship outside the home rather than in it.[75]

The *Dumbarton Herald* editorial discoursed on the education of middle-class girls, female employment and the 'false ideas of rank and station' which marked the case. It reflected the views of first-wave feminism and the educational reform movement in its criticisms of the frivolous nature of middle-class girls' education and its call for schooling of 'a more intellectual, ennobling, and practical character'.[76] However, it went a good deal further in its criticisms of middle-class education by censuring not only boarding schools but also single-sex education, which, it argued, 'cannot be productive of healthy moral feeling in either sex'. It launched an onslaught on 'fashionable' ideas which proscribed useful employment for 'young ladies' and thus created idle hands and idle minds 'prone to mischief' and 'evil thoughts'. The final criticism was directed at 'that love of keeping up a certain rank and position in society'. It was pointed out that the root of the problem was Madeleine's parents' rejection of L'Angelier as an unfitting suitor because of his station in life. The editorial ended with a trenchant attack on the wealthy classes for their love of social position which led to 'much anguish, misery, and guilt'.

The same points were made by the *Glasgow Sentinel*, which also denounced Madeleine for casting L'Angelier aside because of 'love of social position'. The *Glasgow Sentinel* was in no doubt that L'Angelier had been rejected because he was a 'poor clerk with a small salary and had no rich relations'. Its frequent allusion to Madeleine's being 'highly connected' and moving in the 'so-styled respectable circles of our city'[77] was the closest that any of the newspapers came to offering a class analysis of the case and reflected the *Glasgow Sentinel*'s political sympathies with the 'labouring classes'. In keeping with mid-Victorian working-class radicalism, the language and message of the *Glasgow Sentinel* drew much from biblical teachings and it frequently affirmed the view that all men are equal before God.

Other newspaper commentators expressed more general anxieties about the state of the nation or, more particularly, about the sanctity of the domestic sphere, which was regarded as the cornerstone of moral life. While others might have unshakeable confidence that the moral heart of society was beating as strongly as ever, they suggested that there might be a dislocation between appearance and reality. Given that there was nothing obvious to differentiate either Madeleine or the Smith family from the rest of 'respectable society', they raised the spectre that underneath the apparently calm and decorous surface of bourgeois society there might be a seething cauldron of vice and depravity. The *Manchester Guardian* saw Madeleine as typical of her peers, as a young woman who was 'snatched at random from the companionship of thousands of her age and fortune', and speculated whether 'such unsuspected dramas as this may underlie the calm and decorous aspect of society'. Similarly, the *Saturday Review* suggested that the case 'only shows what may be going on in the inmost core of all that is apparently pure and respectable'.[78] These views may have reflected newly emerging anxieties about the solidity of the British way of life and the regulatory efficacy of the public–private divide. Or they may have been an expression of anxieties about the perennial fragility of social order and the need for eternal vigilance.

The Madeleine Smith trial unleashed a deluge of newsprint which ranged from reasoned debates and arguments to unedifying prejudice and bigotry. It raised numerous issues which reflected either widespread contemporary concerns or merely individual fixations. However, central to the debates were questions about gender relations, the meaning of masculinity and femininity, class, social order, national identity and human nature. Given the importance of separate spheres and the domestic ideal to the discursive context of the period, one might have expected a more straightforward reading of a case in which a young woman had so radically breached the fundamental principles of Victorian social order. Instead, there was a multiplicity of interpretations as old, new and rival meanings of key cultural concepts jostled to gain dominance. For what was at stake for all commentators was the social order. Usually the source of disorder was located in working-class life, which for decades had been subject to surveillance, investigation and regulation. However, the Madeleine Smith case trained the spotlight on the most private corners of 'respectable' society as middle-class life came under an unprecedented degree of scrutiny. For those who cast Madeleine as a young woman who had been sinned against by a duplicitous lover, the lessons to be drawn were clear: British society had to protect itself against intrusion from foreigners with different and inferior standards. There was an element of 'Stands the Church clock at ten to three? And is there honey still for tea?' in an interpretation which sought both reassurance and to reassure that all was well with the British way of life. For others, the case signalled newly emerging anxieties about the social relations of bourgeois society and the need to address these social ills so as to avoid a breakdown in social order. Surprisingly, there was no outright condemnation in the press of the 'Woman Question' and those who sought fundamental changes in women's role, even although Madeleine herself had admitted to being a reader of the *Waverley Journal*, a proto-feminist publication. What is interesting is that, in the time of Victorian equipoise, when social and political stability were more assured than they had been for fifty years, these issues were the subject of such intense debate, contestation and negotiation.

Notes

1 *Glasgow Herald*, 3rd April 1857.
2 Quoted in ibid.
3 Douglas MacGowan, *Murder in Victorian Scotland: The Trial of Madeleine Smith* (Praeger, 1999), p. 95.
4 Ibid.
5 Letter from John Inglis, 13th July 1857, McGrigor Donald, Solicitors, Glasgow.
6 *Glasgow Examiner*, 11th July 1857.
7 Ibid.
8 Quoted in F. Tennyson Jesse, *The Trial of Madeleine Smith* (William Hodge and Co., 1927), p. 410.

9   Ibid., p. 412.

10 *Glasgow Courier*, 7th July, 1857.

11 Tennyson Jesse, *The Trial*, p. 32.

12 *Glasgow Courier*, 7th July 1857.

13 Ibid.

14 Tennyson Jesse, *The Trial*, p. 97.

15 Ibid., p. 67.

16 *Glasgow Herald*, 3rd July 1857.

17 *Glasgow Sentinel*, 4th July 1857.

18 *Glasgow Courier*, 7th July 1857.

19 Quoted from The Lord Justice-Clerk's Charge to the Jury, Tennyson Jesse, *The Trial*, p. 295.

20 Quoted in MacGowan, *Murder in Victorian Scotland*, p. 128.

21 *Glasgow Herald*, 6th July 1857.

22 *The Times*, 7th July 1857.

23 *Glasgow Sentinel*, 11th July 1857.

24 Ibid.

25 *Glasgow Herald*, 10th July 1857.

26 *Glasgow Examiner*, 11th July 1857.

27 Ibid.

28 Tennyson Jesse, *The Trial*, p. 179.

29 Ibid., p. 180.

30 Ibid., p. 188.

31 Ibid.

32 Ibid., p. 195.

33 Ibid., p. 228.

34 Ibid.

35 Ibid., p. 143.

36 Ibid., p. 231.

37 Ibid., p. 233.

38 Ibid., p. 234.

39 Ibid., p. 237.

40 Ibid., p. 272.

41 Ibid., p. 273.

42 Ibid., p. 274.

43 *Daily Telegraph*, 9th July 1857.

44 Quoted in Tennyson Jesse, *The Trial*, p. 295.

45 Ibid., p. 295.

46 Ibid., pp. 300–1.

47 *Paisley Herald and Renfrewshire Advertiser*, 18th July 1857.

48 *Daily Telegraph*, 11th July 1857.

49 Quoted in ibid. and in *Edinburgh Evening Post and Scottish Record*, 11th July 1857.

50 See Sheila Sullivan, '"What is the Matter with Mary Jane?" Madeleine Smith, Legal Ambiguity, and the Gendered Aesthetic of Victorian Criminality', *Genders*, 35 (2002), p. 2 for the view that the Not Proven verdict suggests 'a failure of controlling structures'.

51 *Glasgow Sentinel*, 11th July 1857.

52 *Saturday Review*, 11th July 1857.

53 *Glasgow Courier*, 11th July 1857.

54 *Glasgow Sentinel*, 11th July 1857.

55 Ibid.

56 *The Era*, 9th August 1857.

57 *Glasgow Courier*, 11th July 1857.

58 *Edinburgh Evening Post and Scottish Record*, 11th July 1857.

59 *Edinburgh Evening Courant*, 11th July 1857.

60 *Morning Post*, 10th July 1857.

61 *Glasgow Citizen*, quoted in *Paisley Herald and Renfrewshire Advertiser*, 18th July 1857.

62 *Saturday Review*, reprinted in the *Dumbarton Herald*, 16th July 1857.

63 *Daily Telegraph*, 10th July 1857.

64 *Glasgow Courier*, 11th July 1857.

65 *Saturday Review*, quoted in the *Glasgow Herald*, 13th July 1857.

66 *The Witness*, quoted in the *Glasgow Herald*, 20th July 1857.

67 *Lancet*, quoted in the *Glasgow Herald*, 20th July 1857; *Spectator*, quoted in the *Glasgow Herald*, 20th July 1857.

68 *The Witness*, quoted in the *Glasgow Herald*, 20th July 1857.

69 Ibid.

70 *Glasgow Citizen*, quoted in *Paisley Herald and Renfrewshire* Advertiser, 18th July 1857.

71 *Glasgow Chronicle*, quoted in *Paisley Herald and Renfrewshire Advertiser*, 18th July 1857.

72 *Glasgow Sentinel*, 11th July 1857.

73 *Glasgow Chronicle*, quote in *Paisley Herald and Renfrewshire Advertiser*, 18th July 1857.

74 Ibid.

75 *Spectator*, 11th July 1857.

76 *Dumbarton Herald*, 16th July 1857.

77 *Glasgow Sentinel*, 11th July 1857.

78 *Saturday Review*, quoted in the *Dumbarton Herald*, 16th July 1857.

6

Stories of Madeleine Smith

The whole of Britain – and some European countries too – was scandalised by the trial and what it revealed of the relationship between Madeleine and L'Angelier. Henry James later recalled reading about the case in Boulogne, where, as a 14-year-old boy, he was staying with his parents.[1] Nathaniel Hawthorne, touring the Scottish Highlands, reported that the latest newspaper accounts of the trial were being read aloud to groups of ladies and gentlemen in hotels.[2] Susan Smith, from a well-to-do Glasgow family that was not related to Madeleine's, wrote from London to her mother, who was staying in Paris: 'All England and Scotland have been so intensely interested in Madeleine Smith's trial.'[3]

Susan Smith agreed that both parties were 'bad' and that the verdict was a correct one – like many others she felt little pity for L'Angelier: 'How little sympathy one feels with the victim in this case! Generally one feels an interest and sympathy with the murdered man, but as Mr Chapman remarked one really almost feels that he deserved to be poisoned!' Edinburgh publisher John Blackwood wrote to George Eliot that Madeleine 'is a nice young woman but I really doubt whether she did poison the beast and at all events he deserved anything.'[4]

Other contemporaries were less well disposed towards Madeleine. For Jane Carlyle, she was 'a cockatrice' and 'a little incarnate devil'.[5] This is despite a belief that Madeleine was not guilty of the poisoning: so it was the rest of her behaviour that was so wicked. Carlyle's views may have been coloured by snobbery, for she confused Madeleine's very eminent Glasgow grandfather with another David Hamilton of Edinburgh whose mother, 'Mealy Janet', had sold flour.

George Eliot's own unconventional morality did not prevent her from roundly condemning Madeleine, whom she found 'One of the least fascinating of murderesses.'[6] Her partner, George Lewes, was even more robust: he found it 'a hideous case' and could not 'feel the slightest approach to sympathy with her. I see absolutely no trace of goodness in her. From first to last she is utterly bad.' Worse, indeed, than L'Angelier: 'He *had* good feelings. She has none.' So the Eliot-Leweses condemned Madeleine as much for her morals as for the murder which they were convinced she had committed.

The spate of pamphlets which were issued in the wake of the trial cashed in on the interest, prurient and otherwise, aroused by the case, the potent mix of sex, alleged murder and poison guaranteeing healthy sales. Most of these publications reprinted or rehashed newspaper accounts of the trial, usually quoting from Madeleine's letters; others simply bundled together cuttings garnered from various newspapers; some included an introduction which set out the author's interpretation of the events in order to inject some novelty into what was basically recycled material. Usually these pamphlets were partisan in their summing up of the trial, mounting either a spirited defence of Madeleine or an excoriating attack. Typical of the latter approach was the pamphlet published in Glasgow, London and Edinburgh entitled *The Story of Minie L'Angelier or Madeleine Hamilton Smith*.[7] This account of the trial is laced with comments about the depths of Madeleine's depravity: 'her letters divest her of the least pretension to virtue, and robe her with an effrontery and a prurient and disgusting licentiousness such as witches old in vice might sincerely blush to wear'.[8] This was counterpoised by a portrait of L'Angelier as industrious, 'warm-hearted, well-principled, well-behaved and religious'. The pamphlet took a sideswipe at those who were sympathetic to Madeleine, accusing them of a morbid and 'profane sentimentalism'. This was a view shared by *The Era*, in an article written one month after the trial. It was equally perturbed by the extent of sympathy extended to Madeleine and the unhealthy tendency to portray her as either victim or martyr. Both of these publications were clear that Madeleine Smith was corrupt, unchaste, immoral and beyond redemption. For *The Era*, she had strayed far over the line of prescribed female behaviour, with her letters so devoid of feminine reserve that 'it makes us ask in doubt, is the writer a woman?'[9] The author of the *Story of Minie L'Angelier* thought that the whole episode struck an ominous note about the state of society, female education and 'the economy of the home and parental guidance'.

The diverse opinions of Madeleine's contemporaries and the variety of accounts and interpretations of the case suggest that Victorian society was far from being complacent and morally rigid. Only a few contemporary accounts conformed to the version one would have expected of a society which has been represented as the acme of moral inflexibility and cant.

Admittedly, the story was largely represented as a moral tale. However, there was no consensus about who was morally tainted, nor indeed about the moral lessons to be drawn from the episode. Other versions of the case opted for a romantic reading which portrayed Madeleine as the persecuted victim of male villainy, and some even elevated her status to that of heroine or martyr. The many letters which Madeleine received proposing marriage suggest that the Victorians were as capable as eighteenth-century Georgians of celebrating sentiment, extending sympathy to transgressors and exonerating them of all responsibility for their actions.

Over the ensuing 150 years the case has been revisited many times by biographers, crime writers, playwrights, novelists and film makers and the story has been retold in numerous genres, including a musical. The unique Scottish verdict of 'Not Proven' has left space to allow speculation and creative imagination free rein to interpret and reinterpret the story and for people to draw their own conclusions on the question of Madeleine's guilt or innocence. The body of work generated by the Madeleine Smith trial may or may not shed light on her culpability. It certainly can tell us a good deal about the assumptions and prejudices of the authors. E.H. Carr's observation that historians make history can be extended to all storytellers who write about the past. In telling their version of the past they will invest the story with meanings which resonate with their own histories, preoccupations and prejudices. However, deconstructing the different versions of the case can tell us much more than personal stories. The present and the past are intimately linked, and each recounting of the Madeleine Smith case will be influenced by dominant narratives of the past.[10] Oral historians have deconstructed personal testimonies of past events and revealed the ways in which contemporary public discourses have shaped personal accounts.[11] The same process can be applied to the different versions of the Madeleine Smith story. By uncovering the assumptions and the social contexts of the ways in which the story has been told in different epochs we can gain an understanding not only of how the Victorians have been represented at different times but also of how different times saw themselves in relation to the Victorians.

The Victorian era had barely drawn its last breath when Lytton Strachey's *Eminent Victorians* was published.[12] This biographical work lambasted four eminent Victorians who previously had been accorded almost saintly status and were seen to embody all that was good in Victorian society. Strachey's denunciation of these paragons for having base motives and of Victorian culture as deeply hypocritical had a lasting influence on twentieth-century popular perceptions of the Victorians. The sexual double standard, sexual repression, rigid moral codes, religious hypocrisy, public probity and private vice, separate sexual spheres, the patriarchal family and women's subordination became familiar short-hand terms to represent Victorian society. This view of the Victorians was neither unchanging nor unchallenged throughout the twentieth century. Popular representations and academic studies have variously celebrated, been contemptuous of, or attempted to rehabilitate different aspects of Victorian society.[13] However, each version has, to some extent, been shaped by the preoccupations and concerns of the times in which it was written.

The first thoroughgoing account of the Madeleine Smith case was published in 1927, one year before Madeleine's death. The author, Fryn Tennyson Jesse, was born in 1888. She was the grandniece of the poet Alfred, Lord Tennyson, a crime journalist and, as a young woman, had been a war correspondent on the front-line. Her account, which was part of the *Notable British Trials* series, is a succinct summary of the details of the case, with fewer embellishments and fewer errors than some later ones. Nevertheless, her commentary on the events she describes is shaped by the fact that she chose to plot the story in what she viewed as 'typically' Victorian terms. Mary Perry, a spinster, is described as 'an elderly lady', though she was in her thirties. William Minnoch, the respectable businessman favoured by Madeleine's parents, is 'much older' than L'Angelier, though he was born in November 1820 and Emile in April 1823 – so in fact there was a mere two and a half years between them. But casting Miss Perry as a sentimental old lady and Minnoch as an older and steadier suitor than L'Angelier conformed to what had become established Victorian stereotypes.

By the time Tennyson Jesse was writing her account of the trial, Strachey's anti-Victorianism had become the dominant interpreta-tion of the period in popular imagination, and pejorative connotations of 'Victorian' were well entrenched. Victorians were hypocritical and sentimental. Tennyson Jesse claimed that Madeleine displayed 'typical' Victorian sentimentality 'which was hers in full measure' in her attrac-tion to L'Angelier. He fitted the bill as a romantic figure for Madeleine: he was virtually a foreigner, he was poor, he was handsome and he was charming. Tennyson Jesse drew from the stock representations of the Victorian period when describing other members of Madeleine's family. Her father is described as a quintessential Victorian patriarch, 'the very figure of the awful and august Victorian father'.[14] Madeleine's mother, on the other hand, is described as a 'shadowy figure' and 'the true type of Victorian mother – mild in comparison to with "Papa", yet inflexible in her very subservience to him'.[15]

A product and beneficiary of first-wave feminism, Tennyson Jesse was dismissive of the high Victorian period, which, she claimed, confined women to the home and domesticity. Indeed Tennyson Jesse portrays Madeleine as a victim whose vitality and passion were constrained by stultifying conventions which decreed that a young, single, middle-class woman's only role was to seek a husband: 'In those days there was nothing for her to do but to get engaged, a very tame state of affairs for a character like hers, unless she could add to it a set of strange circumstances to give it interest.'[16] Tennyson Jesse celebrated Madeleine's strength of character, her passion, determination and even her ruthlessness, which she interpreted benignly: 'hers was a nature which had to have adventure'. The problem was not Madeleine, but her times, which penned her into an endless round 'of decorous visits paid with her mother and sister ...'.[17]

No doubt influenced by her own experiences during the First World War, Tennyson Jesse envisaged Madeleine, with her courage and spirit of adventure, driving an ambulance in the 'late war', both fulfilled and useful. Even without the war, education or games 'might have saved her': the regime advocated for late-Victorian boys was now seen as the potential saviour of girls too. Madeleine's chief problem, then, lay in her being born at the wrong time. The Victorian era might have suited anodyne personalities such as Madeleine's sisters, she says, but it had little to offer a strong character like Madeleine, who would have found a suitable niche in a more colourful society: 'Had she been a mediaeval Italian she might have been a successful intriguer and removed people whom she wished to seduce without any loss of social standing. As it was, she was born in that period of the world's history which was the most hopeless for a nature such as hers.'[18]

Transposing Madeleine to her own times, Tennyson Jesse imagined her enjoying the new-found freedoms of the modern woman: 'She could have become a business woman, or gone on the stage, or lived in a bachelor flat and had affairs, without the end of the world having resulted.' Had she been a 'modern' girl, living more independently of her family, dashing off to her job as a typist, all would have been different. She suggests that the intense physical ardour, followed by disillusion and rejection, that characterised Madeleine's side of the relationship with L'Angelier would have presented no problem to the flapper and her short-lived affairs – nor indeed to the ambulance driver and her 'sentimental little affairs with wounded officers'. Women who have jobs, Tennyson Jesse suggests, have independence and can dump lovers when they tire of them. But she also sees a career as an outlet for Madeleine's energies, and seems to suggest that she would thus not have needed the lovers in the first place. For

Tennyson Jesse, the panacea was a career; what is not clear is whether a rewarding job prevented the need for unsuitable affairs, or merely enabled one to extricate oneself from them without resorting to poison.

When it came to discussing Madeleine's attitude to sex, Tennyson Jesse drew on the relatively new language and concepts of Freudian psychology. Madeleine must have been 'an unconscious Masochist' to put up with L'Angelier's sanctimonious upbraiding. They were playing a game which Emile 'must have known would end in self-disgust'. She refers to Madeleine's enjoyment of sex: 'she let loose the pagan side of her nature, which was perhaps its most admirable quality'. This is a remarkable – almost Lawrentian – statement: by the 1920s the very aspect which had repulsed Victorians was the most admirable thing about Madeleine.

Tennyson Jesse was part of a metropolitan circle of writers and artists and was expressing new ideas about sexuality which developed among intellectuals, bohemians and radicals in the first decades of the twentieth century. Political enfranchisement, increased economic activity and educational opportunities, at least for some women, laid the foundations for what was self-consciously viewed as a new sexual morality which acknowledged and celebrated the legitimacy of female sexual desire and vitality. In order to emphasise the novelty of these ideas, older patterns of sexual behaviour were condemned as repressive and Victorian women were characterised as passionless. Tennyson Jesse's comment on Madeleine's fulsome expressions of sexual enjoyment in her letters contrasted them with 'typical' Victorian restraint: 'Candour such as this was felt to be perfectly shocking from a young woman, and to do the spirit of that time justice it would probably have been felt to be just as shocking had the parties been married. Love-making was a mysterious arrangement on the part of Providence, which was necessary to gentlemen and which a good wife accepted as her bounden duty.'[19]

Tennyson Jesse's sympathetic interpretation of Madeleine, despite the fact that she believed she had poisoned L'Angelier, stems from the fact that she laid the blame at the door of Victorian gender relations and sexually repressive mores, rather than of Madeleine's temperament: 'Madeleine Smith was born before her time. She had all the profound physical passion with which the northern woman so often makes her southern sister seem insipid; and this passion, of the essence of her being, was a thing supposed at that particular date not to exist in a "nice" woman.'[20]

The idea that Madeleine was born in the wrong era was taken up and continued by practically all other commentators on the case. Her other interwar biographer, Geoffrey Butler, certainly took this view. For him too, Madeleine was 'a misfit, not only in her family but in her generation'.[21]

Her 'instincts, moods and emotions were at variance with those of her age'.[22] For this generation of authors, Madeleine's story served to emphasise their distance from the Victorians: Butler too contrasts attitudes of his own day to those of the 'repressed' Victorians: 'the modern age does not condemn her for her early frailties, and cannot but admire her for her courage'.[23] The only way to fit Madeleine into the prevailing rhetoric about the Victorians was to see her as *untypical*.

The first fictionalised version of the case appeared in the year of Madeleine's death, 1928. The play, *Madeleine Smith: A Tragi-Comedy in Two Acts*, written by Winifred Duke, shared the anti-Victorianism of the biographical accounts of the case. Indeed it was even more comprehensively anti-Victorian in its characterisation of the period. There is a thinly disguised contempt for everything Victorian in this narrative: nothing of the period was deemed worthy of praise or sympathetic consideration. In the introductory scene-setting even the material culture of the period is derided:

> The Scene represents a thoroughly middle-class drawing-room of the 1850s. All the atrocities of the period are displayed and represented, i.e., lustres, gilt-edged albums of the family photographs, antimacassars, screens, large fat sofas and armchairs, beaded footstools, and a multitudinous collection of dust-gathering, useless ornaments.[24]

The author's stage directions also manage to gibe at the religiosity of the Victorians as well as foregrounding the patriarchal nature of gender relations: 'The pictures are principally portraits in gilt frames of Presbyterian divines ... Mr Middleton, a minister of the United Presbyterian Church, is standing with his back to the mantelpiece, talking down to his wife.'

The characters in the play serve as a series of tropes with which to represent the Victorian period: the patriarchal husband and father; the subservient, domesticated wife; frivolous, superficial, sexually repressed or oppressed daughters; the puritanical and hypocritical Presbyterian minister; the sentimental old maid. There is nothing redeeming about them; they are hypocritical, xenophobic, snobbish and prudish. L'Angelier is 'a low foreigner', characters police the topics and language of conversation by deeming them too 'indelicate' for discussion in a drawing room, and Madeleine's father is appalled not by her 'black guilt', but by 'her immorality, her want of proper feeling, her immodesty'.

Madeleine is portrayed as a strong character, scornful of the conventions of her time. She dismisses old spinsters as 'dessicated virgins', the wife of a family friend is 'a dried up married creature ... whose ideas of love-making are bounded by tepid courtship', while her friend Mary Jane is described as 'a young priggish girl'. Madeleine, by contrast, views herself as passionate and self-determining: '[I] knew life and love', 'I have done of my own free will'. This language has more in common with Winifred Duke's and Tennyson Jesse's era than with Madeleine's time and place. Again, Madeleine is positioned outside her culture and speaks with a twentieth-century voice, particularly with regard to how she views her contemporaries. However, she is denied the sympathetic treatment given by her biographers. Rather than being represented as a victim, she is characterised as a manipulative schemer lacking any conscience. Her final soliloquy has her resolving to forget her 'little slip' and observing that she was 'well rid of Emile L'Angelier'. She stretches out her feet to admire her 'pretty ankles' and comments how clever she was to ensure that the jury got a good view of them.

The interwar generation was particularly scathing of the Victorians and saw its own day as more enlightened, more honest and more tolerant. It drew sharp contrasts between the hypocrisy of Victorian sexual mores and its own openness and tolerance. Interwar commentators on the Madeleine Smith case were unequivocal in their belief that the life of a young Victorian woman was stultifying and confined. Madeleine had 'no possible outlet for her repressed energies'.[25] She quaked under the authoritarian regime of her father, a 'typical strict Scotsman of the fifties' whose 'terrifying Victorian presence' dominated his household. According to Butler, young women like Madeleine were bored, browbeaten and practically imprisoned.

Although later generations would not always represent the Victorians quite so negatively,[26] a recurrent theme in most popular writings about the period is the belief that in the mid-Victorian period young women led sheltered, almost incarcerated lives, their spirits crushed by a rigid code of prescribed gender roles and relations. Howard Lockhart's play *The Story of Madeleine Smith: A Dramatic Fiction Founded on Fact*, first performed in 1947, takes this as its theme. Unlike the 'factual' biographies of Madeleine, Lockhart's play is less interested in the issue of Madeleine's guilt or innocence than in her character. Lockhart chose to describe his play as 'a dramatic fiction founded on fact' because much of the dialogue was lifted from the letters and the evidence given at the trial. However, as a 'dramatic fiction' the play is not bound by the same rules as the biographies, and Lockhart does change essentials to suit the staging: the whole action, for instance, takes place in Blythswood Square, although it covers the period from 1855. The situations he creates are the product of dramatic invention, although he appealed to producers of the play not to take dramatic licence and alter the character's conduct to suggest either Madeleine's guilt or her innocence:

> It would be grossly presumptuous as well as historically inaccurate to distort her conduct in this play so as to suggest that she was either 'Guilty' or 'Not Guilty' [...] in the interests of the justice we owe to the dead as well as to the living, no one has a right to set aside the decision of a Court of Law.[27]

The story Lockhart creates is an almost noble tale of rebellion and sacrifice. As with other narratives, Madeleine is presented as a young woman 'born in the wrong century': a rebel spirit who, in refusing to conform to society's prescriptions, sacrificed everything yet remained with her integrity intact. Lockhart's representation of Madeleine's family is drawn from the familiar stereotypes: Mrs Smith was a 'typically negative Victorian mother'; Mr Smith was 'the normal Victorian father – stern and dour but having a genuine affection for his family', although he was also 'typically Scottish and therefore completely undemonstrative'. Despite Lockhart's claim to base the details on fact, when the facts do not fit with familiar tropes they are conveniently altered. In order for her to conform to the stereotypical Victorian spinster, Mary Perry's age is given as 50 rather than 38; Christina Haggart is in her late 30s (she was at least ten years younger) and speaks in almost incomprehensible stage Scottish;[28] while Madeleine's mother is portrayed as the epitome of the weak and frail 'angel in the house', despite the fact that she had a full social diary and rarely missed the opportunity to attend a ball or to travel.

L'Angelier and Madeleine's relationship is shorn of any traces of prurience and is presented as a tragic tale of true romance doomed by vulgar materialism and snobbery. Madeleine's father maps out his expectations of her, pronouncing that he wants her to be 'an ornament in my household. And some day, when the right man comes along, I shall give my consent and you shall be his wife. But he must be a man of substance to give my daughter the position for which I have brought her up.' L'Angelier clearly does not fit the bill. The Smiths and their class are not only preoccupied by wealth and social status: they compound their sins with their xenophobia and philistinism – L'Angelier's name is always coupled with 'foreigner' and at one point Madeleine's father refers to him as 'French vermin'. Operas are dismissed as 'high-coloured love tragedies [which] depict so often a sordid side of life which is best not to see the light of day'.

Lockhart's version is as a feminist story of a woman resisting male power. Madeleine is a great admirer of Florence Nightingale and a defender of women's right to work. She explains her transgressions to her mother: 'I had to have more power, more to occupy my mind and body', telling her that she believes that it would not have happened 'if you and Papa had allowed me to take up some work, like a man'. Perhaps because it was written in the midst of the political and social changes wrought by the Second World War, Lockhart's story contains a dimension missing from other accounts. His references to the hypocrisy, snobberies and vulgar materialism of the Smith circle read more as a criticism of the Victorian class system than as a criticism of an era. By and large, the characters in the play are portrayed as narrow-minded, judgemental and self-interested. Madeleine, who is the flawed heroine of this tale, embodies the virtues of tolerance, respect for all humanity and a commitment to the 'common good', values which echoed post-Second World War beliefs in achieving the New Jerusalem of democracy, equality and freedom for all.

In all of these narratives Madeleine is portrayed as 'out of her time'. In some versions she is a victim, in others a feminist heroine and in yet others a self-willed, manipulative egoist. In creative genres she always speaks with a twentieth-century voice (and language) and displays twentieth-century sensibilities. In Lockhart's play she tells her father that '[some people] haven't got the courage to go out and grab hold of what life has to offer in both hands'. In defying her father's orders to break all contact with L'Angelier she tells him: 'I respect your feelings but I also respect my own and Emile's.' Winifred Duke has her proclaiming: 'My God, My God! No, there is no God to help me out.'[29] All of these narratives appropriate the Madeleine Smith story, and sometimes her voice, to condemn Victorian hypocrisy and intolerance and contrast them with the more enlightened sensibilities of the twentieth century.

The first author to quote at any length from those letters which were not introduced at the trial was Peter Hunt, whose biographical account, *The Madeleine Smith Affair*, was published in 1950 and thus was contemporaneous with Lockhart's play.[30] Hunt departs from previous accounts in his interpretation. He uses these additional quotations to advance his discussion of the relationship between Madeleine and L'Angelier, which he sees as characterised by Madeleine's manipulation of the situation and the man. The preface by William Roughead echoes Tennyson Jesse by presenting Madeleine as 'not a maiden of her time' but belonging spiritually to an earlier, pagan age, 'stifled' and 'confined' by Victorian restrictions.[31] Hunt too sees Madeleine as suffering under Victorian hypocrisy, yet he points out that the Victorians did not have a monopoly on 'humbug'. He presents his own day not as Tennyson Jesse, Butler, Duke and Lockhart do, as a step forward, an era in which a Madeleine might have happily thrived, but as one where 'our pessimism takes immorality in it stride', and where 'we accept any form of beastliness in the headlines of our papers'.[32] Readers in the 1950s, he argues, would have been less shocked than were the Victorians, inured as they had now become to 'beastliness'. 'Today, her brand of morality would have been unnoticed,' he felt; but this was a sign of contemporary decadence, not healthiness. Yet, in 1955 the case of Ruth Ellis demonstrated that morality and murder were still intertwined in the public view.[33]

Hunt's interpretation displays a more sympathetic attitude to the Victorians than most other earlier accounts. There is a belief that the lost innocence and lack of a strong moral code in contemporary society could be found in Victorian times. Hunt's view is not unalloyed nostalgia, for he recognises the flaws of the Victorians. His attitude reflects a waning of pre-war, rabid anti-Victorianism, and also a moral conservatism which harks back to an earlier age of supposed moral certainties. Yet he still clings to the same old assumptions about the people he describes. Papa Smith was 'everything the Victorian father is so often imagined to be'; and Mama 'had surrendered to her husband's mastery'.[34] Evidence of Mama's subservience is that she did not attend Madeleine's trial. Hunt fails to point out that Papa, Jack, Bessie and James did not attend either.

A chapter on the Madeleine Smith case appeared in a collection of accounts of murders over the previous century by John Rowland, also published in 1950.[35] Madeleine was 'a typical Victorian miss ... nervous of her father'. She was burdened with the running of two households on account of her Mama's invalidism. Yet Rowland had clearly read at least those letters produced at the trial, and so knew that Madeleine wrote often of social activities. He reconciles this with the picture he has drawn of her industrious and dutiful life by telling us that she 'was allowed such decorous gaieties as came the way of a Victorian lady of the middle class'.[36] At first sight, this view of Madeleine seems at odds with all those earlier assertions that she was *not* typical, not of her time. But it seems that her typicality, for Rowland, lay in her relationship with her domineering father and the narrow and 'decorous' confines of her daily life, an interpretation universally acknowledged by other commentators. Elsewhere he speaks of her passionate and reckless love for L'Angelier. His views are, in fact, part of the canon that sees Madeleine's life as typical but her personality as not.

Nigel Morland's biography, written later in the same decade, follows much the same path. He depicts Madeleine as hemmed in by 'the constricting walls of middle-class Victorianism'.[37] He points to the double standards and hypocrisy of Victorian sexual mores. He portrays Papa as a martinet, in the way of Victorian fathers, and Mama as 'guileless and innocent', utterly dominated by her husband.[38] Mrs Smith was 'completely effaced by her husband's strength of character. She was obedient and passive ... humourless and easily perturbed'.[39] Her appearance – about which we actually have no clue – is inferred from her supposed character: she was 'small, rather timorous, and blonde fading to brown'. It is enough to sum Mr Smith up as 'the grim Victorian paterfamilias': no more need be said.[40]

The Smith case continued to excite interest and, it seems, to encourage illicit hoarding of material. In 1889 a clerk at the Justiciary Office in Edinburgh had removed some of Madeleine's letters which remained with the trial papers and sold them to a bookseller. These were largely recovered (and the clerk gaoled); but some remained unaccounted for, and at least one surfaced as late as the 1970s in private hands.[41] Henry James bemoaned the lack of any photograph of Madeleine and felt that he would give anything for a sight of her 'then face'. But the photos of Madeleine and of Emile that had been used at the trial had disappeared. However, the frontispiece of Hunt's 1950 book is a fine line drawing which is an exact copy of the missing photograph of Madeleine – which only surfaced when a bookseller sold it (and that of L'Angelier) to Glasgow's Mitchell Library in 1991. Someone had hoarded it in the mean time.

Morland, in particular, had tried to research his topic carefully, and some of his correspondence with the Mitchell Library survives. He was following a fifty-year-old tradition, for extensive 'digging' had gone on in the early years of the twentieth century. Local agents were employed to search notices in the *Glasgow Herald* for the births of Madeleine and her siblings. Neighbours and alleged ex-servants of the Smiths in Falkirk were interviewed, and a potpourri of truth and embroidery emerged, to be drawn upon and repeated over the decades. This came to a head in the 1950s. Some useful material, such as a photograph apparently of the Clapton home of Mrs Gorton's school, was deposited in the Mitchell Library. A William Glen also donated a photograph of 'the Smith family', which has been widely reproduced ever since.[42] The original photo is completely anonymous. It shows a couple and their children, dressed in the fashion of the 1850s. The oldest child is a teenage daughter, a pretty girl of perhaps 15 or 16. This, we are told, is Madeleine. A major problem is that there are seven children, when we know that only five Smith children survived infancy. Furthermore, it is impossible, even discounting any two children to taste, to square the ages and sexes of the remainder with the known family. The photograph is not of Madeleine Smith. It does, though, demonstrate how her case has attracted wishful thinking, gullibility and careless research which can transform fiction into 'fact'.

The flurry of 'discoveries' and surge of interest in the case in the early 1950s may have had something to do with David Lean's film *Madeleine*, made in 1949. In many ways the film version is truer to the facts of the case than are many of the factual versions appearing in print. The film takes the form of a courtroom drama and Lean, remaining true to the 'Not Proven' verdict, refuses to settle decisively for either guilt or innocence. This may have been a dramatic device designed to leave the audience guessing. However, it did not satisfy popular tastes, which would have preferred an unambiguous verdict and a solution to the mystery. Despite the courtroom drama form, Lean's tale is not based around the question of whether or not Madeleine 'did it'; rather, it is a story of male power and female subordination. He emphasises this by portraying Madeleine's father as a formidable patriarch and L'Angelier as bullying and domineering, while Madeleine's arrival at the courthouse is greeted by a haranguing male mob. Although Lean focuses on the theme of male domination and power, Madeleine is represented neither as victim nor as proto-feminist. Although she is spirited and neither cowed by society's rigid moral codes and rules nor bowed by her predicament, lacking the feminist conscious-ness of Lockhart's Madeleine, her resistance takes the form of deviousness and subterfuge rather than outright defiance.

It was not until the 1970s that the case was revisited by popular writers. By this time, Britain was experiencing significant social and polit-ical transformations. The late 1960s through to the early 1970s have often been viewed as a period of rapid and far-reaching social changes. These years saw the emergence of student protests, counter-culture movements, the women's liberation movement, as well as gay and lesbian movements. In popular memory, one of the defining features of the period is its association with a revolution in sexual mores. The introduction of oral contraception, legal changes relating to abortion, sexuality, relaxation of censorship and women's rights both reflected and facilitated changing social attitudes. Although these changes were not universally welcomed and their impact is perhaps exaggerated, they did usher in a period of unprecedented openness with regard to frankness of expression about sexuality. Consequently, in the two narratives of the case which appeared in the 1970s sex and sexuality are accorded a more central role.

Henry Blyth's factual account of the case, published in 1975,[43] was the first to speculate freely in print on some of the more 'shocking' details from the letters – the loss of Madeleine's virginity and the nature of the couple's sexual intimacy. Madeleine:

had no doubt whatever that she could prove herself in bed to be every bit as ardent as any lover whom she might take. Her desire no doubt sprang partly from a healthy sensuality, but also from her desire to dominate her lover in bed and make him her slave. She was the type of woman who frightens hesitant males.[44]

This reading of Madeleine is of a sexual dominatrix, assertive and in control of her relationship with L'Angelier, inside and perhaps outside the bedroom. The ambivalence of Blyth's interpretation of Madeleine's sexuality – on the one hand, she demonstrates 'a healthy sexuality', but on the other, an unhealthy desire to dominate – may reflect Blyth's ambivalence to second-wave feminism, which was flourishing at the time. It was to be welcomed if it encouraged women to more freely express their sexuality, but not at the expense of any erosion of male power.

Blyth's musings on the nature of female sexuality permeate his narrative. He extrapolates from Madeleine's sexuality to share his insights into 'the female character' in general: 'women who stand up to male dominance are just waiting to become willing slaves of the right man. It is a curiosity of the female character that women who show the greatest defiance in the face of male domination so often become the willing slaves of the one man who really attracts them. It is then that they develop a masochistic submission …'. However, he warns, 'It must be remembered that once a dominating woman has been thus tamed, she will only continue to admire her lover for so long as he maintains this ascendancy over her.'[45] Blyth thus sees Madeleine's sexual adventure beginning in domination and ending in masochistic submission: 'Madeleine … soon showed herself ready to accept this domination, and even to wallow in it.'

Blyth's interpretation, his use of sexual imagery and his willingness to foreground sexuality suggest a familiarity with coffee-table-book Freudian analysis. More important, the sexual script he writes of the case reflects contemporary concerns and preoccupations. The meanings with which he imbues the story are ones which have a cultural resonance for the 1970s, where newly found sexual candour, encouragement of female sexual expression and women's search for personal autonomy in their reproductive choices and their relations with men engendered fears as well as possibilities.

Yet, for all the novelty of this narrative, he falls back on the usual tropes of the Victorian period. The same old assumptions and stereotypes appear: Mr Smith was a patriarch whose word was law, dogmatic and pompous – a 'typical Victorian father in the authority which he exerted over his wife and family'; Mrs Smith was 'chaste and dutiful', submissive and in delicate health.[46] It is worth quoting Blyth's description of Mama further. She was 'small, self-effacing and unsure of herself'. She had a 'dominating husband, who had married her when she was too young to know anything at all about the facts of life'. By the time of Madeleine's affair, Mama had become 'little more than a small brown mouse about the house'. All this seems to owe more to Blyth's reading of Victorian and later novels than to the evidence at his disposal.

Unlike the earlier writers who had seen Madeleine as not of her time, Blyth argues repeatedly that she was a typical Victorian. This is not incompatible with his view of her as 'over-sexed' and as the deliberate seducer of a rather overwhelmed L'Angelier. Blyth's view of female sexuality is an essentialist one which owes little to the specific context of time or place. He sees nothing remarkable in what he characterises as Madeleine's sexual voraciousness. Her typicality resided in the disproportionate importance she placed on public probity and the fact that she was driven to murder to maintain the veneer of outward respectability: 'She was, after all, a typical Victorian, and the typical Victorian, especially if male, believed in the principle that it really did not matter what one did so long as one took steps to ensure that one was never caught doing it.'[47] Once again, hypocrisy is seen as a defining Victorian characteristic.

Glen Petrie's novel *Mariamne*, also published in the 1970s,[48] is similar to Blyth's biographical account in the centrality given to sexual themes. Petrie makes no claims as to his novel's representing with any accuracy the historical facts of the case, although he draws liberally from Madeleine's published letters for his material. He is uninterested in exploring the question of Madeleine's guilt and makes it clear from the outset that his central character, Mariamne, murdered her lover. Petrie claims that his theme is 'the fascination with the problem of evil'. Yet there is little exploration of Mariamne's character other than the fact that she is passionate and sexual. The real fascination seems to be with lesbianism. This fictionalised account has a lesbian theme and the content is distinguished by its strong undercurrents of repressed lesbianism. Almost all of the women, including Mariamne's mother, the servants and female friends are depicted as having lesbian desires, although there are no sexually explicit passages in the novel. Sexual activity among women is restricted to tender kisses on the cheek or shoulder and references to the sexual frisson enjoyed by both parties while servants dress or undress their mistresses. The novel is also riddled with female sexual jealousies and rivalries. Petrie attributes all this repressed lesbian sexual energy to women's subordination to male patriarchal power; it is this which subverts and distorts the expression of unsullied heterosexual love. Women's suppressed hatred of male power is expressed in either a distorted heterosexual desire which seeks domination and masochistic submission, as in the case of Madeleine, or, alternatively, love is displaced onto other women.

The case has been revisited most recently by biographers primarily attracted to the Smith case because of its 'whodunnit' features.[49] It is this 'unsolved mystery' aspect that has been in large part responsible for the continued interest in the Madeleine Smith story. Most commentators seem to be of the opinion that Madeleine was indeed guilty of poisoning L'Angelier – though many apparently agree with her contemporaries that 'he deserved to be poisoned!' Jack House was unequivocal: 'My own opinion is that she poisoned L'Angelier.'[50] Of the most recently published analysts of the case, Douglas MacGowan is reluctant to accuse Madeleine outright, but is clearly uncomfortable with any other explanation for L'Angelier's death, while Jimmy Campbell is a passionate defender of her innocence. For Campbell, Madeleine was a 'caring and loving' girl who 'had no idea that she was in the coils of a reptile'.[51] His argument is that L'Angelier had laid elaborate plans to poison himself in such a way as to incriminate Madeleine and to lead to her ultimate execution. Despite the fact that Campbell's book claims to be a 'myth-shattering new account' which uncovers new forensic evidence, it too draws on standard representations of the period, including gender relations.

All the genres of the post-war period, whether factual or fictional, rely on a view of the Victorians that can be traced back to Tennyson Jesse in 1927. They structure their accounts in a common setting: Victorian middle-class life was dull and snobbish, peopled by overbearing fathers, meek and downtrodden mothers, daughters who were cramped and curbed. The Victorians were unhealthily repressed and hypocritical, especially about sex. Confronted by the dissonance between what they knew (or thought they knew) of strait-laced Victorian women and Madeleine's passionate responses, commentators could only reconcile these by seeing her as 'out of her time'. Characters are judged by how much or how little they can be made to conform to the stereotypes. Details which resonate with ideas of restriction, boredom, hypocrisy, sentimentality – and they can be found – are seized upon, while the numerous features of the story which do not are glossed over. Most writers use a system of shorthand to represent the Victorians, fashioned from previous accounts and dominant narratives of the past. However, each retelling of the story which draws on this stock of representations has solidified them and, in turn, shaped successive popular cultural perceptions of the era.

A common feature of most commentators on the case is to differentiate clearly their own period from that of the high Victorians. Almost invariably, the Victorian past is represented as more backward, less enlightened and less tolerant. Those writers who have not been condemnatory have been motivated by a reactionary nostalgia which damns the perceived decadence of their own times, celebrates 'Victorian values' and harks back to the supposed innocence and moral rectitude of the Victorians. Each account is coloured, inevitably, by the interests and dispositions of the writers and their times. The emotional landscape of the present is transposed to the past in ways which tell us as much about the times in which they were written as they do about the Victorians. These stories of Madeleine Smith are the constructions of authors who have composed their tales in ways which reflect the social context and social concerns of their times and therefore can themselves be viewed as a subject of history.

Most treatments of the Madeleine Smith story have been for a general audience. There have been fewer academic studies. Those that have been published share to a surprising extent this same range of assumptions about Victorian social life and gender relations. This is despite the fact that intellectual and academic interpretations of Victorian values, politics and culture offer a complex picture rather than a comprehensive, Stracheyan censure of the period.[52]

Mary Hartman's article in *Victorian Studies* was the first feminist academic account of the Madeleine Smith case.[53] Written when second-wave feminism was becoming influential in both popular politics and academic writings, it frames the story within a rigid and fairly simplistic application of the separate spheres thesis, at that time the dominant conceptual category for understanding gender relations in the nineteenth century. This approach took as its starting point that the nineteenth-century belief that men and women should occupy separate and complementary spheres was fundamental in structuring and shaping people's experience and identity in the Victorian period. Historians have interpreted separate spheres differently and have attributed different meanings and significance to their operation. Hartman's version of this thesis is an almost literal interpretation of the concept which equates separate spheres with a physical rather than a symbolic separation: women occupied the private world of home and family, men the public world of the marketplace, citizenship and civil society.

Although Hartman concedes that women were beginning to achieve more authority within the home, she argues that women's lives remained constrained by being confined to the domestic sphere; their education was token. She states that the curriculum at Madeleine's boarding school consisted merely of piano lessons, walks, needlework and deportment. (In fact we do not know what subjects were taught, though there were resident teachers for English, music and French.) In particular, the period between the end of schooling and the achievement of marriage is seen as provoking boredom, restlessness and discontent, for there was nothing permissible for young women to do. Thus, according to Hartman, those women who attended the trial were vicariously breaking free of the ideological shackles that bound them, savouring the actions of a woman who had done what they had barely dared to imagine. Madeleine is no longer seen as untypical: in fact, for Hartman she 'can usefully be considered as perhaps an uncomfortably representative specimen of her class'. Although influenced by feminism, Hartman does not see Madeleine as a feminist heroine, rebelling against patriarchal power. Her interpretation of the story sees her as a prisoner of contemporary views of gender relations. Although she has transgressed, Madeleine does not proudly proclaim it. Rather, she is driven to murder by desperation to maintain the appearance of public respectability, stemming from the deeply embedded belief that public expression of women's sexuality seriously breached moral codes.

Writing almost thirty years later, Sheila Sullivan is influenced by post-structuralism and the cultural turn in history, and exemplifies the inter-disciplinary approach to gender studies which emerged in the 1990s.[54] Despite the very different intellectual influences of Hartman's and Sullivan's approaches, they are remarkably similar in their conclusions. Sullivan's view of Madeleine's motive, if indeed she did kill L'Angelier, is that it was primarily to protect her privacy. To her contemporaries, Sullivan argues, 'Wanting to maintain the separation of spheres, to remain private, was a realistic reason for respectable women to kill.' For both Hartman and Sullivan, Victorian notions of appropriate gender roles could be powerful enough to provoke murder: Hartman titles an article on the case 'Murder for Respectability'; while for Sullivan it was the embeddedness of discourses of public and private that provided the motivation.

Of course, our own story of Madeleine can be deconstructed in the same way. It too is of its time. Eclectic in its influences, it draws on a range of perspectives from the lexicon of gender history which we have absorbed in the thirty years or so of our involvement in the researching and writing on the subject. The history of the different approaches to women's history can be traced in our narrative: the importance placed on women's agency and the mutually constitutive natures of class and gender relations which have their genesis in the 1970s. One can also see the influence of recent developments in cultural history, with our emphasis on the cultural and social aspects of Madeleine's letter writing, the importance of the discursive context in shaping identities, the role of the historian in the creation of history and the influence of public discourses on the writing of history. Perhaps most important, we identify with an increasing body of work which has developed since the late 1980s and which questions the continued usefulness of the separate spheres thesis as the key to understanding the gendered nature of the Victorian world.

There have been many interpretations of the separate sphere thesis: those which have been sensitive to the porous nature of 'public' and 'private' acknowledged that these categories were ideological constructs rather than physical spaces, and emphasised the inconsistencies and contradictions of the dualism. Many of these approaches have extended significantly our understanding of the Victorians and how they may have organised their mental universe. However, we need to acknowledge where they do not help us to fully understand the complexity of Victorian society. There were different constructions of femininity and a matrix of circulating discourses. Privileging one of these discourses above all others at all times can impede our understanding of the formation of individual subjectivities and the diverse influences shaping how Victorians thought and acted.

Like all historians, we are seeking to make sense of the past. While we have tried to convey the complexity and diversity of this brief moment in Victorian history, in doing so we have almost certainly simplified, omitted, emphasised or overlooked evidence in order to construct a coherent narrative which 'fits' with our view of the past. However, we have at least laid bare our conscious intentions and influences, rather than concealing them under the cloak of a 'truer' and more 'objective' reading of the Madeleine Smith story.

Madeleine can be all things to all people – the independent 'free spirit' born before her time; the sexually alluring vamp; the victim of an ideological straitjacket; the prisoner of powerful discourses; the epitome of female duplicity; 'the hero of her own life'. There have been different scripts written for her and different roles assigned to her, many conforming to cultural stereotypes or myths. Sometimes the myths become tangible, as with the photograph of the 'Smith family'. At other times, as when Hartman bases her account of Madeleine's schooldays on unreferenced quotes given by Morland, there is a kind of 'Chinese whispers' game, where 'facts' are passed on, perhaps distorted, and given an authority which they never deserved. The first biographers were writing when those who had seen Madeleine Smith were still alive and able to pass on snippets of gossip. Some bore a kernel of truth, others were pure invention. Subsequently, even the more 'serious' commentators on the case have perpetuated these *canards*, so that fact and fiction imperceptibly merge.

The Victorians have been represented in many different ways since the early twentieth century. Academic histories have moved from comprehensive criticism and censure, to re-evaluation and rehabilitation, to more nuanced accounts which focus on the complexity of Victorian society and the impossibility of viewing it as monolithic.[55] There have also been many shifts in the way that Madeleine Smith's story has been told. What has remained remarkably enduring is the power of the discourse of separate spheres to influence all these accounts. Despite changes of emphasis and viewpoint over time, and despite plentiful evidence to the contrary, there has been extraordinary unanimity in the way that Madeleine's story has been viewed through this prism, and a picture of what her life, her relationships and her motives 'must have been' has been universally accepted.

Notes

1   Richard Altick, *Victorian Studies in Scarlet* (Dent, 1972), p. 189.
2   Ibid., p. 186.
3   GCA TD 1/1053, Letter, 11th July 1857.
4   Altick, *Victorian Studies in Scarlet*, p. 187.
5   Ibid., p. 188.
6   Ibid., p. 187.
7   *The Story of Minie L'Angelier or Madeleine Hamilton Smith* (Edinburgh, Myles Macphail; Glasgow, T. Murray and Sons; London, Simpkin, Marshall and Co., 1857).
8   Ibid., p. 10.
9   *The Era*, 9th August 1857.
10 John Brewer's *Sentimental Murder* (Harper Collins, 2004) offers a novel interpretation of a celebrated eighteenth-century crime by focusing on the ways that the story has been told and retold in subsequent accounts and genres, rather than attempting to fill in the historical gaps in the story or unravel the 'truth' of the case.
11 Anna Green and Kathleen Troup (eds), *The Houses of History* (Manchester University Press, 1999), chapter 9.
12 Lytton Strachey, *Eminent Victorians* (Continuum, 2003.)
13 Miles Taylor and Michael Wolf (eds), *The Victorians since 1901* (Manchester University Press, 2004).
14 F. Tennyson Jesse, *The Trial of Madeleine Smith* (William Hodge and Co., 1927), p. 4.
15 Ibid., p. 4.
16 Ibid., p. 7.
17 Ibid., p. 8.
18 Ibid.
19 Ibid., p. 13.
20 Ibid., p. 7.
21 Geoffrey L. Butler, *Madeleine Smith* (Duckworth, 1935) p. 9.
22 Ibid., p. 172.
23 Ibid., p. 183.

24 Winifred Duke, *Madeleine Smith: A Tragi-Comedy in Two Acts* (William Hodge and Co., 1928).

25 Butler, *Madeleine Smith*, p. 11.

26 Taylor and Wolf, *The Victorians since 1901*, passim.

27 Howard Lockhart, *The Story of Madeleine Smith: A Dramatic Fiction Founded on Fact* (H.W.F. Deane and Sons, Ltd, 1949), author's Introduction.

28 'Och I ken fine. Ma certes, you don't need to mind me. I've a laud o' my ain, ye ken … I got a rale fleg the noo …', Lockhart, *The Story of Madeleine Smith*, p. 26.

29 Winifred Duke, *Madeleine Smith*, p. 28.

30 Peter Hunt, *The Madeleine Smith Affair* (Carroll & Nicholson, 1950).

31 Ibid., p. vii.

32 Ibid., p. 20.

33 Ellis, a nightclub hostess, was hanged for shooting her lover outside a London pub.

34 Hunt, *Madeleine Smith*, pp. 36–7.

35 John Rowland, *A Century of Murder* (Home & Van Thal, 1950).

36 Ibid., p. 36.

37 Nigel Morland, *That Nice Miss Smith* (Frederick Muller Ltd, 1957), p. 49.

38 Ibid., p. 62.

39 Ibid., p. 37.

40 Ibid., p. 57.

41 Henry Blyth, *Madeleine Smith: A Famous Victorian Murder Trial* (Duckworth, 1975). Blyth reproduces a letter, undoubtedly genuine, 'in the author's possession', p. 191 and plate 5.

42 Most recently in William Knox, *Lives of Scottish Women* (Edinburgh University Press, 2006) and Jimmy Campbell, *A Scottish Murder: Rewriting the Madeleine Smith Story*, Tempus, 2007.

43 It also appears in the second edition of Jack House, *Square Mile of Murder*, also published in 1975. House adds the refinement that the photo was taken in 1852 'when Madeleine was 15'. Of course Madeleine, born in March 1835, was not 15 in 1852.

44 Blyth, *Madeleine Smith*, pp. 52–3.

45 Ibid., p. 47.

46 Ibid., pp. 2–3.

47 Ibid., p. 50.

48 Glen Petrie, *Mariamne* (Macmillan, 1977).

49 Douglas MacGowan, *Murder in Victorian Scotland* (Praeger, 1999); Jimmy Campbell, *A Scottish Murder*. A musical version of this book first appeared at the Edinburgh International Festival in 2003.

50 Jack House, *Square Mile of Murder* (Richard Drew Publishing, 1984), p. 78.

51 Campbell, *A Scottish Murder*, p. 212.

52 Taylor and Wolff, *The Victorians since 1901*, Parts I and III.

53 Mary Hartman, 'Murder for Respectability: The Case of Madeleine Smith', *Victorian Studies*, 16, 4 (1972–73), pp. 381–400; and Mary S. Hartman, *Victorian Murderesses: A True History of Thirteen Respectable French and English Women Accused of Unspeakable Crimes* (Schocken Books, 1977).

54 Sheila Sullivan, '"What is the Matter with Mary Jane?" Madeleine Smith, Legal Ambiguity, and the Gendered Aesthetic of Victorian Criminality', *Genders*, 35 (2002), pp. 1–44.

55 Martin Hewitt (ed.), *An Age of Equipoise? Reassessing mid-Victorian Britain* (Ashgate, 2000).

7

Afterwards

New York in 1928: the jazz age, the age of prohibition, flappers and speakeasies; the world of the great Gatsby. In the Bronx, a sprightly old lady lives out her last months. She had convinced her doctor that she was 64: her family, who must have known she was much more, indulged her by going along with the pretence. In this most modern of eras, she was an anachronism. Although refusing to admit it, she could recall visiting the Great Exhibition of 1851. She had danced in the company of Napoleon's nephew Lucien Bonaparte when the waltz, rather than the Charleston, was shocking. Lena Sheehy was in fact 93 – a *pre*-Victorian. To knock thirty years off one's true age is an amazing feat of dissimulation, and would have required constant vigilance. Mrs Sheehy was aided by her continuing vivacity, mental alertness and, apparently, hennaed wigs.

She was, of course, Madeleine Smith, seventy years on from her notoriety. After the trial she vanished from view and, over the ensuing years, flits in and out of our sight. Contemporaries wrote of her continued existence until about the end of the century. For Henry James the point was that 'she precisely *didn't* squalidly suffer, but lived on …'.[1] In fact, Madeleine outlived James himself, and practically everyone else who had commented on or been involved in her trial. A couple of years before her death, Madeleine's survival was 'discovered' by the press, although it got little right beyond this simple fact. Yet it was not a discovery at all. An old-established firm of solicitors in Glasgow (and another in Bath) knew full well where Madeleine was until the very end.

David Lean's film of the Madeleine Smith story ends with Madeleine being whisked away from the court in Edinburgh while a decoy occupies the crowds at the front of the building. A similar incident was reported in contemporary newspapers. She and Jack took a cab to Slateford, and then the Glasgow train to Stepps Road station. From there they went straight to *Rowaleyn*.[2] No one knows what happened next. Newspapers dressed their ignorance up as high-mindedness: 'It is scarcely fair to follow her to her home, and again reveal what ought never to be known beyond the family circle.'[3]

There were numerous 'sightings', as there always are in such circumstances. The *Aberdeen Herald* reported that Madeleine reached the city on Friday by the south train on the way to Orkney.[4] This would seem a singularly inappropriate hiding place. More plausibly, especially in light of her subsequent emigration, rumour placed Madeleine on a steamship bound for New York. This tale seems to have originated with some hysterical passengers who pointed to an unknown young woman for no good reason: the woman's own sister denied that she was Madeleine.

More sober accounts tell us that she remained at *Rowaleyn* for at least a short time, not leaving the grounds even to go to church. Madeleine herself, in the last words we have directly from her, wrote to the Matron at Edinburgh prison that she would have to go away for some time. It would certainly have been difficult for her family to live under the glare of publicity that Madeleine brought, even if they had wanted her company. Bessie, for one, certainly did not: she never forgave Madeleine, whether or not she believed her sister guilty, for the shame she had brought and the blight she had cast on her sister's prospects. It must have been an uncomfortable homecoming, even for one with Madeleine's thickness of skin.

However, the family did not completely disown Madeleine and arrangements were made for her to go quietly away. Although she was to remain in touch with family members for the rest of her life, Madeleine never again lived in Scotland. Hunt, writing in 1950, asserted that she went to stay with a clergyman friend of the family in Plymouth. He does not supply a reference for this, but it is eerily accurate. The 1861 Census (not available until 1961) confirms that Madeleine – or Lena Smith as she was calling herself – was living at 39 George Street, Devonport. This was the home of the Rev. George Mason, curate of St Stephen's church. Madeleine was understandably chary of disclosing her real identity, and gave her birthplace as London rather than Glasgow, and her age as 23 rather than 26.

The Rev. Mason and his wife, Ellen, were newcomers to the busy and sometimes rough dockyard town in the late 1850s, having come from the more genteel setting of Dorset. In the autumn of 1859 they set up a home for 'fallen women' – though these were of a much lower social class than Madeleine, who may have lost her honour but retained her middle-class status.[5] On census night Ellen was staying at the home, of which she was 'lady superintendent', with three helpers and twenty-six young women, all described as 'penitents'. They came largely from the south-west, although a few originated further afield, in Wales or in eastern England.

Was George Mason indeed a family friend? There is no mention of him in any of the correspondence, and no apparent link between the Oxford-educated clergyman from the south of England and the Smiths of Glasgow. Ellen Mason was born Ellen Jones in Kent, and no likely avenues lead to a connection between her and Madeleine: she does not seem to have been a school friend, for instance, although they were the same age. Besides, Madeleine rarely made female friends. In all probability, Madeleine was another of 'the fallen', although living in the vicarage rather than the nearby home, on account of her class.

When did Madeleine join the household? Where had she been from 1857 to the spring of 1861? London may simply have been the most anonymous birthplace to choose; or it may be that she had spent some of the interval in that city. She was clearly trying to conceal her identity: Smith was blessedly anonymous – but that 'Madeleine'! So, for the first time, she adopted the diminutive 'Lena'. Later writers assert that this 'hated pet name' was originally bestowed by Bessie. This is not the case. Bessie said that in the family Madeleine was known as Maddie or Maggie.[6] The trial had been so sensational that the name Madeleine Smith was known throughout Britain, and indeed beyond. Even those who believed her to have been innocent of murder knew about the letters, knew intimate details about her physical life, knew that she had broken the ultimate taboos of Victorian morality and – worse – had done so with relish. Despite her show of insouciance at the trial, she may well have wanted to hide. The family, too, although not withdrawing financial support, were clearly keen for her to 'disappear'.

L'Angelier had wanted Madeleine to take painting lessons, and she had pestered Papa to pay for them. It seems, though, that she never had actually begun these lessons. Now, during her stay in Devonport, did she revive these artistic ambitions? The days may have been long and dull in the worthy Rev. Mason's household, and any distraction welcome. Nearby, a young drawing master was staying in lodgings at number 5 George Street. He, too, was a long way from home, having been born in Leek in Staffordshire. His name was George Wardle; he was a year younger than Madeleine and his family were involved in the production of silk fabric. Maybe he was learning draughtsmanship in the naval town: but drawing masters give lessons, and we can surmise that Madeleine became a pupil. Vivacious and captivating, she soon became more. However they met, by the time of the census in April 1861 the couple were planning to marry.

The marriage, which took place in London that July, is the first occasion that Madeleine really steps out of the shadows that obscure her after the trial. Suddenly, here she is – in certificated fact, not rumour or fantasy. She married George Young Wardle at St Paul's church, Knightsbridge on 4th July 1861. Her father and Jack were witnesses. Earlier the same day, a marriage settlement had been drawn up, which tells us that Wardle had previously lived in Devonport, and then at Bloomsbury Place. But on the marriage certificate his address is given as 5 Bloomfield Terrace, Pimlico. Madeleine allegedly lived not far away, at 72 Sloane Street, Chelsea. The householder at 72 Sloane Street, Mrs Grace Maxon, did keep lodgers, and the Wardles did live there for a time after the wedding. Madeleine can have been there only briefly before it, perhaps just long enough to estab-lish residence.

George Wardle's sister Elizabeth had married a cousin, Thomas Wardle – later Sir Thomas – whose firm was to work closely with that of William Morris.[7] The Wardle family were of similar social standing to the Smiths, and George was the sort of young man whom Madeleine might have married had there been no L'Angelier, no scandal. She came with £3,000 – no very great dowry – and still with dreadful notoriety. The Wardles can hardly have been pleased, yet they accepted Madeleine, and George remained in close touch with Sir Thomas and his children all his life.

Wardle must have been in love with Madeleine, who was still vivacious, glamorous and, appealingly to one on the fringe of the pre-Raphaelite set, had a romantic past. A daughter, Mary, was born at Sloane Street in 1862, and then the family set off on a tour of Norfolk and Suffolk. George was making drawings of churches there for William Morris. It seems that he had done work on commission for Morris's firm for a while. Lots of tales have been spun around this. Several authors have Madeleine with Janey Morris and her sister Elizabeth Burden, embroidering for Morris's fledg-ling firm in its early days at Red Lion Square.[8] Some date this to a period *before* her marriage and as the means of her meeting Wardle.[9] Sadly, none of them ever cites evidence.

The couple were in Southwold in Suffolk in December 1863 when their son, Thomas Edmund, was born. Shortly afterwards, the church drawings complete, they moved back to London and George began to work for Morris on a more regular basis.[10] After having two children quite quickly, the Wardles – still in their twenties – had no more. The 1860s are acknowledged to mark the beginning of the 'great fertility decline', when middle-class couples began consciously to limit their families. Was this the case with Madeleine and George? Or did something go wrong, either physically with Madeleine at the time of Tom's birth, or even at this early date with the marriage itself?

In 1865 Morris and Co. moved to Queen's Square, Bloomsbury. This was convenient for the Wardles, living in the flat at 4 Bloomsbury Place. In 1870 George became manager of the firm. In 1871 he was away from home visiting the Leek Wardles, but Madeleine and the two children were at home in Bloomsbury Place. Madeleine was still Lena, but did now admit to having been born in Scotland. By 1877 the couple had moved to a house, 9 Charlotte Street, still in Bloomsbury. They moved in artistic and literary circles, where Madeleine's past was not hidden. Most of their acquaintance forbore to mention it, although Rossetti once, in a peevish mood towards Morris, sketched a scurrilous playlet in which the latter is poisoned by taking coffee from the hand of 'Mrs Wardle'.[11] There are also stories of those not aware of her history dining with Madeleine and committing various faux pas by referring to the celebrated case.[12] But in the main, life seems to have been fulfilling and interesting. Madeleine was apparently a chic hostess whose dinner invitations were sought after. As well as Morris and Rossetti, the Wardles knew Burne-Jones, Bernard Shaw and several other luminaries of metropolitan cultural life. In 1879 George, together with Morris and the architect Philip Webb, founded the Society for the Protection of Ancient Buildings (SPAB). Madeleine took some part in the celebrated Leek Embroidery Society set up by her sister-in-law, Lady Elizabeth, in 1879. Both Madeleine and George painted watercolours.[13]

What drew this artistic and fashionable set to the little house in Charlotte Street? They were not the sort to be deterred by Madeleine's notoriety – if anything, that was likely to be part of the attraction. Despite Rossetti's rather spiteful reference, there are suggestions that he and Morris had been her supporters at the time of the trial, long before they had met her. A contemporary of theirs at Oxford reported that 'the artistic set' argued that 'a beautiful young woman, who was on her trial on a charge of murdering her lover, ought not to be hanged, even if found guilty, as she was "such a stunner"'.[14] 'Oh Hill', they cried, 'you would never hang a stunner!' This is generally agreed to have referred to Madeleine Smith.[15] But romantic posturing will only go so far: Morris and his circle must have enjoyed the company of the Wardles. Madeleine was a frequent visitor when Morris moved his home and works to Merton Abbey in 1881. Morris records her calling in November 1882 and entertaining the Morrises with gossip about goings-on at the Globe Theatre the night before.[16]

Morris placed great trust in George Wardle, his works manager. When George left for a business trip to the USA on the firm's behalf in 1880 Morris wrote in his letters of introduction that 'I believe you will find Mr Wardle sympathetic in matters social, political and literary, as well as matters artistic."[17] By this time he had known his manager for nearly twenty years and was confident in his social as well as professional suitability. It had been for Madeleine twenty years of personal and social fulfilment.

All this was in stark contrast to the lives of her parents and siblings, left behind in Scotland. It is always alleged that the Smiths, in their humiliation, sold up *Rowaleyn* immediately and fled to Polmont, three-quarters of the way to Edinburgh. And that Mr Smith equally immediately gave up his architect's business in Glasgow. Neither is quite true. *Rowaleyn* was sold, but not until 1860, three years after the trial.[18] Even then, the 'cottage' Woodcliff that Papa had bought for Mama was retained in the family's ownership. Mr Smith also continued to work as an architect: one of his commissions at this period was Overtoun House in Dumbarton, and he also worked on plans for The Western Club in Glasgow.[19] Nevertheless, it is clear that there were some adverse consequences, socially if not professionally, from the scandal.

By April 1861 the family was living at Westquarter House, Polmont. In 1861 and 1862 Mr Smith's business address continued to be the office in St Vincent Street. However, his health was failing, and it was this rather than shame that caused him finally to give up his practice. James Smith died on 30th December 1863. The cause of death was given as jaundice – his kidneys seem to have failed. His will has sometimes been cited as evidence of a break with his eldest daughter: but in fact he was merely being fair when he left £3,000 each to Bessie and to Janet but 'purposely excluded my eldest daughter Madeline [sic] Hamilton Smith or Wardle' because 'by her contract of marriage I have settled a provision upon her which with other outlays formerly made by me on her behalf will be fully equal to the amount of the provisions hereby made by me upon my other daughters'.[20] It was customary for unmarried daughters to be left more than their sisters who had already received marriage portions; besides, the enormous costs of the trial (Blyth estimates them at £4,000) meant that Madeleine had already had more than her fair share.

Madeleine, having recently given birth to baby Thomas in far-off Suffolk, is unlikely to have attended the funeral. She seems not to have resented the terms of Papa's will, though, and maintained at least some contact with the family. Eventually, too, she did come to inherit from the Smith estate, and continued to receive funds from it until her death.

Jack and James continued to work in Glasgow. Jack was a wine merchant, with premises in West Regent Street, where Madeleine had been born. For some time after Papa's death, the family lived at Cross Arthurlie House in Barrhead, to the west of Glasgow and back in Renfrewshire, where James and Janet had been born.[21] But the family remained peripatetic, as they had always been. By 1880 they had moved house to Bridge of Allan, which they had always favoured as a holiday spot. They lived in Melbourne Villa, a fine suburban house in Charlton Road which was nevertheless not nearly as splendid as Polmont or *Rowaleyn*. None of Madeleine's siblings ever married, although Bessie and Janet lived into old age, James and Jack to middle age. Contrary to what has often been written, none of the family died 'soon after' Papa. (Morland, for example, says that 'Mrs Smith died shortly afterwards, to be followed by Bessie.'[22] MacGowan has Jack moving to London with Madeleine and remaining there after her marriage.[23])

In 1881 Mama, the 'girls' and Jack were together in Melbourne House. They had Mama's annuity of £300 p.a. and the interest on Bessie and Janet's inheritances of £3,000 apiece, as well as Jack's legacy and earnings. They kept two servants and were comfortably off. Yet, compared with Madeleine's exciting life in London, it sounds a dreary existence. Poor flirtatious Bessie: how much more vexed she would have been not to have made a conquest in 1856, had she known it was to be her last chance! While we cannot prove that it was their sister's downfall that prevented Bessie and Janet from marrying, it seems more than likely. For Jack and James it may have been different – after all, William Minnoch was married within a year of the trial and remained a pillar of Glasgow business life.

Mama, the supposed invalid, lived on. James, the family rascal and comic, died of cancer in 1887. By 1891 the rest of the family had moved to Belmont House, 'a good sized mansion with porter's lodge, just at the boundary of Falkirk.'[24] In fact there were a dozen or so rooms in the house – it was large enough to become a hotel at a much later date. Mama was now 76, her children all in their forties. They are reputed to have lived reclusively, although Jack continued his wine merchant's business.

Meanwhile, in London, Madeleine's world – still that of the literary and artistic intelligentsia – widened to encompass the political too. William Morris, of course, was a socialist and, from his recommendation of George Wardle as politically sympathetic, it seems that Wardle's views were at least not incompatible with his. There is no sign, though, that Wardle was ever particularly active in the socialist cause. Indeed, Morris's daughter May described him as 'a man who stood aloof from politics and watched all enthusiasms with equanimity.'[25] His life throughout the 1870s and 1880s revolved around his work with Morris, the activities of the SPAB, and business trips to America. In 1887 he visited Venice on behalf of the SPAB to investigate the nature of the restoration work on St Mark's. Madeleine enjoyed socialising with many of the leading artists of the day, visiting their houses, going to the theatre and bringing up Mary and Tom. The couple were financially comfortable – Morris estimated a little later that George earned £1,200 a year as works manager. In 1881, still at Charlotte Street, they had only one resident servant, although there was probably other help at times. Madeleine was still quite cagey about her past: the census return gives her birthplace as simply 'Scotland'.

The children were more or less grown up. Mary seems to have been independent, possibly headstrong; Tom was turning into a firebrand. Although Morris's influence cannot be discounted, it was apparently her son rather than her husband who led Madeleine to take up the socialist cause. Now Lena Wardle began to appear in the records of the Socialist League. In 1885 a 'Lenia Wardle' was elected Provisional Council member.[26] Thomas Edmund Wardle – her son Tom – was an office bearer in the Bloomsbury branch of the League, and letters and reports written by him to its Council from 1885 to 1888 survive.

In May 1886 Tom was arrested for causing a disturbance at Stratford in the East End by addressing a street meeting. Morris paid £5 17s bail for him.[27] Perhaps his father had refused. That same year, Thomas and Lena (but not George or Mary) were both members of a 'Hall Committee' of the Socialist League. In January 1887 Lena was one of fifteen members of Morris's Council of the Socialist League – and the only woman, which she would have loved.[28] Tom addressed a large open-air meeting in Hyde Park in April that year. He and Lena were moving in exciting and exalted political circles: Eleanor Marx and her husband Edward Aveling were part of the same splinter group within the League and Aveling had been a fellow council member with them in 1887. George Bernard Shaw was a dinner guest at Charlotte Street later in 1887.[29] In fact, his diary records him popping in several times that year, once to pick up a copy of the League manifesto. At a dinner party just before Christmas at 'the Wardles' he 'discussed theatricals with them'.[30]

That Christmas marked a high-water mark in Madeleine's London life. She had a respected role in socialist circles: she was librarian of the League's library, and involved in many of its activities.[31] That October she had been ticket seller for Morris's play *Nupkins Awakened*. In 1888 things began to change. Madeleine was as busy as ever in the socialist cause. Shaw recorded seeing her at 'Cursitor Street', where she advised him about getting a stand-in speaker when he had to cancel an appointment.[32] This was the address from which two socialist journals, *Freedom* and *The Leaflet*, were published, representing the two factions into which the Socialist League had split. The League advocated revolutionary socialism, but members differed over the best means to achieve it. One group favoured a parliamentary route, while the other were professed anarchists. *Freedom*, a 'journal of anarchist socialism' was published from 19 Cursitor Street, where 'a member of the Freedom Group will always be at the office' during the office hours of eight to five every Monday.[33] Morris himself took issue with the Parliamentarians, but was dismayed to find the Anarchists taking over and withdrew from the Socialist League altogether in 1889. It seems that Madeleine's involvement with the League ceased at about the same time. Morris went on to found the Hammersmith Socialist Society in 1890: a photograph of the assembled members exists but it is impossible to tell whether Madeleine was one of their number.

Madeleine always loved being active and busy. She had energy and optimism and threw herself wholeheartedly into her latest enthusiasm. Bernard Shaw, who knew her well enough to see beyond the notoriety, said that she was 'an ordinary, good-humoured, capable woman with nothing sinister about her'.[34] Later reminiscences of her at this time said that 'She was gay, lively and beautiful … and an enthusiastic advocate of the Socialist gospels which the SDC [Social Democratic Club] sought to encourage. No attempt was made to conceal her identity. It was an open secret, well known to the members'.[35] This agrees with another memory of Madeleine at this time as 'a brilliant conversationalist and excellent company', whose past was known to at least some club members.[36]

Outwardly at least, her life was rewarding and successful. She had developed something of a reputation as a chic hostess, although the only proof offered is that she was allegedly responsible for the fashion of using place-mats instead of a cloth at her dining table. Butler paints a picture of the Wardles at this time, George 'wearing a long dark Spanish cloak and a broad hat, with his slightly stooping walk and thin, grey beard', and Lena with her naturally straight, dark hair frizzed to follow fashion.[37] They were a smart and popular couple and certainly in their circles Madeleine's past, with its flouting of conventional morality, to say nothing of possible murder, was no bar to social acceptance.

But change was under way. The householder at Charlotte Street in 1887 was recorded not as George or even as Lena, but as Miss Wardle – their daughter Mary. It appears to be the case that George only retired from the Morris firm in 1890, and we are told that he and Madeleine separated some time shortly after this date. So where was George from the late 1880s? 'Miss Wardle' was the householder in Charlotte Street from 1887 to 1889: in the autumn of that year she married John Scarratt Rigby and they lived together in what had been for so long the family home. Mary's choice of husband reflects the closeness that still existed between George (and no doubt Madeleine) and the Wardles of Leek. John Rigby came from Leek but was working in London as a 'designer for manufacturers and decorators', which sounds very much like Morris and Co.[38] It may not have been a very exalted or lucrative position, for in 1891 the couple had (as well as baby Stephen) three boarders and one servant.

Tom had married in 1888, which seems to have marked the end of his socialist activities. Like his mother (and indeed half the family acquaintance, such as Morris and Shaw), Tom mixed politics with the arts, and now the latter took over as the chief influence in his life. He had been working as a 'dramatic agent' and his bride was a young singer, 20-year-old Annita Bied-Charreton. The couple both gave their professional names too: Tom was rather unimaginatively calling himself Thomas Edmunds, while Annita was Anna di Fiori. Her father Alfonso was Italian, as was one of the two witnesses, Pasquale Novissimo, a well-known jeweller, originally from Naples. The other witness was Lena Wardle.[39]

Not long after, Tom set off for America, leaving Annita on her own in a flat in Bloomsbury awaiting the call to join him.[40] George Wardle had allegedly gone to live in Italy, whose architecture and archaeology had long beckoned him. But where was Lena? She was with neither her daughter nor her son. Tradition has it that she sought financial refuge with Sir Thomas and Lady Elizabeth in Leek. If that is so, it shows that she had forged remarkably close ties with her in-laws and that they did not count her solely responsible for the marriage breakdown. It is never possible to say why a marriage fails; in this case, neither partner sought a divorce or a remarriage. Maybe the marriages of the two children marked a point at which two people who had been held together by little more than shared parental responsibility felt they could go their own ways. Maybe Madeleine's enthusiastic espousal of her son's political cause drove a wedge between them, for George was never a socialist activist. Morris was probably right: George did not embrace enthusiasms and complained that he had to discourage William Morris from talking politics all day.[41] If George was as phlegmatic as Madeleine was mercurial, there may well have come a time when opposites ceased to attract.

It seems that Madeleine was not in Britain at the time of the 1891 Census, taken in April. Perhaps she had initially accompanied George to Italy and it was there that the fissures in their relationship had widened and destroyed it. Or perhaps she was simply on holiday. Although she was not with them at the time of the 1891 Census, it may well have been that Madeleine spent some time with or near her Leek in-laws: certainly a tradition that she did so survives in the Wardle family.[42] She allegedly cut a dramatic figure in the quiet market town, having already taken to dyeing her hair with henna.

Madeleine never lacked courage or resolution. In 1893, at the age of 58, she determined to make another fresh start. She boarded the SS *Arizona* in Liverpool, and on the 11th of September arrived in New York. Taking full advantage of the opportunities offered by such a departure, she declined to give her marital status and stated her age to be 36.

Did she see any of her family one last time before leaving? Mama, Bessie, Jack and Janet were all still alive and living in Falkirk. Perhaps Madeleine took the journey north one final time. Local rumour persisted with all sorts of stories. An early twentieth-century investigator received a report that 'the family at one time consisted of Mr John and Miss Smith, and another lady who although going by another name was supposed to be the Madeleine Smith. I am told that she is dead; at any rate she is not here now.'[43] The 'other lady' is much more likely to have been Bessie: we must hope that she never knew the ignominy of such a misconception, if it was widespread.

Janet continued at least some correspondence with Madeleine, even after she went to New York. Mrs Smith died soon afterwards, in 1894, and Jack followed in 1899. Contemporary reports (for by this time there were those engaged in researching the Madeleine Smith story), although garbled as to the size of the family, were agreed on one thing – they lived quietly and almost reclusively.[44] 'They might as well be in the centre of Africa; they visit nobody and nobody visits them.'[45]

So Janet and Bessie remained together in the 'good-sized mansion'. Observers felt that they hid themselves out of shame: 'They seem to have means as they stay in a big house and I wonder they did not go abroad long ago.'[46] Yet the 1901 Census shows that they were not always so reclusive. As well as three servants (a cook and two general maids) there were two visitors, a brother and sister in their twenties from Glasgow. The sisters were still only in middle age – Janet admitted to 48, though she was in fact 56 – and they were involved with the local church, and probably other activities too. There were still lots of extended-family members in Edinburgh and in Glasgow and it would be surprising if all contact had been lost.

Nevertheless, a quiet life on the outskirts of Falkirk was a far cry from the bustle and excitement of New York. Madeleine stayed in the city at which she had landed. She told the immigration officials at Ellis Island that she was only on a visit. Perhaps she did intend merely to visit Tom and Annita, but it seems more likely that permanent emigration was always in her mind. Although she may have lived with her son and his family for a while, that does not seem to have been a long-term arrangement. Madeleine had enough money to live on: some came from George, and some from her share of the Smith family estate.

By 1901 George Wardle was back in England. Now 65, he was living in a boarding house on the outskirts of Canterbury.[47] He had no occupation, but was probably still engaged in studying church architecture. Mary had separated from John Rigby, and their son Stephen was at a boarding at school in Sussex.[48]

With so little evidence, any comments on Madeleine's relationship with her daughter must be speculative. Morland says that Mary was known as 'Kitten', and that she was a proto-feminist. She definitely had decided views: her will stipulated that on her death (which occurred in 1935) a competent vet should destroy any animals belonging to her. She seems never to have accompanied her mother and brother to socialist gatherings, and it is tempting to see her relationship with Madeleine as lacking closeness. Madeleine was one of those women who relate much better to men than to other women. She had few intimate female friends at school or afterwards, and her defenders tended also to be male. At any rate, she set off for the USA without much apparent thought of seeing Mary again.

Many women might have taken the opportunity to lose a few years from their real age on setting off for a new life in the New World. But few would have dared to lose quite so many as Madeleine did en route. Could she really have passed herself off as so very much younger than she actually was? Her attitude to accuracy about age had always been cavalier. She had written to L'Angelier in December 1855: 'My right age is 20 next March. But if you would like your wife to be a year or so younger I shall say any age.' Even this was incorrect, for she would be 21 in March 1856. In the same way, she gave her age as 30, rather than the true 36, at the 1871 Census. But now she maintained a much bigger and more unlikely fiction, and in her new life in New York even increased the number of years shed. This was in part fuelled by her new relationship with a man over twenty years her junior. He was William Sheehy, a 'concrete contractor' born in New York but of Irish extraction. By 1910 Lena was passing herself off as 45, a staggering thirty years younger than she in fact was. Quite how she explained her son Tom, now 47, is a mystery. She and Sheehy had been together, they said, since 1898, and were living as married, although George Wardle was still alive in England. Their home was at 2099 Eighth Avenue.

Had William Sheehy any idea of his wife's sensational past? Can he really have believed that a woman of 75, however well preserved, was in her mid 40s? The Sheehys were in contact with Tom Wardle and his family; unless there was a pretence that Tom was her brother rather than her son,

Madeleine must have told Sheehy something near the truth. Perhaps he simply didn't care. As to her 'secret past', Madeleine kept her family at least partly in the dark. Since her identity was so well known among their acquaintance in London, Tom at least must have had some knowledge of the circumstances. But later it was not talked of in the family, and future generations knew little beyond there having been some scandal in Grandmother's past. William Sheehy may very well never have known that his wife had been the most scandalous woman in mid-nineteenth-century Britain.

George Wardle died in 1910. He was being cared for in a Plymouth nursing home, though his usual home was in Fowey, Cornwall. His will was scrupulous about honouring the provisions for 'my wife Madeleine Wardle' set out in the marriage settlement drawn up nearly fifty years before. He also made sure that Janet and Bessie (if still alive) would get her share if she had predeceased him. To a certain extent, the terms of the will were dictated by earlier agreements. Nevertheless, there is no whiff of rancour about it, no suggestion that their parting had been especially acrimonious.

Madeleine and William Sheehy were now free to marry. But there is no sign that they ever did. The Smith family solicitors in Glasgow were sending Madeleine her share of Jack and James's estates. After George's death, her interests were safeguarded by Sir Thomas Wardle as the last surviving signatory of the marriage settlement. Perhaps this is where the tradition of Madeleine's throwing herself on the financial mercy of her brother-in-law originated, although it seems that he acted merely in an administrative capacity. The legal papers and the solicitors' accounts continued to refer to 'Mrs Madeleine Smith or Wardle, widow'.[49] After Bessie died in March 1910, only Madeleine and Janet, the oldest and the youngest of the Smith children, remained.

They can only have kept in touch by letter. Always a prodigious letter writer, Madeleine would have loved this, for letters are wonderful for telling an edited tale. Sheehy could disappear if she chose not to mention him. She could for ever remain the vivacious and admired sister of their youth. For Janet, Madeleine was always a glamorous figure, increasingly shadowy with the years. Through Janet we know that Madeleine was still in touch with Tom: supplying her sister's Eighth Avenue address to their solicitors in 1914, Janet added that 'the same will always reach' Tom.

Janet made her will at around this time, making bequests to friends, servants and charities, and demonstrating that she was by no means isolated or friendless. The residue of her estate, though, went to her sister Madeleine and to Madeleine's two children. Although she had several more years to live, even Janet – the loyal, noisy girl who had danced until she fainted – was getting old and frail. She had a faithful housekeeper who looked after her as she and the furnishings of the family home grew faded and dusty together.

In contrast, as it always had been, Madeleine's life was more vibrant. She and William Sheehy were still living on Eighth Avenue in 1920, when Madeleine's age was recorded as 57 rather than the real 85. It must have been getting harder and harder to maintain this fiction: surely even Madeleine must by now have been showing some signs of decrepitude? For years – since before her emigration – she had dyed her hair with henna. Several comments about this have survived, though some commentators thought it was her own hair and others that the startling edifice was a wig. But bright hair and a vivacious manner on their own could not have been enough to convince others that someone who was in fact a very old woman was merely middle aged.

She certainly remained mentally alert, and dealt with her own correspondence. In 1922 the last link with her old life was lost when Janet died at Belmont, aged 78. Janet's will suggests that she was no more reclusive or isolated than any other elderly middle-class spinster of her day. She left money to friends, to servants and ex-servants, to the daughters of her doctor and to charities and her church. But the remainder of her estate was left 'to my sister Mrs Madeleine Smith or Wardle, widow, presently residing in the USA'. Janet seems never to have heard of William Sheehy. Neither had the family solicitors, who got in touch with Mrs Wardle at the address supplied by Janet in a letter written just two months before her death and handed to the solicitor when he went to Belmont two days after it. Janet had also left a silver bowl to the two lawyers, Mr Donald and Mr Reid. Now they wrote to Madeleine to inform her of this, and she replied on 17th June 1922 'expressing the wish that the bequest should be accepted'.

Janet had been only a 'protected tenant' of Belmont, so it seems that the family had never owned it as they did *Rowaleyn*. The household furniture was generally 'in a poor state of repair'. The Smith fortunes had declined sadly over the years. Janet and Bessie's shares of their father's money had been invested in property – some tenements and shops in Blackburn Street, Glasgow. Even so, the sum total of Janet's estate before any deductions was a modest £6,033. Madeleine, still living at 2099 Eighth Avenue, was sent an interim payment of £75 as the life rentrix (the capital was to go to Mary Rigby and Tom Wardle after their mother's death). Thereafter she received annual payments of between £284 and £424, enough to make life more pleasant, perhaps, but not on which to live lavishly.

There were also hints a little later that the Sheehys' life together was less than happy – that William drank and that he spent all her money. In fact, Lena did not have a great deal of money and he, a building contractor, had probably provided for her for years. He may, though, have over-indulged in drink. William A. Sheehy of Eighth Avenue died of carcinoma of the oesophagus on 28th July 1926, aged 64, and was buried in St Raymond's cemetery.[50] Cancer of the oesophagus is prevalent among alcoholics. Ironically, Madeleine's brother James had died of the same cause. Sheehy's real age may well have been 64, for Madeleine seems to have tailored hers to remain just younger than her husband – consistency with her 1920 Census age would have made her 63 by now. If so, his wife was over twenty-five years his senior, and he was exactly of an age with her daughter. He can hardly have expected Lena to outlive him.

The weeks leading up to his death must have been a bad time for Madeleine. Not only was her husband ailing, but the one thing she had dreaded for decades finally happened. The American press broke the story that the notorious Madeleine Smith was still alive and had settled in the USA. Fortunately, there were garbled accounts of her whereabouts. She was settled in Nebraska. She was living in New Orleans. Journalists wrote as if they had spoken to Madeleine, who 'declines to discuss the tragic events of her career', but it seems unlikely that they had. They had no details; but the basic fact that Madeleine was not long dead, as had been assumed, had come from somewhere.

Madeleine moved a little further out of the centre of New York, to Park Avenue in the Bronx. It was not a wealthy area but it teemed with cosmopolitan life, such as she and Tom had always loved. Her grandchildren continued to visit. Although she cannot have been particularly well off, there is little sign of that isolation or penury which the newspapers and some subsequent writers have alleged were her lot. Madeleine Hamilton Smith Wardle died on 12th April 1928. Her granddaughter Violet arranged for her to be buried at Mount Hope Cemetery.

Once again, the newspapers carried stories that mixed fact and fantasy. Madeleine was said to have remarked that she would do the same thing again; she had long paid for masses to be said for [Protestant] Emile; she was exposed by 'film people' angered by her refusal to play herself in a movie and threatened with deportation. The idea of 91-year-old Madeleine acting convincingly as her 21-year-old self is an indication of how wild the stories got. In reality, Madeleine never broke her silence about L'Angelier. With her ability to put unpleasantness behind her, she had probably not given him a thought in decades.

Why did newspapers insist that Madeleine died lonely and broke?

Or that her marriage to Sheehy was 'disastrous'? Faced with the facts of her life after the trial, which was, unarguably, long and full of interest, was there a need to see Madeleine as at last getting her come-uppance? Madeleine Smith had been immoral and possibly a murderer – yet she had enjoyed a life of reasonable prosperity among a literary and artistic elite in London, and a further thirty-five years in the vitality of early-twentieth-century New York, with a much younger husband and with grandchildren and great-grandchildren nearby. Consciously or not, she had sought out exactly those circles where her notorious past could be accepted. She mixed with artists, radicals, writers. They knew who she was. This must have been a decision taken by George and Lena, for it would have been possible to conceal any links between Lena Wardle and Madeleine Smith. It was a brave decision; but they must have known their circle well, for the press was still publishing nonsense about her whereabouts, and clearly, no one who knew the truth had talked.

Henry James, although getting the details of Madeleine's subsequent career wildly wrong, did in his ironic comments on the case hit the nail on the head: 'She precisely *didn't* squalidly suffer, but lived on to admire with the rest of us, for so many years, the rare work of art with which she had been the means of enriching humanity.'[51]

The story of Madeleine Smith is at least in part a murder mystery. The 'whodunnit' aspect, while only one element of a wider and richer story, is one that continues to fascinate those who learn about the case. Although not the sole focus of this book, it is an aspect that cannot altogether be ignored. But we have no easy resolution, no clear-cut explanation to offer. Emile L'Angelier died by swallowing arsenic: that much is certain. He must have either done so accidentally or by his own hand, or been given it by another. If the latter, it is hard to imagine anyone else but Madeleine being responsible. Unfortunately, there are problems with all these scenarios.

L'Angelier experienced three episodes of gastric illness, and there is dispute as to whether he had met Madeleine immediately before any of them. The day before his death L'Angelier came back from Bridge of Allan to see Madeleine. He went out that night and was gone for some hours. He returned dying from arsenic poisoning. The crucial missing link in the chain of evidence that might otherwise have convicted her was the absence of any proof that he had seen her that night. However much it was argued that he had returned from Bridge of Allan specifically to see her and that thus it was unlikely he had failed to do so, no meeting between the pair could be proved.

There was a widespread view at the time of the trial that Madeleine was probably guilty. For the *Scotsman*, 'It was a miracle that the circle of proof was not completed.'[52] The *Glasgow Sentinel* agreed: Madeleine had 'escaped' through 'the absence of one little link in a chain of evidence which report says could now be supplied, otherwise the most conclusive of its kind ever offered in a court of law.'[53] Rumours continued to circulate that evidence of the couple's meeting on the fatal night had been suppressed out of either chivalry, class deference or a view that L'Angelier had in any case deserved to die.[54]

Yet there are objections to this view, and Madeleine has retained her partisans.[55] At first sight her motive would appear plain: she was, in effect, being blackmailed by L'Angelier, who threatened to show her incriminating letters to her father. But her defenders point out that l'Angelier's death was almost bound to result in the letters being revealed. Similarly, it was shown that Madeleine had bought arsenic; but she was so open about it, even taking Mary Jane Buchanan with her to the chemist's, that this too seems incompatible with guilt.

Nevertheless, it is conceivable that Madeleine might have poisoned her lover, simply not thinking of the consequences with regard to the letters. Certainly she was not a logical thinker, and her desperate letter of 9th February 1857 – 'Oh for God's sake for the love of heaven hear me' – speaks of panic. It is less easy to explain her nonchalance over buying arsenic. However, Madeleine shows herself in her letters as often narrowly self-centred and lacking in any imaginative empathy. So maybe she was the kind of person to buy arsenic quite openly, not seeing how it would appear; or perhaps, in a rather patrician way, she imagined that shopkeepers would not be consulted or credited. It is difficult, nevertheless, to see Madeleine's actions as those of a calculating killer.

Her defenders have, of necessity, fallen back on L'Angelier and argued that he committed suicide. Some add the twist that he intended Madeleine to be accused of killing him. Friends of L'Angelier's reported that he was 'excitable' and had threatened suicide in the past – although perhaps not with very serious intent. One problem is that, although Madeleine could be shown to have bought arsenic, Emile could not. This is a difficulty for those who see him as a suicide and for those who argue that he was simply a regular arsenic user who miscalculated his dose.[56] Furthermore, if he was intent on incriminating Madeleine, why did he not do so during the hours when he lay dying and had several conversations with his landlady and the doctor?

The evidence of Mary Perry and of Emile's own pocket book suggested that he may have suspected Madeleine was trying to poison him. But in that case, why would he have taken a fatal drink from her on the night that he died? If he did suspect that his lover had poisoned him and yet kept silent, he would have shown a previously well-hidden selfless devotion. In short, his behaviour, too, is hard to explain and riddled with inconsistencies.

It is not our intention to rehearse yet again the minutiae of the evidence: that has been done repeatedly, and yet never conclusively. It is difficult to envisage a scenario that encompasses all the facts and makes some kind of cohesive sense. Yet people do not always behave with logical consistency. L'Angelier may have killed himself, whether intending to incriminate Madeleine or not. Madeleine may have poisoned him: neither her youth, sex nor class made it impossible, and in her letters she shows on occasion a ruthless detachment with regard both to pets and to people. She was in a desperate situation and it is hard to see how she might have been able to extricate herself. But L'Angelier too must have seen that his affair with Madeleine was over, and that they would never be married. He was not a man to take such reversals calmly.

The jury in the case can only be commended, for they did not allow themselves to be swayed by its shocking aspects or by what they must have seen as Madeleine's terrible moral lapses. The judgement of hindsight can only confirm what was found at the time: that there was a case to answer against Madeleine Smith, but that it could not be proved. It still cannot.

Notes

1 Letter to William Roughead, 16th June 1914, quoted in Richard Altick, *Victorian Studies in Scarlet* (Dent, 1972), p. 189.

2 *Paisley Herald and Renfrewshire Advertiser*, 18th July 1857.

3 Ibid.

4 Quoted in the *Paisley Herald and Renfrewshire Advertiser*, 18th July 1857.

5 A. Clifton Kelway, *An Early Chapter in the History of the Catholic Revival* (Longmans, Green and Co., 1905).

6 NAS AD 14/57/255/3, Precognition of Bessie Smith.

7 Anne Jacques, *The Wardle Story*, Churnet Valley Books, 1996.

8 For instance P. Henderson, *William Morris His Life, Work and Friends* (Thames & Hudson, 1967). Sometimes Georgiana Burne Jones is added to the group.

9 Violet Hunt, *The Wife of Rossetti: Her life and death* (Bodley Head, 1932), says that Madeleine was already one of two embroiderers working for Morris in 1860. She adds that Madeleine, having been abandoned by her family, was 'living in a London boarding house very miserably'. This is echoed by Judith Flanders, *A Circle of Sisters* (Penguin 2002), who alleges that Madeleine Smith 'moved to London under an assumed name, and eventually got work with The Firm as an embroiderer' (p. 84fn).

10 The drawings are in the Victoria and Albert Museum.

11 Fiona McCarthy, *William Morris: A lifLe for Our Time* (Faber & Faber, 1994) reproduces it. It was titled 'A Drama of the Future in one Unjustifiable Act', and was written in the early 1870s.

12 Altick quotes one about the journalist George R. Sims allegedly expressing concern for the husband, whoever he might be, of the notorious poisoner – whose dinner table he was at that moment sharing. Altick, *Victorian Studies in Scarlet*, pp. 185–6.

13 Paintings by George seem still to be in existence. We are grateful to Mr Bill Greenwell for this and other details about Madeleine's later life.

14 G.B. Hill, *Letters of Dante Gabriel Rossetti to William Allingham 1854–1870* (T. Fisher Unwin, 1897), p. 144.

15 Jan Marsh, *The Pre-Raphaelite Sisterhood* (Quartet Books, 1985), p. 119.

16 Norman Kelvin, *Collected Letters of William Morris*, vol. IIA (Princeton University Press, 1987), p. 137.

17 Ibid., p. 563.

18 Dunbartonshire Register of Sasines, no. 1700 (May 1860) and no. 1886 (September 1860).

19 He was still owed money on both of these commissions at the time of his death. NAS SC 67/36/48, Will of James Smith, 13 August 1864.

20 Ibid.

21 They were all there at the census in 1871.

22 Nigel Morland, *That Nice Miss Smith* (Frederick Muller Ltd, 1957), p. 183.

23 Douglas MacGowan, *Murder in Victorian Scotland: The Trial of Madeleine Smith* (Praeger, 1999), p. 153.

24 Mitchell Library, Madeleine Smith collection no. 19, report on inquiries at Falkirk.

25 Florence Boos (ed.), 'William Morris's Socialist Diary', *History Workshop*, Spring 1982, p. 73.

26 Archives of Socialist League, International Institute of Socialist History, www.iisg.nl/archives/en/files/s/10769755full.php.

27 Nick Salmon, *The William Morris Chronology* (Thoemmes Press, 1996).

28 Boos (ed.), 'William Morris's Socialist Diary', p. 21.

29 S. Weintraub (ed.), *Bernard Shaw: The Diaries 1885–1897* (Pennsylvania State University Press, 1986), p. 262.

30 Ibid., p. 325

31 Kelvin, *William Morris Letters*, vol. IIA, p. 704n. The editor assumes that 'Lena' was Thomas Edmund's wife, but this was clearly Madeleine.

32 Weintraub, *Bernard Shaw: Diaries*, p. 419.

33 *Freedom: A Journal of Anarchist Socialism*, 2, 19, April 1888.

34 Quoted in Jack House, *Square Mile of Murder* (Richard Drew Publishing, 1984), p. 80.

35 Remarks attributed to 'Odell' in *T.P.'s Weekly*, 1928, cutting in Mitchell Library.

36 Mr W. Blair, letter to newspaper, 2nd May 1928, cutting in Mitchell Library.

37 Geoffrey L. Butler, *Madeleine Smith* (Duckworth, 1935).

38 1891 Census.

39 We are very grateful to Mr Bill Greenwell, who generously shared with us much information about this period of Madeleine's life.

40 She was there in April 1891 but left for the USA soon afterwards.

41 Boos (ed.), 'William Morris's Socialist Diary', p. 73.

42 Jacques, *The Wardle Story* and personal communication.

43 Mitchell Library collection no. 4, letter to Thomas Wilson from Robert Guy, Falkirk, 1906.

44 Mitchell Library collection no. 19, a report stating that an ex-servant remembered four daughters and two sons; and that Madeleine had married a clergyman and lived in London.

45 Mitchell Library, S.R.349 MSS VIII, letter from James Robertson, Burgh Chamberlain of Falkirk.

46 Mitchell Library, Madeleine Smith collection no. 4, letter to Thomas Wilson from Robert Guy, Falkirk, 1906.

47 1901 Census.

48 John later emigrated to South Africa, and died in 1952. Stephen lived in London until his death in 1967. We are grateful to Bill Greenwell for this information.

49 We are extremely grateful to Colin Aldebert, formerly keeper of the records at McGrigor Donald, Glasgow, for his help in identifying and supplying this material.

50 MacGowan, *Murder in Victorian Scotland*, and personal communication.

51 Henry James, letter to William Roughead, quoted in Altick, *Studies in Scarlet*, p. 189.

52 *The Scotsman*, 18th July 1857.

53 *Glasgow Sentinel*, 18th July 1857.

54 One such even surfaced in 1928, when 'A respected member of the Liberal Club said he and three others had been passing the Smith house and saw her speaking from a window with a young man. All four later agreed not to report this, in view of evidence about L'Angelier's general character.' Newspaper cutting, unidentified, 2nd May 1928, Mitchell Library.

55 Jimmy Campbell, *A Scottish Murder: Rewriting the Madeleine Smith Story* (Tempus Publishing, 2007).

56 As was argued at the trial, arsenic could be deliberately taken by women as a beauty aid; it has also been suggested that men saw it as an aphrodisiac. It has recently been suggested that arsenic was used at the Botanic Gardens, where L'Angelier had lodged until July 1856. He continued to visit his old landlady there until early in March 1857, the month that he died. Campbell, *A Scottish Murder*.

Bibliography

Primary sources

Mitchell Library, Glasgow
Glasgow Post Office Directory, 1840.
Glasgow Post Office Directory, 1856–57.
Madeleine Smith collection no. 4, letter to Thomas Wilson from Robert Guy, Falkirk, 1906.
Madeleine Smith collection no. 19, report on inquiries at Falkirk.
Newspaper cutting, unidentified, 2nd May 1928.
S.R.349 MSS VIII, letter from James Robertson, Burgh Chamberlain of Falkirk.
Scotland 1841, 1851, 1861, 1871, 18881, 1891, 1901 census returns.
T.P.'s Weekly, 1928, cutting.

Glasgow City Archives
GCA AGN 256, Birkenshaw land sales.
GCA T-BK 165/9, Testamentary papers of John Wilson, 1868.
GCA TD 559/4, Inventory of valuation of John Stewart, 10 Monteith Row, 1845.
GCA TD 66/5/9, House Plans.
GCA TD 862/70, Inventory of valuation of William Houldsworth.
GCA T-HB/493, Trust of Mrs Agnes Adam or Logan, Victoria Place, West Regent St., 1866.
GCA TD 1/1053, Smith of Jordanhill family papers.

Glasgow University Library Special Collections
Bh12-g.5, Full report, of the extraordinary and interesting trial of Miss Madeleine Smith ... on the charge of poisoning, by arsenic her late lover, Emile L'Angelier, including the whole correspondence.
Bh11-y.20, Papers illustrative of the trial of Madeleine Smith, for the alleged murder of P. Emile L'Angelier, before the High Court of Justiciary at Edinburgh, on the 30th day of June, 1857.
MU18-h7, The Story of Mini L'Angelier or Madeleine Hamilton Smith.
F13²-b.17, Report of the trial of Madeleine Smith before the High Court of Justiciary at Edinburgh, June 30th to July 9th, 1857, for the alleged poisoning of Pierre Emile L'Angelier.

National Archives of Scotland
NAS AD 14/57/255, Precognition of Robert Oliphant, Helensburgh.
NAS AD 14/57/255, Precognition of Mary Jane Buchanan.
NAS AD 14/57/255/3, Criminal precognitions of James Smith.
NAS AD 14/57/255/3, Precognitions against Madeleine Smith, evidence of Christina Haggart.
NAS AD 14/57/255/3, Precognition of Bessie Smith.

NAS AD 14/57/255/19, Precognition of Janet Hamilton Smith.
NAS AD 14/57/255/49, Precognition of Janet Hamilton Smith.
NAS AD 14/57/255/80, Precognition of Augusta Walcot nee Giubelei.
NAS JC 126/1031/1 Box 3.
NAS JC 126/1031/1/152, Madeleine Smith trial papers: Murdoch's poison register.
NAS JC 126/1031/1/156, L'Angelier's pass book with J. Chalmers, provision dealer.
NAS JC 126/1031/1/157, L'Angelier's pass book with John Stewart, butcher.
NAS SC 67/36/48, Will of James Smith, 13 August 1864.

McGrigor Donald Solicitors
Letter from John Inglis, 13th July 1857, McGrigor Donald, Solicitors, Glasgow.
Inventory of Janet Smith, 1922.

Contemporary publications

Daily Telegraph
The Dumbarton Herald
Edinburgh Evening Courant
Edinburgh Evening Post and Scottish Record
The Era
The Extra
Freedom: A Journal of Anarchist Socialism
Glasgow Chronicle
Glasgow Citizen
Glasgow Courier
Glasgow Daily Times
Glasgow Examiner
Glasgow Herald
Glasgow Punch
Glasgow Sentinel
Glasgow Time and Daily Advertiser
Hamilton Advertiser
Manchester Guardian
Morning Bulletin
Morning Post
Paisley Herald and Renfrewshire Advertiser
Saturday Review
The Scotsman
Scottish Daily News
Tartar
The Times
The Witness
The Story of Minie L'Angelier or Madeleine Hamilton Smith (Edinburgh, Myles Macphail; Glasgow, T. Murray and Sons; London, Simpkin, Marshall and Co., 1857).

Secondary sources

Books

Adburgham, Alison, *Shops and Shopping, 1800–1914* (London: Barrie and Jenkins, 1989).

Altick, Richard, *Victorian Studies in Scarlet* (Dent, 1972).

Bell, J.J., *I Remember* (Porpoise Press, 1934).

Black, J. Anderson and Garland, Madge, *A History of Fashion* (Orbis Publishing, 1975).

Blyth, Henry, *Madeleine Smith: A Famous Victorian Murder Trial* (Duckworth, 1975).

Branca, Patricia, *Silent Sisterhood: Middle Class Women in the Victorian Home* (Croom Helm, 1975).

Brewer, John, *Sentimental Murder* (Harper Collins, 2004).

Brown, Callum G., *The Death of Christian Britain* (Routledge, 2001).

Butler, Geoffrey L., *Madeleine Smith* (Duckworth, 1935).

Calder, Jenni, *The Victorian Home* (Batsford, 1977).

Cameron, Alistair, *See Glasgow See Theatre: A Guide to Glasgow Theatre Past and Present* (The Glasgow File, c. 1990).

Campbell, Jimmy, *A Scottish Murder: Rewriting the Madeleine Smith Story* (Tempus, 2007).

Craig, Mary, *French Letters: The True Story of Madeleine Smith* (Black and White Publishing, 2007).

Davidoff, Leonore, *The Best Circles: Society, Etiquette and The Season* (Croom Helm, 1973).

Davidoff, L. and Hall, C., *Family Fortunes: Men and Women of the English Middle Class, 1780–1850* (Routledge, 1987).

Davis, Dorothy, *A History of Shopping* (Routledge & Kegan Paul, 1966).

Davis, Natalie Zemon, *The Return of Martin Guerre* (Harvard University Press, 1983).

Duke, Winifred, *Madeleine Smith: A Tragi-Comedy in Two Acts* (William Hodge and Co., 1928).

Evans, Bill and Lawson, Andrew, *A Nation of Shopkeepers* (Plexus, 1981).

Gillis, John, *A World of their Own Making* (Oxford University Press, 1997).

Flanders, Judith, *A Circle of Sisters* (Penguin, 2002).

Flanders, Judith, *The Victorian House* (HarperCollins, 2003).

Flanders, Judith, *Consuming Passions: Leisure and Pleasure in Victorian Britain* (Harper Press, 2006).

Foreman, Carol, *Lost Glasgow* (Cromwell Publishing, 2002).

Gay, Peter, *The Bourgeois Experience: Victoria to Freud*, vol. 1: *Education of the Senses* (Cambridge University Press, 1984).

Gernsheim, Alison, *Victorian and Edwardian Fashion: A Photographic Survey* (Dover Publications, 1981).

Ginzburg, Carlo, *The Cheese and the Worms: The Cosmos of a Sixteenth-century Miller* (Routledge & Kegan Paul, 1980).

Gleadle, Kathryn, *British Women in the Nineteenth Century* (Palgrave, 2001).

Gordon, Eleanor and Nair, Gwyneth, *Public Lives: Women, Family and Society in Victorian Britain* (Yale University Press, 2003).

Green, Anna and Troup, Kathleen (eds) *The Houses of History* (Manchester University Press, 1999).

Hamish Fraser, W., *The Coming of the Mass Market* (Archon Books, 1981).

Hartman, Mary S., *Victorian Murderesses: A True History of Thirteen Respectable French and English Women Accused of Unspeakable Crimes* (Schocken Books, 1977).

Henderson, P., *William Morris His Life, Work and Friends* (Thames & Hudson, 1967).

Hewitt, Martin (ed.), *An Age of Equipoise? Reassessing mid-Victorian Britain* (Ashgate, 2000).

Hill, G.B., *Letters of Dante Gabriel Rossetti to William Allingham 1854–1870* (T. Fisher Unwin, 1897).

Hill, Thomas E., *Manual of Social and Business Forms: A Guide to Correct Writing* (Hill Standard Book Co., Chicago, 1882).

House, Jack, *Square Mile of Murder* (Chambers, 1961).

House, Jack, *Square Mile of Murder* (Molendinar Press, 1975).

House, Jack, *Square Mile of Murder* (Richard Drew Publishing, 1984).

Hunt, Peter, *The Madeleine Smith Affair* (Carroll & Nicholson, 1950).

Hunt, Violet, *The Wife of Rossetti: Her Life and Death* (Bodley Head, 1932).

Jacques, Anne, *The Wardle Story* (Churnet Valley Books, 1996).

Jalland, P., *Women, Marriage and Politics 1860–1914* (Oxford University Press, 1986).

Kelvin, Norman, *Collected Letters of William Morris*, vol. IIA (Princeton University Press, 1987).

Kelway, A. Clifton, *An Early Chapter in the History of the Catholic Revival,* (Longmans Green and Co., 1905).

Kenna, Rudolph, *Old Glasgow Shops*, (Glasgow City Archives, 1996).

King, Elspeth, 'Popular Culture in Glasgow', in R. Cage (ed.), *The Working Class in Glasgow 1750–1914* (Croom Helm, 1987).

Knox, William, *Lives of Scottish Women* (Edinburgh University Press, 2006).

Ladurie, Emanuel Le Roy, *Montaillou* (Penguin Books, 1990).

Lancaster, William, *The Department Store: A Social History* (Leicester University Press, 1995).

Lansdell, Avril, *Fashion a la Carte, 1860–1900* (Shire Publication, 1985).

Lockhart, Howard, *The Story of Madeleine Smith: A Dramatic Fiction Founded on Fact* (H.W.F. Deane and Sons, Ltd, 1949).

Lystra, Karen, *Searching the Heart: Women, Men and Romantic Love in Nineteenth-Century America* (Oxford University Press, 1989).

McCarthy, Fiona, *William Morris: A Life for Our Time* (Faber & Faber, 1994).

MacGowan, Douglas, *Murder in Victorian Scotland: The Trial of Madeleine Smith* (Praeger, 1999).

MacGowan, Douglas, *The Strange Affair of Madeleine Smith: Victorian Scotland's Trial of the Century* (Mercat Press, 2007).

Maloney, Paul, *Scotland and the Music Hall* (Manchester University Press, 2003).

Marsh, Jan, *The Pre-Raphaelite Sisterhood* (Quartet Books, 1985).

Mason, Michael, *The Making of Victorian Sexuality* (Oxford University Press, 1995).

McKendrick, Neil, Brewer, John and Plumb, J.H., *The Birth of a Consumer Society: The Commercialization of Eighteenth-century England* (Harper Collins, 1984).

Midgley, Clare, *Women against Slavery: The British Campaigns, 1780–1870* (Routledge, 1992).

Miller, Michael B., *The Bon Marche: Bourgeois Culture and the Department Store, 1869–1920* (George Allen & Unwin, 1981).

Morland, Nigel, *That Nice Miss Smith* (Frederick Muller Ltd, 1957).

Morland, Nigel, *That Nice Miss Smith* (Souvenir Press, 1988).

Nead, Linda, *Victorian Babylon: People, Streets and Images in Nineteenth-Century London* (Yale University Press, 2000).

Peterson, M. Jeanne, *Family, Love, and Work in the Lives of Victorian Gentlewomen* (Indiana University Press, 1989).

Petrie, Glen, *Marianne* (Macmillan, 1977).

Pols, Robert, *Family Photographs 1860–1940* (Public Record Office, 2002).

Rappaport, Erika Diane, *Shopping for Pleasure: Women in the Making of London's West End* (Princeton University Press, 2000).

Rowland, John, *A Century of Murder* (Home & Van Thal, 1950).

Ruddick, James, *Death at the Priory: Love, Sex and Murder in Victorian England* (Atlantic Books, 2001).

Salmon, Nick, *The William Morris Chronology* (Thoemmes Press, 1996).

Stobart, Jon and Owens, Alastair, *Urban Fortunes: Property and Inheritance in the Town 1700–1900* (Ashgate, 2000).

Strachey, Lytton, *Eminent Victorians* (Continuum, 2003).

Taylor, Miles and Wolf, Michael (eds), *The Victorians since 1901* (Manchester University Press, 2004).

Tennyson Jesse, F., *The Trial of Madeleine Smith* (William Hodge and Co., 1927).

Vickery, Amanda, *The Gentleman's Daughter* (Yale University Press, 1998).

Walkowitz, Judith, *City of Dreadful Delight* (University of Chicago Press, 1992).

Weintraub, S. (ed.), *Bernard Shaw: The Diaries 1885–1897* (Pennsylvania State University Press, 1986).

Whitaker, Wilfred, *Victorian and Edwardian Shopworkers* (David and Charles, 1973).

Wilson, Elizabeth, *Adorned in Dreams: Fashion and Modernity* (Virago, 1985).

Articles and essays

Boos, Florence (ed.), 'William Morris's Socialist Diary', *History Workshop*, Spring 1982.

Daggers, Jenny, 'The Victorian Female Civilising Mission and Women's Aspirations towards Priesthood in the Church of England', *Women's History Review*, 10, 4 (2001), pp. 651–70.

Davin, Delia, 'British Women Missionaries in Nineteenth-Century China', *Women's History Review*, 1, 2 (1992), pp. 257–71.

Gordon, Eleanor and Nair, Gwyneth, 'The Economic Role of Middle-Class Women in Victorian Glasgow', *Women's History Review*, 9, 4 (2000), pp. 791–814.

Gunn, Simon, 'The Public Sphere, Modernity and Consumption: New Perspectives on the History of the English Middle Class', in Alan Kidd and David Nicholls (eds), *Gender, Civic Culture and Consumerism: Middle-Class Identity in Britain 1800–1940* (Manchester University Press, 1999), pp. 12–29.

Hartman, Mary, 'Murder for Respectability: The Case of Madeleine Smith', *Victorian Studies*, 16, 4 (1972–73), pp. 381–400.

Hartman, Mary S., 'Crime and the Respectable Woman: Toward a Pattern of Middle-Class Female Criminality in Nineteenth-Century France and England', *Feminist Studies*, 2, 1 (1974), pp. 38–57.

Innes, Sue and Rendall, Jane, 'Women, Gender and Politics', in Lynn Abrams, Eleanor Gordon, Deborah Simonton and Eileen Janes Yeo (eds), *Gender in Scottish History since 1700* (Edinburgh University Press, 2006), pp. 43–83.

Lyons, Martin, 'Love Letters and Writing Practices: On Ecriture Intimes in the Nineteenth Century', *Journal of Family History*, 24, 2 (April 1999), pp. 232–9.

Mitchell, Sally, 'Sentiment and Suffering: Women's Recreational Reading in the 1860s', *Victorian Studies* 21 (1977), pp. 29–45.

Nenadic, Stana, 'Middle Rank Consumers and Domestic Culture in Edinburgh and Glasgow, 1720–1840', *Past and Present*, 145 (November 1994), pp. 122–56.

Rappaport, Erika Diane, '"A New Era of Shopping": The Promotion of Women's Pleasure in London's West End, 19091914', in Leo Charney and Vanessa R. Schwartz (eds), *Cinema and the Invention of Modern Life* (University of California Press, 1995).

Simon, Sherry, 'The Paris Arcades, the Ponte Vecchio and the Comma of Translation', *Meta*, XLV, 1 (2000), p. 75.

Sullivan, Sheila, '"What is the Matter with Mary Jane?" Madeleine Smith, Legal Ambiguity, and the Gendered Aesthetic of Victorian Criminality', *Genders*, 35 (2002), pp. 1–44.

Vickery, Amanda, 'Golden Age to Separate Spheres? Review of the Categories and Chronology of Women's History', *Historical Journal*, 36, 2 (1993), pp. 383–414.

Vickery, Amanda, 'Women and the World of Goods; A Lancashire Consumer and Her Possessions, 1751–81', in John Brewer and Roy Porter (eds), *Consumption and the World of Goods* (Routledge, 1993), pp. 274–304.

Walker, F.A., 'Glasgow's New Towns', in Peter Reed (ed.), *Glasgow: The Forming of the City* (Edinburgh University Press, 1993).

Walker, L., 'The Feminist Re-mapping of Space in Victorian London', in I. Borden et al. (eds), *The Unknown City: Contesting Architecture and Social Space* (MIT Press, 2000), pp. 297–309.

Unpublished sources

Smitley, Megan, '"Women's Mission": The Temperance and Women's Suffrage Movements in Scotland c.1870–1914 (unpublished PhD thesis, University of Glasgow, 2002).

Internet resources

www.amostcuriousmurder.com/Story.htm.
Archives of Socialist League, International Institute of Socialist History, www.iisg.nl/archives/en/files/s/10769755full.php.
Wall, Cynthia, 'Window Shopping', University of Virginia, online publications, 2001.

Index

Lightning Source UK Ltd.
Milton Keynes UK
23 February 2011

168080UK00001B/15/P